THE INDIAN OCEAN

Regional and International Power Politics

Ashok Kapur

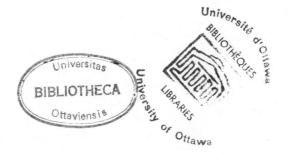

PRAEGER

PRAEGER SPECIAL STUDIES • PRAEGER SCIENTIFIC

Library of Congress Cataloging in Publication Data

Kapur, Ashok
  The Indian Ocean.

  Bibliography: p.
  1. Indian Ocean Region—Politics and government.
2. Indian Ocean Region—Foreign relations.   3. Indian
Ocean Region—Strategic aspects.   I. Title.
DS341.K36   1983   327'.09182'4   82-16703
ISBN 0-03-058641-0

589 413

DS
341
.K36
1983

Published in 1982 by Praeger Publishers
CBS Educational and Professional Publishing
a Division of CBS, Inc.
521 Fifth Avenue, New York, New York 10175 U.S.A.

© 1983 by Praeger Publishers

3456789 052 987654321
Printed in the United States of America

Preface

This study will explore the strategic perspectives of the Southern Indian Ocean world as they relate to northern strategic norms and policies, and as they express changing international tendencies and world power relations. The discussion is not exhaustive and the perspective is southern. It is intended to be un-northern (un-northwestern or North American and un-northeastern or Soviet); a critic may even choose to describe it as anti-Western and anti-Soviet.

The task of a scholar is to provoke rethinking, which often results in the development of psychological discomfort. The exercise is intended to halt the recycling of sterile, repetitive, and boring ideas that neither explain nor predict changing international tendencies. Recycled ideas have a use: they reinforce and increase the psychological comfort of like-minded people. However, that is the task of the propagandist, not of the scholar. I will regard this book as a success if the following pages provoke discussion about: the characteristics of the Indian Ocean world; the factors that shape South/North relations; the international relations of strategic buffers and conflict zones in the arc that stretches from Southern Africa to Southeast Asia with its links and discontinuities; the strategic relationships between erstwhile centers and their peripheries; about middle power-superpower interactions in crisis and non-crisis situations in the preceding three decades; and the meanings of strategy and power in the world today.

The definition of the "South" and the "Indian Ocean world," like that of the "third world," is imprecise. Much work remains to be done to formulate precisely the particular relationships that have emerged, and are still emerging, in the world beyond the North—that is, beyond NATO/WTO countries, and beyond the northern strategic cores represented by North America/North Atlantic, the two Europes, the Soviet Union, People's Republic of China, and Northeast Asia. My rough working definition of the "South" includes the following components:

Countries located south of the northern states and, in particular, south of the northern strategic cores;

States that are not members of the major military alliance systems;

States that are outside the alliance systems, but nevertheless function as strategic buffers and conflict zones for the
competing superpowers and other industrial and military powers;

States that reject a dependence on military alliances in a
formal sense, and in a declaratory manner, for purposes of their
national security but nevertheless rely on the use of force to
enhance and to protect their national security. Economic and
military development, not disarmament and formal membership
in military alliances, is the cohesive norm in the behavior of
these states;

Many southern states belong to the nonaligned movement.
This does not necessarily imply an ideological, diplomatic, and
strategic unity in the collective behavior of these states, but
it implies the existence of an attitude that international relations
is something significantly more than the study and practice of
East-West and particularly Soviet-American relations;

Southern states believe that international security policy
has cultural roots and cultural consequences; that strategy is
culture-bound; and consequently there is a need to examine
the relationship between strategy (strategies) and culture (cultures). Strategy is not simply a relationship between military
force levels or structures, military technology, military doctrines, and verifiable arms control. It has a cultural component,
a cultural base, and there are cultural consequences of particular
strategic doctrines and concepts. "Cool, analytical strategists"
mask the cultural bases and cultural consequences of their advocacy. Cross-cultural communications between hostile pairs
must be increased and made explicit rather than being kept
frozen if strategic dialogues are to become the basis of rethinking national security policy and international security policy
development. The crisis in Iran after the fall of the shah and
the Falklands crisis cannot be completely understood and addressed unless the cultural component is recognized and brought
forward on the academic and policy agenda; and

Southern states are also distinguishable by their emphasis
on economic security along with military security in their definition of national security. In urging third world states to reduce
their arms expenditures and to reduce and perhaps to eliminate
the purchase of modern weapons, the northern advocates are
perilously close to practicing double standards. Furthermore,
there is an element of hypocrisy in northern advocacy of southern restraint in arms acquisition in that it is the established
view of northern elites that arms sales serve northern political
and commercial goals and therefore are necessary and desirable.
Southern states urge a distinction between northern over-

armament—which ought to be reduced by meaningful and not cosmetic negotiations and agreement—and the problem of southern under-armament or uneven-armament, which ought to be corrected with appropriate upgrading of existing forces and with the acquisition of new and modern forces until decisionmakers perceive that they are able to raise the risks of superpower and great power military intervention, and generally are able to escape diplomatic isolation and forcible military intervention. For the South it appears that security has two pillars: economic and military development to protect the weaker states against the dangers of great power and superpower intervention, conflict from hostile neighbors, and conflict that is a product of regime instability. For the southern states, arms reduction, deceptive international (superpower) arms control agreements that raise ceilings rather than entail risk taking and sacrifice, and disarmament talk are not the system-changing avenues of international action.

This definition of the "South" is generally representative of the attitudes and policies of the major powers in the Indian Ocean world, such as, India, Pakistan, Egypt, Algeria, Iran, Israel, Nigeria, and South Africa. It is not limited to the military powers only or to near-nuclear states. Indeed, it is the argument of this study that the nuclear diplomacy of the near-nuclear state is qualitatively different from that of the five nuclear-weapon states in the North. The nuclear factor is one of a number of factors that account for the crisis and noncrisis behavior of Southern states.

Chapter 5 was originally prepared for the XIIth World Congress of the International Political Science Association held at Rio de Janeiro in August 1982. I am indebted to the participants for their valuable comments, and to the office of International Relations, the Social Sciences and Humanities Research Council, Ottawa, for travel support.

Acknowledgments

The preparation of this study was interrupted during 1980-81 because of my appointment to the United Nations Committee on Israeli Nuclear Armament. Nevertheless, the delay had its use. It gave me an opportunity to consult many experts on a variety of topics. I would like to express my deep gratitude to the many delegates to the United Nations, international civil servants, and academic specialists in the New York and Washington, D.C. areas who gave freely of their time and who shared their thoughts with me. As many are still working in official capacities, it would be inappropriate to mention them by name. It goes without saying that the responsibility for the ideas in this book is solely mine.

I would like to thank my wife Deepika and my two sons for their support during this period. Naim Shaikh provided valuable research assistance. Janice Love typed most of the manuscript with great care and speed. Finally, my students gave me a chance to test my ideas in the classroom, and I would like to thank them for this opportunity.

Contents

Introduction

The contemporary international relations literature views the Indian Ocean world as a peripheral area in world politics. The neglect of Indian Ocean studies is the result of a general bias in international studies. There is an overemphasis on the study of the security and diplomatic behavior of states that constitute strategic cores of power in the northern half of the globe: North America, North Atlantic, the two Europes, the Soviet Union, China, and Northeast Asia. In post-1945 studies the focus has been on East/West relations. In recent years the focus has broadened to study North/South and West/West relations. In all cases, the emphasis is on the centrality of the North in the contemporary international system. South/South relations are not studied as a phenomenon of potential or actual international significance. Middle powers and regional powers in the South are not studied as a new structural phenomenon in international relations. International politics is not viewed as a study of superpower, middle power, and regional power interactions.

The study of third world international relations, of international relations of the southern half of the globe, is usually cast in terms of third world development and regional conflict management. With regard to the latter, the premise is that the superpowers are the two international principals, the two security managers. Insofar as the literature deals with military and diplomatic aspects of the Indian Ocean region, the prime concern is to analyze the behavior of, and implications for, the superpowers in regional politics and conflicts. Self-centeredness or ethnocentricity is a hallmark of U.S. and Soviet strategic thinking and policies.[1] Studies of different military crises in South and Southeast Asia, the Middle East, and Africa are written in terms of superpowers' attitudes and interests.[2]

Moreover, the examination of superpowers' behavior in the Indian Ocean area does not reveal an agreement about the character and scope of the relationship.[3] Many suggest that superpower behavior is globally competitive (because of a presumed conflict of interests) and expresses itself in the Indian Ocean region as a diplomatic and military rivalry. A variation of this theme is that the conflict is land based and not significantly naval; that is, the Soviet Union seeks political and strategic power and diplomatic alignment in areas that border the Indian Ocean.[4] The superpower competition has moved southward toward the Middle East, Africa, and Southern Asia; and superpower naval activities are meant to strengthen superpower constituencies in the third world states. In the North there is a definite sense that the territorial status quo has been established and accepted by the superpowers in the Helsinki Agreement of 1975. But the third world is a gray area where the superpowers compete. The challenge is to acquire power and to formulate the strategy to beat the Soviet threat.

This perspective sees the third world as a helpless plaything, an arena where superpowers' rivalries are played out. The theme of regionalism—the development of regional interests, regional cooperation, and regional institutions—is not seen as a factor in the study of regional international relations. Autonomous regional international relations are not seen as important in the study of the structure of contemporary international relations.

There is no accurate overview of the international relations of the Indian Ocean world, but there should be one, as this area deals with the political life of three continents. It includes an ocean that links with other oceans and seas (see Map 1 and Table 1).[5] The area is inhabited by peoples who have distinctive cultural norms and strategic interests. They aspire to change their domestic and international condition in a world of unequal powers. Autonomous regional power centers are emerging in South Asia, the Middle East, and Southern Africa. They can escape forcible intervention and diplomatic isolation vis-à-vis the superpowers and the international community. They can manage select crises—particularly ones they initiate. They not only survive punishment by the superpowers but can also project power beyond their own frontiers and can become a voice in international security debates. If they cannot succeed in influencing regime formation, they have the power to deny success to those great powers who seek to impose their regime.

The regional powers are middle powers because they form a layer of secondary states in the system of states. They are able to formulate horizontal relations among regional enemies and vertical superpower-middle power interactions. They are active participants in regional and international life, and their policy is to alter the structure of international relations. They are successful because regional international relations in the Middle East, South Asia, Southern Asia, Africa, and South America reveal the emergence of attitudes and policies to gain upward mobility for regional powers and to minimize extraregional intrusiveness into regional affairs.

MAP 1

The Indian Ocean World

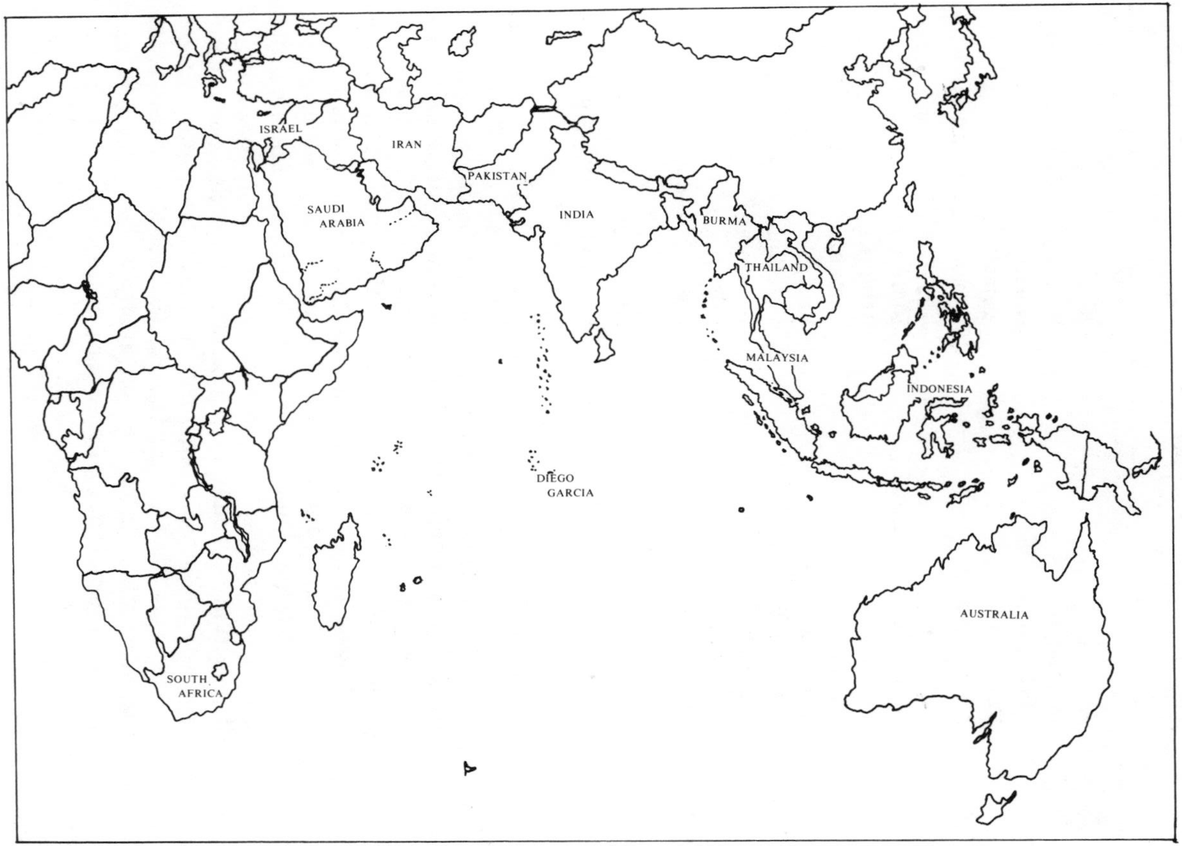

TABLE 1

List of Countries in the Indian Ocean World
(not in alphabetical order)

Australia	Kuwait
Indonesia	Saudi Arabia
Philippines	Oman
Malaysia	Yemen
Singapore	Democratic Republic of Yemen
Vietnam	Egypt
Cambodia	Sudan
Thailand	Ethiopia
Burma	Somalia
Bangladesh	Kenya
Sri Lanka	Tanzania
India	Mozambique
Pakistan	Malawi
Gulf Kingdoms	Mauritius
Iran	Zimbabwe
Iraq	South Africa
Israel	Malagasy Republic
Lebanon	

Note: This list has the following basis: all countries geo-graphically touch the Indian Ocean or contiguous seas such as the Red Sea, Persian Gulf, and Suez Canal. There is explicit or latent consciousness of diplomatic, economic, cultural, and historical links with peoples and countries in the Indian Ocean area. In many instances the consciousness became suppressed due to the development of North/South colonial ties in the preceding 300 years. These North/South ties froze South/South interactions. Today South/South interactions are being developed through unilateral, bilateral, and multilateral diplomacy in various fields, and the basis of the old (pre-1945 and pre-1970) North/South relations is being continually revised through crisis and noncrisis diplomacy of southern states.

The rise of regional powers points to the emergence of a southern orientation in international relations. A number of features broadly distinguish the South from the North. "South" deals with countries located south of North America, Europe, the Soviet Union, and China. Apart from the geographical aspect, the southern states are outside the normal sphere of NATO and Warsaw alliance relations and influence. Politically, militarily, and culturally they are outside the mainstream of northern international relations or East/West relations. They are alienated from the North but see themselves forced to achieve temporary and tacit alliances with northern partners. These partners, however, are not reliable. Consequently, the southern states seek self-reliance and a capacity to manipulate the northern states for their own advantage.

The southern states are secondary powers with proud cultural and political heritages. They are conscious of the cultural roots and implications of strategic theory and behavior, and sense that strategic conflict is also cultural conflict. The economic status of the southern states is not necessarily the crucial determinant of the definition of the South. Most of them are viable economies. Their GNP is less than that of the superpowers or several other northern states (particularly FRG and Japan) but they are not less developed. These societies are economically and politically unevenly developed. Their strategic and political behavior flows more from their cultural and strategic perceptions and less so from their economic life.

Practitioners in the North tend to ignore system-changing trends in Indian Ocean regional politics. The bias is toward the system-maintenance behavior of the northern states, particularly the superpowers. It takes a crisis to attract the attention of northern practitioners and thinkers. The normal behavior in the foreign policymaking process is best described by the phenomenon of ethnocentricity, inertia, busy-ness, and anti-intellectualism (see note 1). Furthermore, Western students of third world foreign policy have also developed anti-intellectual, anti-empirical tendencies. Conceptual sterility is the consequence of a failure to seek out evidence because that evidence may cause psychological discomfort to a pet theory. Among Western students of third world international relations (or Indian Ocean international relations), there is no deep consciousness, let alone a consensus, about the nature of the change, its direction, and its implications for the future of international and regional order. There is no systematic study of the interrelatedness of issues, the multiplication of actors, or the significance of events, processes, attitudes, and policies of the regions. The following questions are often ignored: What is the impact of strategic and cultural norms in the northern international system on the Indian Ocean region? In what sense is the Indian Ocean region a system and is its emergence a sign of a changing international system? What is the impact of current Indian Ocean regional international relations on the meaning and the pattern of power politics in the international system? Should regional power centers be defined as autonomous manipulators of international power centers whose task is to arrange their upward mobility and the downward mobility of the superpowers? If so, are the parameters of conflict and cooperation taking shape in the gray areas? Will the 1980s see the emergence of regional cores in the Indian Ocean arc from Southern Asia to Southern Africa (with varying degrees of success)?

The literature fails to address such questions. It has a number of distinct orientations or ideological biases, but it lacks the capacity to explain and predict the characters of change—its systemic implications. There is "high" advocacy and "low" analysis. Consider the following examples.

Third world writers complain about the dangers of superpower intervention in regional conflict. They argue that the presumed difference in motives underlying the intervention of superpowers in regional affairs is insignificant, and that their rivalry and military buildup is a threat to peace.[6] This view is not wrong, but it is incomplete. If threats to peace emanate from linkages between regime instability, regional conflict, and international conflict, then the third world emphasis on the consequences of superpower behavior intervention is one-sided.

The analysis of several Western writers also suffers from one-sidedness. They emphasize the danger of Soviet penetration in regional affairs and argue that a stronger Western (particularly U.S.) response is needed. Soviet behavior is portrayed as a mixture of many motives. The Soviet Union, historically expansionist, seeks domination and access to strategic resources-- partly to deny these to the West and partly because it may become an importer of resources in the future. Soviet expansionism is a product of its organizational history of conspiracy, Byzantine intrigue, and preoccupation with geopolitics and balance of power. Finally, Soviet expansionism is a consequence of its anti-Western attitude and anti-imperialism since 1917.[7]

Alternative perspectives remain untapped. The Soviet Union has used military force in Africa, the Middle East, and the Americas during the 1970s (directly or in collaboration with Cuba and East Germany). But to what extent is Soviet expansionist behavior a consequence of insecurities that derive from

its historical experience and its assessment of current developments in the international environment? How permanent or
successful is Soviet military intervention beyond Eastern Europe?
Superior Soviet military force can establish a temporary military
and political presence in the third world, but does it lack the
capacity to control political and cultural relations in the crisis
spots in the Middle East, South and Southeast Asia, Africa,
and South America? How successful have Soviet military moves
been in Africa (1975) and Afghanistan (1978-79)? The questions
imply that Soviet expansionism could be a consequence of Soviet
insecurity about the world outside its borders. Soviet intervention may result in a failure of policy as, for instance, in the
ouster of USSR advisers from Egypt, the defeat of Nkomo in
Zimbabwe elections, the failure to acquire a naval base in India,
and the mistrust among Africans of the Cuban presence in Africa
and of the Cuban role in the nonaligned movement. If "success"
means "domination," then USSR interventionist behavior in
Africa and the Middle East is not necessarily successful. An
alternative perspective of Soviet behavior should be studied,
taking into account the following.

First, the Soviets have an undeniable "historical memory"
of fear derived from almost ten centuries of foreign invasion.
The search for military and political security may be a consequence of fear.

Second, the Soviet leadership is aware that it lacks domestic
and external legitimacy, that it is perceived as the illegitimate
successor of the tsars. This factor is important in a system
that faces internal dissent and economic problems.

Third, Soviet foreign policy in 1917 was based on the view
that the Bolshevik revolution was the first step to a world revolution that would surround the Soviet Union with friendly states.
When world revolution failed, foreign policy had to be based on
military force rather than the premise of a friendly strategic
environment.

Fourth, the Soviet leadership faces a learning problem.
Its self-image is that its intervention occurs for a good cause
(socialism) and is likely to be welcomed. Yet Soviet experience
(the 1920s to the present) suggests otherwise in Poland, Czecho-
slovakia, Hungary, Afghanistan, and elsewhere. This self-image
cannot change because no other self-image can replace it. Yet,
the greater the discrepancy between self-image and actual behavior, the greater will be the tension between the two, and
the greater will be the resort to military force that is seen as
likely to occur.

Fifth, both superpowers were (and probably still are) un-
prepared for the responsibility of world leadership and did not

have a well-defined relationship between commitments and power.
Their external policies lack elite consensus. Consequently,
their behavior is a continuous pattern of clumsy ad hoc responses
to an international environment they can neither understand
nor control.

Lastly, the Soviet Union is heading toward serious economic
and social strains in its domestic life. This is due to a structural problem with Soviet agriculture and changing demographic
and industrial indicators with respect to the 1980s.[8]

The approach to the study of regional conflicts in the U.S.
literature is in many instances one-sided and self-serving.[9]
Regional conflict is attributed to regional rivals: Israel and the
Arabs, India and Pakistan, South Africa and Black Africa, and
others. Studies of regional arms races and regional nuclear
proliferation are structured around this premise. However, it
is rarely defended or tested empirically and is usually overstated.
A number of alternative perspectives may be noted.

First, the superpowers have an interest in international
system maintenance. They do not seek revolutionary change
that could shrink their power in international relations. Their
commitment to the doctrine of two principals in international
security is a common interest and is of far greater importance
than their limited competitiveness.

Second, the superpowers must maintain a pose of an ideological struggle to satisfy domestic intra-elite struggles. Disharmony in intra-elite relations in the United States and the
Soviet Union is the basic factor in superpower decisionmaking
processes. Domestic enemies are hidden but are more dangerous
because they are a threat to the elite in power, particularly in
a democracy. External enemies are explicit but are less dangerous
because their power and interests are predictable and the parameters of external threats are knowable and manageable. Foreign
policy is a continuation of hidden, intra-elite power struggles.
It is an action-reaction phenomenon that flows from an unsettled
authority structure at home. It is not simply action-reaction to
external threats from beyond one's territorial frontier.

Third, a pose of global competition precludes formal agreement, but this is not significant. Formal agreements raise definitional issues and these become subject to bureaucratic vetoes.
The image of a superpower competition keeps domestic bureaucratic vetoes latent. This image is necessary as it serves two
functions: it diverts subnational attention away from in-house
debates and struggles, and it may also be the catalyst to reorient
domestic debate, as external inputs into a domestic threat can
produce a new elite consensus with a "new" definition of the

problem. Moreover, formal agreements are unnecessary if informal restraints exist and the limited competition is manageable and predictable.

Fourth, more issues unite the superpowers than divide them. The rules of the game provide for limited competition in different issues and spheres of the world on a nonexclusive basis.[10] Nonexclusivity requires superpower involvement in regional life through the management of regional elites' competition and of regional crises. The primary concern of the superpowers is not to achieve regional peace, even though their public communications stress this commitment. They wish to foster instability because it allows them to be involved in regional issues. With regional peace (defined as the existence of social harmony and the absence of social conflict), the superpowers would lose their access to regional life—its resources, markets, elite contact, and military activities. With true regional peace, the superpowers would be out of business.

Lastly, both superpowers have interests in regional life, but these do not always require competitive responses. In the third world, even if one superpower left, the other would still be there to maintain its interests. So the superpowers must do something to remain involved at all times in regional international relations. Their involvement is usually meant to achieve regional peace and security as per their own requirements.

Staying involved rather than achieving peace and security for others is the superpower norm. The superpowers are selfish. Regional peace and security is subordinate to their definition of international security and their own interests. The post of global and permanent competition between the superpowers is a ruse that is meant to throw dust into the eyes of half-educated third world elites. This pose facilitates the penetration of third world elite structures by the superpowers in their guise as protectors of local clients. But this guise obscures an overriding fact. Even when they speak on opposite sides in visible international fora and in third world capitals, they are nevertheless in a position to make a deal utilizing the self-serving premise that both have a special responsibility for world peace. To them there is no difference between national security and international security, and the latter depends on a stable superpower relationship.

Soviet academic writings are also one-sided and self-serving. Soviet international relations theory after Stalin reveals an anti-third party orientation.[11] Soviet writers speak the language of anti-imperialism, peaceful coexistence, anticolonialism, and wars of national liberation. The Soviet contributions to the armed struggles in Vietnam, Cuba, Mozambique, Angola, and the Horn of Africa, as well as in conventional interstate crises in the Middle East, South Asia, and Southeast Asia are well known. Soviet writers voice their support for third world aspirations against foreign domination. However, Soviet theory rejects the concept of the third force in international relations. The Soviet Union uses nonalignment and peaceful coexistence to promote its own aims, and uses third world movements to support the context of bipolar international relations.

To the superpowers, regionalism is the development of regional institutions that respond to their interests and strategies. They see the regional powers as subimperial agents in regional life. The general public equates political nationalism with independence, but collaboration between the regional and international elites is the real basis of policymaking. Collaboration between like-minded domestic and external elites is facilitated by the existence of intra-elite competition in most societies. Thus, intra-elite competition and instability among regional decision structures provide the opportunity for foreign-linked intervention. In this view of regional-international collaboration, foreign-linked subnational domestic factionalism was (is) the principal unit of behavior and analysis of regional life.

This view of regionalism is the starting point for our study. However, we will argue that tendencies to rethink attitudes and policies that could shape bilateral detente in regions with deep-seated and historical disputes are emerging. In Indian Ocean regional international relations, we will probe such possibilities in relation to Southern Africa, the Middle East, and South Asia from the perspective of three regional powers in the Indian Ocean arc: India, Israel, and South Africa. It will be argued that the new orientation in regional thinking is to shrink super-power influence in erstwhile areas of regional instability and crisis, and to replace these with new approaches that develop regional orders. The premise is that indigenous solutions must be found for indigenous problems.

MAJOR QUESTIONS IN THE STUDY

At present, our literature inadequately studies the sources of conflict, the patterns of power politics, and the relationship between potential, mobilized, and applied power in the arc that stretches from Southern Africa to the Middle East, the Persian Gulf, and South and Southeast Asia. To cover the deficiency, we propose to examine the following questions.

- Is the Indian Ocean region an arc of permanent instability in the international system? Is this permanence revealed by the movement since 1860 of international conflict (war, civil violence, revolution, coup d'etat, regime instability, territorial dispute, and ethnic conflict) from the North to the South? Or does the international politics of regions in this arc contain the seeds of regional detente in the 1980s, based on the superpowers' system of cold war and detente? Is conflict being toned down in the North and South, or is it growing in the South and taking on a different character?
- Is the Indian Ocean region an arena for the superpowers to work out their rivalries in the periphery of the international system so that the central balance in the North is protected from unmanageable tension? Must superpowers' rivalry be exported to the periphery because superpower conflict in the central balance could threaten their peace? Does superpower conflict in the periphery release tension in the North? Is superpower competition in the third world essential for super-power detente in the North? Is superpower rivalry in the Indian Ocean region a sign of the globalization of superpower conflict—from Europe to Asia to the rest of the world? Do third parties and regional powers in the Indian Ocean area reject the above alternatives? What is their approach to check superpower intervention in regional affairs, to develop regional order, and to seek international influence?
- Does the Indian Ocean arc have a moderate constituency or has it been overtaken by radical and anarchical forces? What is the balance between the forces of order and disorder in Indian Ocean international relations?
- Are the forces of disorder (such as Libya, PLO, Cuba, Iran) a threat to the status and the power of one or both super-powers? Or is the threat directed primarily against the theory of a secular state and the system of states?
- Does the emergence of ethnic and religion-based revolutionary and anarchical forces mean that Indian Ocean international relations are becoming retribalized? If so, is groupism, not statism and nationalism, the new motive force behind change in the Indian Ocean regional politics?
- Does an ethnic, insular, and retribalized foreign policy process point to the emergence of subnationalism as the principal unit of behavior and analysis of the international environment? If so, do states and the relevant subnational entities react only to external threats, or is their behavior mainly a reaction to internal enemies? Could it be argued that state relations are not simply an interstate phenomenon but that relevant sub-

national elites have interests and policies of their own, that
intra-elite dynamics are the significant sources of conflict in
interstate relations? And even if the public enemy left the
international scene, would the "other side" still be there?
- Is international politics after 1945 a study of cold war politics
  and controlled militarization of the international environment,
  particularly that of the South?
- Has a gap emerged between mobilized and applied power so
  that failure to convert mobilized power into applied power is
  to transform strength into weakness? When a second or a
  third party is able to create or to manipulate a gap between
  mobilized and applied power in the adversary's behavior, does
  such a situation make the strong weak? Under what conditions
  does strength (possessed capability) become weakness (inability
  to influence the outcome)?

The Indian Ocean region is ripe for intellectual inquiry
because world crises today are crises in the Indian Ocean arc.
The structure of political, military, and economic interaction is
established in the North: North Atlantic, North America, and
in international relations of Eurasia and Northeast Asia. Northern international relations are alliance relations. The rules of
the game are defined and understood by the principals in the
northern world. Global war is out. Arms race is in, as is cold
war politics and a shaky detente. Informal and formal arms
control allows controlled arms racing and lucrative arms trade.
All major powers are to have access to regions of their choice
on a nonexclusive basis. Territorial frontiers are not to be
changed in the European state system. This norm is being
applied to Sino-Soviet, Sino-American, USSR, Japanese, and
Sino-Indian relations. In the North, border conflicts are political
and strategic disputes. In a broad sense, a territorial dispute
is a consequence of a deteriorating political relationship. Both
are negotiable.

In the Indian Ocean region, no such rules of accepted
behavior exist in the encounter between the superpowers and
the regional states. This study will argue that despite the ups
and downs of the superpower relations, their interests are
globally parallel. There is a high degree of parallelism in their
behavior in the Indian Ocean area, as in their naval interactions
in the Indian Ocean itself. So the real debate is not between
the superpowers; it is between them and the lesser powers—
the emerging regional power centers. The South/North debate
represents a fundamental change in third world thinking, at
the level of strategy, culture, and economics. It is expressed

by the centers in the Indian Ocean arc. This is a new process
in Indian Ocean and global international relations and it has
implications for the superpowers in the 1980s.

NOTES

1. G. T. Allison, The Essence of Decision (Cambridge,
Mass.: Little, Brown, 1971), particularly the discussion of
"organizational process"; I. L. Janis, Victims of Groupthink
(Boston: Houghton Mifflin, 1972); K. E. Boulding, ed., Peace
and the War Industry, 2d ed. (New Brunswick, N.J.: Trans-
actions Books, 1973), particularly essays by I. L. Horowitz and
R. J. Wolfson; J. G. Stoessinger, Nations in Darkness, 3d ed.
(New York: Random House, 1978); and Ken Booth, Strategy
and Ethnocentrism (London: Croom Helm, 1979).
2. The literature is extensive and the interested reader
may wish to see the following in studying regional crisis. On
South Asia: W. J. Barnds, India, Pakistan and the Great Powers
(London: Pall Mall, 1972); and Robert Jackson, South Asia
Crisis: India, Pakistan and Bangladesh (London: Chatto and
Windus, 1975). On Southeast Asia: Leslie H. Gelb with R. K.
Betts, The Irony of Vietnam: The System Worked (Washington,
D.C.: Brookings Institution, 1979). On the Middle East and
the Persian Gulf: various Adelphi Papers published by the Inter-
national Institute for Strategic Studies in London are useful
background (see bibliography for titles). On Africa: Colin
Legum et al., eds., Africa in the 1980s: A Continent in Crisis
(New York: McGraw-Hill, 1979); and C. P. Potholm and R. Dale,
eds., Southern Africa in Perspective (New York: Free Press,
1972), for general background.
3. The works by Michael McGwire and G. Jukes are
particularly recommended. For Jukes see The Soviet Union in
Asia (Australia: Angus and Robertson for the AIIA, 1973), and
The Indian Ocean in Soviet Naval Policy, Adelphi Papers, no.
87 (London: IISS, 1972). For McGwire see his edited works
Soviet Naval Developments: Capability and Context (New York:
Praeger, 1978) and (edited with John McDonnell) Soviet Naval
Influence: Domestic and Foreign Dimensions (New York: Praeger,
1977). Also consult A. J. Cottrell and R. M. Burrell, eds.,
The Indian Ocean: Its Political, Economic and Military Importance
(New York: Praeger, 1972); Indian Ocean Arms Limitations and
Multilateral Cooperation on Restraining Arms Transfers, hearing
before a panel of Committee on Armed Services, House of Repre-
sentatives, 95th Congress, October 3, 10, 1978; Paul H. Nitze,

L. Sullivan, Jr., et al., Securing the Seas, Atlantic Council Policy Study (Boulder, Col.: Westview Press, 1979); Admiral S. G. Gorshkov, Red Star Rising at Sea, translated by T. A. Nelly, Jr. and edited for publication by H. Preston (Annapolis, Md.: Naval Institute Press, 1974), and Seapower of the State (New York, Pergamon, 1979).

4. W. A. C. Adie, Oil, Politics and Seapower: The Indian Ocean Vortex (New York: Crane, Russak, 1975).

5. The effort to convert the Indian Ocean into a peace zone originated with the nonaligned states and expressed itself in U.N. diplomacy. It resulted in several reports prepared under the auspices of the U.N. secretary-general. Deliberations on the Ad Hoc Committee on the Indian Ocean still continue and are discussed in summary form in the Appendix.

6. Indian writers are prominent in this regard. For an academic view see K. R. Singh, Politics of the Indian Ocean (Delhi: Thompson Press, 1974). For a senior Indian naval officer's view see Admiral S. N. Kohli, Seapower and the Indian Ocean (New Delhi: Tata McGraw-Hill, 1978). Some prominent U.S. writers have begun to explore the link between antinationalism and interventionism in U.S. thinking. For this aspect see Melvin Gurtov, The United States Against the Third World (New York: Praeger, 1974).

7. See Chapters 3 and 4.

8. The foregoing points are drawn from L. J. Halle, Cold War as History (New York: Harper Torchbook, 1975), and M. Schwartz, The Foreign Policy of the USSR (California: Dickenson, 1975).

9. For general perspectives see B. M. Russett, International Regions and the International System (Chicago: Rand McNally, 1967); L. J. Cantori and S. L. Speigel, eds., The International Politics of Regions (Englewood Cliffs, N.J.: Prentice-Hall, 1970); R. A. Falk and S. H. Mendlovitz, eds., Regional Politics and World Order (San Francisco: Freeman, 1973), particularly part V; J. N. Rosenau et al., eds., World Politics (New York: Free Press, 1976), particularly part III; for regional conflict and regional arms race aspects see R. J. O'Neill, ed., Insecurity: The Spread of Weapons in the Indian and the Pacific Oceans (Canberra: Australian National University Press, 1978), particularly the essays by F. A. Vali and M. Ayoob; for the regional nuclear proliferation focus see E. W. Lefever, Nuclear Arms in the Third World (Washington, D.C.: Brookings Institution, 1979).

10. The notion of "shared access" or shared power was expressed explicitly by Richard Nixon, U.S. Foreign Policy for

the 1970s: Building for Peace, message to Congress, February 25, 1971, in the sections dealing with East Asia and South Asia in particular (pp. 34 and 41 respectively). Alastair Buchan, The End of the Postwar Era (London: Weidenfeld and Nicholson, 1974), provides an academic discussion of the concept of non-exclusive spheres of influence for the major powers.

    11. N. I. Lebedev, A New Stage in International Relations (New York: Pergamon, 1976).

1

The New Patterns of
Power Politics

During the past 100 years the patterns and processes of international relations have changed substantially. This chapter discusses four alternative international systems.

The first system refers broadly to pre-1945 international relations. It roughly describes the pattern of international politics of the European powers up to their decline in the early and mid twentieth century. The second system refers to the rise of two superpowers by 1945 and the image of superpower hostility since 1947.

The third system refers to the superpower relationship since 1945. It rests on the proposition that superpowers are locked into a unique relationship (system) that is part conflict and part cooperation. It is based on the thesis that there are but two international principals: both are military equals; neither can pursue its interests unaided—without taking into account the views and interests of the other superpower; despite the public stance of hostility both share a common interest, which is to preserve their international position and dominance in formulating the rules of the game. The image of superpower hostility hides the self-serving notion that the superpowers have the power and the responsibility to keep international and regional peace. There is a structural link between the image of superpower competition and their private cooperativeness. The image of competition is a necessary prerequisite of foreign policy because intra-elite competition is the central factor in the decision structure of the superpowers, particularly in the United States. Only when foreign policy is conceived as an expression of unsettled domestic elite struggles does the image of superpower competition assume a significance that is different from what it is commonly assumed to be.

The fourth system is a post-1945 development that is still in a formative stage. It points to the emergence of secondary powers--middle powers and regional powers—in the contemporary international system. These powers are located geographically outside the normal sphere of operation of the NATO and Warsaw military alliances. Diplomatically and strategically these powers interact with alliance members and leaders in the North, but the interaction is based on a sense of dependence and vulnerability to pressures in the outside environment. The quest of the secondary powers is to alter the condition of inequality and vulnerability, and to make the northern states vulnerable to southern states' interference. The southern states are ideologically dissimilar (for example, India, Israel, South Africa, Arab states, and Islamic states). But there is a strange similarity in their attitude to shape strategies that avoid forcible overseas military intervention and diplomatic isolation, and that are calculated to locate opportunities for regional order and to contribute to international security debate.

Table 1.1 outlines the features of these four systems. The cold war and detente systems represent the contemporary reality which was marked by high tension in U.S.-USSR relations. The cold war and detente system represents the contemporary reality of northern international relations, the period of controlled, institutionalized tension in U.S.-USSR relations since 1953. This system has demonstrably absorbed tensions in U.S.-USSR relations including events like the USSR invasion of Afghanistan in December 1979. The South versus North cold war and detente system is an emerging system. This view flows from the proposition that international relations today are undergoing a structural change comparable to the change in U.S.-USSR relations since 1953. Two broad approaches are taking shape. The first, expressed by the superpowers, speaks the language of international security. In this approach the events, attitudes, processes, and policies point to the central role of the superpowers in the management of international conflict. The second approach is expressed by regional and middle powers, and they speak the language of regional security. A primary premise in this approach is that the system of states can no longer tolerate superpower intervention into regional life. Instead of being a source of stability, superpower intervention and self-interest favors instability in regional life. The superpowers are interested in staying involved in regional affairs, not in seeking regional peace. Their interest in regional peace is limited at

TABLE 1.1

Four Alternative Old and New International Systems (Past and Present)

Features of International Systems	1 Old: Westphalian System	2 New: Superpowers Cold War System	3 New: Horizontal Northern Cold War and Detente System	4 New: Emerging South Versus North Cold War and Detente System
Operative law (a) about state (b) about war and peace	(a) sovereign equality of states is emphasized (b) law of war and peace exists; the two are separate	(a) sovereign equality is legal norm but is ignored (b) international law about war/peace is mostly irrelevant	Same as in column 2	Same as in column 2, except that weaker states emphasize state equality
Primary institutions (a) states system (b) war (c) diplomacy	(a) the states system is the policy framework (b) war is primary instrument (c) diplomacy is primary instrument	(a) same as in column 1 (b) military threats replace general war-fighting; limited war and intervention is needed (c) diplomacy means crisis diplomacy	(a) same as in column 1 (b) same as in column 2 (c) same as in column 3	(a) same as in column 1 (b) same as in column 2 (c) same as in column 3
Pattern of capability distribution (equality/inequality)	Equality among great powers; inequality for the majority of states	There is equality between superpowers and increased stratification of military and industrial/economic power world-wide.	Equality between superpowers; growth of multiple power centers in the North; growing rich-poor gap between North and South	Same as in column 3, except South engages in resources diplomacy
Definition/perception of power and power politics	Strong dominate the weak; military and economic power means influence	Same as in column 1 except that there are two international power centers.	Same as in column 2	New patterns of power politics emerge because of third party emergence after 1945.
Pattern of international communications (horizontal/vertical)	Horizontal interstate great power communications are primary ones; vertical ones are meant to socialize and manage the weak	Same as in column 1	Same as in column 1	South seeks to develop southern content in international communications
Importance of territoriality and nationalism	Very important because power means territorial power	Territoriality declines in importance because of the bombers, missiles, and MNCs; subnational elitism is key.	Same as in column 2	Territoriality and nationalism are important to newly emerging states.
Impact of global environment and global communications	Great powers shape the global environment	Superpowers shape global environment; each superpower represents the environment to the other.	Same as in column 2	There is high impact of North on the South, but this is changing.

(continued)

Table 1.1 (continued)

Features of International Systems	1 Old: Westphalian System	2 New: Superpowers Cold War System	3 New: Horizontal Northern Cold War and Detente System	4 New: Emerging South Versus North Cold War and Detente System
Impact of domestic politics on foreign policy	Nil or insignificant	Significant but hidden; foreign policy is seen as interstate action-reaction, as externally directed and externally induced.	Foreign policy is a consequence of subnational elite competition, and intra-elite factionalism is foreign-linked.	Pattern of decisionmaking is same as in column 4; the northern system goes South.
Relationship between peace and force	Force is prerequisite for peace (meaning stable military relations between enemies).	Same as in column 1	Same as in column 1	Same as in column 1
Number of essential actors in the system	Four or five according to European experience	Two	Five (United States, Soviet Union, People's Republic of China, Japan, and West Europe	Same as in column 3, and third parties became important depending on the policy issue(s).
Quest for disarmament	There is disarmament talk (1899–) but actual militarization.	Same as in column 1; arms control is meant to achieve stable arms racing	Same as in column 2	Same as in column 1 with likelihood of movement toward pattern of column 2.
Role of violence and revolution	There is high incidence of interstate violence; elites fear revolution because it threatens elite structure.	Revolutionary states become traditional, stability-oriented, and self-serving superpowers; however, revolutionary rhetoric continues; arms race replaces interstate war.	Incidence of war shifts from North to South; there is a significant increase in arms spending, military mobilization in peacetime, and trade between North and South.	Incidence of civil (nonstate) and interstate violence is high in the South.
Quest for noncoercive social international relations	The Marxist perspective is not adopted in international relations; instead, statism is strengthened.	The national security system rejects notion of universal social nonstate relations.	Same as in column 2	Same as in column 2
Quest for world federalism	Kantian perspective is not adopted as state policy.	Concept exists in public consciousness but is rejected as state policy.	Same as in column 2	Same as in column 2

Source: Compiled by the author.

best to a desire to avoid regional wars that could involve the superpowers. Their loyalty to their regional allies is temporary and depends on their own economic or strategic interests, not on ideological commitments. The superpowers are capable of discarding local regional allies so it is up to their temporary allies to manipulate the superpowers to stay involved. There is a growing tension between the superpower concept of international security and the third world concept of regional security. The two are not compatible. Mistrust is the basis of South/North interactions.

THE FIRST SYSTEM: THE WESTPHALIAN SYSTEM

The first system is based on the existence of a system of states that came into being with the Treaty of Westphalia in 1648. This treaty ended the period of religious wars that had characterized European political and social life in the preceding years. The Westphalia system securalized the political process by separating the authority of church and the state. The prince was to be the guardian of sovereignty in his land. The state and the sovereign became a legal person. The state's domestic life was, legally and theoretically, to be immune from the foreign policy process. The state was the essential unit in the international environment, and collectively the states constituted a system. There was common recognition by all states that they functioned as a community. Undoubtedly there were conflicts and cooperation between states, but the state was regarded as a social institution. It was meant to be the highest form of social organization, and the loyalty of the people was primarily to a higher territorial and political entity, beyond the local group and the tribe. As such, the state was meant to detribalize politics. Detribalization occurred because the subjects were required to respect the territorial organization, the state. In its original conception the Westphalian system made statism the basis of international relations. The role of nationalism emerged later to strengthen the state system.

The states-system has two major features: the states have a legal personality and sovereign equality of states is the basis of international life. Thus, the United States and Fiji are legal equals. Excluding exceptions like the veto right assigned to the permanent members of the U.N. Security Council and voting rights in the World Bank, international organizations are based on the doctrine of one vote for one state.

In practice, the states-system works differently and is amoral. Why? Self-help is the main rule of action. In the states-system, nothing succeeds like success. Even though a state has the right to speak about its rights and justice, its only real right consists of policies it can enforce. Having the capacity to secure or to deny gain to the adversary is the only real basis of right in interstate relations. Might is right even though the use of power and force is often justified by reference to a higher moral or legal principle. Power, not right, is the source of order or disorder in international life.

The states-system is amoral and interstate relations usually rest on a creative tension between power and noncoercive norms. It is arguable that a state (and the states-system) has some moral content. Although there is no absolute right or justice in the relations between states, morality plays a role in several ways. Despite different policies, states commonly share a desire to preserve the system of states because it is only through this system that a society can find the ultimate legal and political defense for its existence. Even though states are willing to tolerate military aggression, they frown on acts that could mean the end of a particular state. To the extent that a states-system facilitates the existence of different entities, it is moral. Second, states speak the language of morality and peace even when they practice power politics. Cosmetically, this is morality. Third, moral questions are raised by constituents within a state and these affect the definition of choices in a state's external behavior. Finally, the system is moral insofar as it repudiates the domination of one state (empire) as the basis of international life. Nonetheless, the system is deficient in moral terms because it rejects in practice the notion of equality and democracy as the basis of interstate relations. Since 1815 great responsibility to manage world order has rested with the great powers; inequality in the distribution of power in the states-system has been the basis of regime formation and international rule-making.

Overall, the Westphalian states-system is built on a tension between legal equality, morality, and actual inequality of power in international life. Inequality produces two types of arguments. The weak states usually plead the importance of sovereignty and equality. What they are saying in effect is that "We are weak, we are vulnerable to external economic, military, cultural, and political penetration, and we should get a better deal; might should not be right." Weak states usually emphasize the legal and moral doctrine of sovereign equality. The weaker the state, the greater is the declaratory emphasis on law and equality in interstate relations. On the other hand, the militarily and economically powerful states have little dependency on law unless they are in a weak situation; when they are strong they write

the law or influence its content. In the latter case, they use
law to their advantage and argue that inequality is a fact of
life. They argue that the quest for absolute equality for all
states is impractical. There should be "undiminished security"—
for the strong. There is nothing wrong with inequality provided
states seek stability in international and regional life. Therefore, international hierarchy is not only a fact of life but it is
also the best available method to secure stability in international
relations. Stability requires hierarchy, otherwise there will be
disorder among equals. Peace (defined as order and not necessarily justice) can be secured if the strong curb their ambitions,
if they act collectively (that is, by showing mutual respect for
each strong state's interests), and if all major powers in the
states-system agree not to create crises that could destroy
everyone or make the world unstable. The concert of Europe
(1815 to 1848) and the superpowers' cold war and detente diplo-
macies have been based on this approach.

The tension between legal equality and actual inequality
is permanent and necessary in international relations. It is
permanent because the distribution of power among states changes
over time, but inequality among states is unavoidable. States
with less power are likely to remain dissatisfied, and so alteration
in the status quo is possible and thinkable for them. Over time
there is upward and downward mobility in the international hierarchy for particular states: some states will be at the top, some
will be in the middle, and some will be at the bottom. Military,
economic, and human resources will invariably be unequally
distributed among states. The tension is necessary because
the doctrine of sovereign equality is a theoretical defense against
the assertiveness of the strong. It can be a basis for self-help
or collective action by the weak states against the strong powers.
The doctrine of sovereign equality is not significant as a quest
to democratize international life because no one sees merit in a
world where everyone has some power but all are equally insecure.
Rather, it is significant as a theoretical base for a strong secondary power that is weak in relation to the strong power and sees
itself able to move upward in the international system.

THE SECOND SYSTEM: THE COLD WAR BETWEEN
THE UNITED STATES AND THE SOVIET UNION

Advocates of the cold war point out that a cold war is not
merely a ritual. It is a product of a fundamental disharmony
of interests between two ideological, economic, social, and military

systems. Nuclear weapons are a product of this perceived disharmony. The centralization of international power in two conflicting poles means that the Big Two are the principals in
international life. They must shape a delicate balance to keep
peace between themselves and the world; superpower peace is
world peace and international and national security are inseparable. Post-1945 international relations deal primarily with con-
flictual interstate action-reaction. The central premise and
thesis is that superpowers behave the way they do to maintain
their international position and in response to threats (primarily
from each other) in the international environment. The detente
is of a limited character because of the disharmony of interests.
The conflict is cold because a hot war could mean the end of
the world. The conflict can be managed but it cannot be resolved.

This system studies events in U.S.-USSR relations that
created and intensified the hostility between the two superpowers
after 1945. It dwells on the declaratory policies of the two international power centers, the United States' wishing to contain
communism and roll it back, and the Soviet Union's desire to
bury the capitalists, liberate the oppressed, and promote revolution. Military and diplomatic events are studied in this system
in the framework of the image of relentless ideological hostility
between two opposite economic and social systems. Foreign and
military policy is regarded as a consequence of the internal
organization and structure of the antagonistic systems. The
public enemy is the enemy in the cold war system. The enemy
is fixed. Negotiations are based on mutual mistrust and military
strength. It is a Hobbesian world in which two superpowers
are engaged in a continuous struggle. There is no alternative
to struggle. War is a continuation of politics by other means,
and politics is a continuation of war by other means. The struggle never ceases, but its methods may vary in time and space.

The prime evidence of the cold war system consists of the
national postures, the arms race, and international crises that
mark the U.S.-USSR relationship since 1945. The focus is on
the military balance, which is represented by an assessment of
quantitative, qualitative, and geographical factors as perceived
by the major antagonists.

The cold war system may be visualized as the "Z" phenomenon
(see Figure 1.1). Here communication, socialization, and struggle
occur first horizontally within the elite structure—represented
by the top side of the "Z". This is intra-elite activity. Then
communication and socialization travel from the elite vertically
downward to the public. The content of the message is shaped
and controlled by the elite—the independent managers of inter-

FIGURE 1.1

The "Z" Phenomenon in the Cold War System

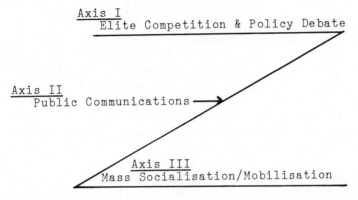

Notes: Axis I refers to intra-elite power struggle and policy debate using the presence of a foreign enemy to justify preferred solutions and policy outcomes that favor a particular group in society. The intra-elite fight is about solutions, not about precise threat definitions. The preferred solution shapes the threat definition, not vice versa.

Axis II is structurally linked to Axis I for the following reasons. First, access to media is power for the winning elite group. Second, the media are a vehicle of elite opinion and elite divisiveness. The parameters of the debate and, indeed, the definition of the issues are in the hands of in-house elite groups, and not of the media "out there." The media lack expertise to evaluate specialist information and formulate issues and choices, but the media have the technology to broadcast and magnify the desired elite messages to the external and domestic audiences. Third, elite control over the national policy agenda is power. The power to determine the agenda is the power to shape the decision. Finally, the elite control over secrecy concerning vital information is exercised in the name of national security. Information control is power that lies in the hands of in-house elite groups.

national communications. The Walter Cronkites are not able to
alter the parameters in the content of communications established
in horizontal intra-elite decisions. The non-specialist public is
half educated and it lacks the intellectual background and the
skills to question the basic parameters of the message and it
absorbs the message—written and oral—without resistance.
Once the elite is able to achieve some sort of public identification
with elite images, communications, and threat definitions, then
the extension of the message occurs horizontally through the
media, instruction, mass socialization, rumor, and face-to-face
communication. The cold war system is like the "Z" phenomenon.
The cold war ideology travels throughout the "Z". It shapes
the perception of the public enemy, the external environment,
and the means necessary to control or manage the environment.
It provides the methodology to assess external events and enemy
actions. Attitudes, events, processes, and policies reinforce
each other and revolve around the definition of the enemy's
behavior and its significance.

THE THIRD SYSTEM: COLD WAR AND DETENTE RELATIONS BETWEEN TWO OR THREE INTERNATIONAL POWERS

The third system of international relations is a combination
of cold war and detente relations between two international power
centers: the United States and the Soviet Union. The first and
third systems share similarities, but are also different.

The first similarity is that power (capacity) is unequally
distributed among states and is hierarchically organized. Post-
1945 international hierarchy has several distinguishing features.
A great and growing gap marks the distribution of military and
economic power between the superpowers and the lesser powers.
The erstwhile European international powers are either weak or
reluctant to accept the opportunities and obligations of world
power policies. Third world states have yet to transform world
politics.

The second similarity lies in a continued consensus about
the definition of power. Being a superpower means a state can
mobilize and use the resources of its territorial and extraterri-
torial (global) environments to meet its goals and still have a
reserve for future contingencies. Power is defined as the ability
to impose one's will by force if necessary and yet possess spare
power. "Superpower" means great power and great mobility.
There is a relationship between potential, mobilized, and applied
power.[1] Possession of power also creates an image of strength.

The third similarity is that decisionmaking about international security in both systems is collaborative among the great powers and is elitist from a third world viewpoint. Superpowers speak a similar (parallel, if not identical) language about world order, and advocate stability and peace through controlled use of their arms. Their behavior is interventionist and is not supportive of third world aspirations to decrease foreign intervention against weaker societies and to improve the third world's economic and social condition.

A recent study suggests a classification of interstate behavior that differentiates between the nature and form of human and state behavior and its international goals and methods. Martin Wight sees differences between "realism," "reform" or "rationalism," and the "revolutionary" schools of thought in the study of international relations. The features of each school are set out in Table 1.2. The categorization implies that each approach is mutually exclusive. This, however, is not necessarily so. When schools are examined as descriptions of processes rather than as terminal conditions, superpowers' international relations are a shift from revolutionary to realism in the case of the United States and the Soviet Union. Revolutionary international society (of any kind) is a future utopia and hence not relevant here.

Consider the following. The United States and the Soviet Union were the two main revolutionary states of the twentieth century. Their goals and methods differed. The United States entered the world scene in the twentieth century from a position and sense of prosperity and security. The Soviet Union came on the world scene from a position and sense of insecurity and economic weakness. The United States sought the growth of capitalism and a world society based on self-determination, democratic ideals, and a rejection of power politics. The Soviet approach was that of Byzantine intrigue and power politics. Today both states have transformed themselves into parochial, militaristic, ethnocentric, self-serving, and decaying empires that must deal with each other because they need each other.

Their relationship is one of limited conflict and limited cooperation. This indicates a dual transformation: from revolution to realism to reform-style conduct. International communications between the powers differ between the first and the third, and the second and the third international systems. However, the movement away from the revolutionary approach reveals continuity between the old (pre-1945) balance of power approach among great powers (except Napoleon and Hitler) in Europe and the new quest for stability through arms race, threat making, and crisis diplomacy expressed by the superpowers. In a sense,

TABLE 1.2

Martin Wight's Study of International Relations

Realism	Rationalism/Reform	Revolutionism
Pessimistic view of human nature	Duality in man	Emphasizes idea of world state
Preoccupation with power for its own sake	Optimistic/pessimistic about human nature (duality in man)	Has two meanings: universal imperialism or community of mankind
Likening of international society to the jungle—in effect, the denial of any such society	Life is not a state of savage nature; it is not a condition of competitive survival; it has goodwill and mutual help	Examples are views of Kant and Marx
Belief in the primacy of foreign policy, the aims of which should be freedom of action, self-sufficiency, and self-reliance	Political power should be pursuit of justice	Could mean a world federation of states or an international society of individuals
Opportunistic approach to international law	Aim of politics was good life; hence foreign policy took back seat to domestic politics	Premise: all men are good and perfectable
Belief in the immanence and inevitability of war and a penchant for ruthlessness in its conduct	Harmony is goal of foreign policy	Includes revolutionary war doctrine (Islam, Marxism) in name of higher principle
Exploitation of "barbarians" (that is, those of an alien culture)	To achieve harmony, vital interests should be minimized	
In the realm of ethics, justification by necessity and justification by success	War was breakdown of politics	
	"Barbarians" should be under trusteeship	

Source: Brian Porter, "Patterns of Thought and Practice: Martin Wight's International Theory," in M. Donelan, ed., The Reason of States (London: George Allen, 1978), Chapter 3.

international relations of the third system as practiced by the superpowers reveal an old mode of behavior: namely, the superpowers seek international stability and regime formation in terms of great power values and interests. To devise and maintain this system it is necessary not to equalize power, but to seek stability at the top of the international hierarchy with inequality below. Inequality below is necessary to preserve the centrality of the top in political, military, economic, and intellectual-cultural power and communications.

Contemporary China's behavior also confirms the shift away from the revolutionary approach to power and international change. Initially, Maoist China appeared on the world stage as a revolutionary state and society. It claimed to oppose super-power hegemony and imperialism. China was the countryside that was going to liberate the city represented by modern indus-trial empires. China was going to be the anticapitalist spark of world revolution that would liberate the human spirit. How-ever, rhetoric is not principle and "principled" talk can be opportunism. Before his victory in China in 1949, Mao went on record seeking a deal with U.S. capitalism. According to U.S. foreign service officer John Service, Mao told him in Yenan on August 23, 1944:

> China must industrialize. This can be done—in China—only by free enterprise and with the aid of foreign capital. Chinese and American interests are correlated and similar. They fit together, eco-nomically and politically. We can and must work together.
>
> The United States would find us more coopera-tive than the Kuomintang. We will not be afraid of democratic American influence—we will welcome it. We have no silly ideas of taking only Western mechanical techniques. . . .
>
> America does not need to fear that we will not be cooperative. We must cooperate and we must have American help. This is why it is so important to us Communists to know what you Americans are thinking and planning. We cannot risk crossing you—cannot risk any conflict with you.[2]

This attitude set the stage for the Mao-Nixon handshake in 1972. Yet our images of U.S.-Chinese relations in the past are made of events like the spurning of Premier Chou en-Lai by John Foster Dulles in Bandung, the military encounter in

Korea, the war of words between the two elites, and so on.[3] Historically, such encounters are footnotes that obscure a hidden process. Bureaucratic politics in Peking and Washington have worked to develop a tangible relationship along lines sought by Mao in 1944. Today China seeks Western capital and technology. With its entry into the United Nations, it seeks the opportunity, obligation, and parliamentary experience to engage in international power politics. The East—first Moscow and then Peking— looks more and more toward the West; there is hardly an East-West issue that cannot be negotiated, given the time and the will. Even when issues cannot be brought to maturity by formal agreement, they can be, and are, defined. Expectations can be, and are, refined to provide for manageable encounters with external enemies. Parallel but structured expectations between public enemies make formal agreement unnecessary. This process of structured and stable parallelism is accompanied by a cold war song-and-dance act. It is the new name of international power politics. Practitioners in Washington, Moscow, and Peking play it well.

These similarities between the first and third systems suggest that cold war and detente should be examined as two sides of the same coin rather than as opposites. The alleged disharmony of interests among the superpowers and China is not the real issue in their behavior and relationship. Disharmony exists but it is devoid of significance. It neither helps explain nor predict the factors and consequences of the behavior of these powers. When the superpower armies met for the first time in international history in Europe in the mid 1940s they did not fight each other. They made a deal to work out a relationship—however troubled that would be. Soviet and U.S. security establishments have clashed in various gray conflict zones in the peripheries—beyond regions where their central interests are involved. A cold war/detente system has emerged between the two international actors. The significance of this system is conceptualized in Table 1.3.

The war system (first column) emphasizes the application of military power to win. The capacity to mobilize power and to possess potential power is also related to the notion of applying power to win. It means that war fighting, not simply threat making, is the major policy instrument. The war system is excluded because a superpower war would probably mean global destruction, and this is not in the interest of either superpower. The peace system (third column) implies the emergence of non-coercive international social relations. Because of the disharmony of interests between the United States and the Soviet Union,

TABLE 1.3

The Superpowers' Cold War and Detente System Compared to the War System and the Peace System

Attributes of the War System	Attributes of the Cold War and Detente System	Attributes of the Peace System
1. Fighting general war is necessary to preserve international stability and the security of the great powers	1. General war is usually avoided by the major powers because of the fear of a breakdown of the international system	1. Pacifism and social harmony should be the basis of international relations
2. Military victory is necessary and possible in the system of states	2. Because of widespread hostility among states, a system of peace—defined as the development of noncoercive international relationships—is not possible in the foreseeable future	2. The use of force, and the threatened use of force, breeds mistrust and hostility among states and the peoples
3. There is constant, non-negotiable struggle in world politics. The world today is Hobbesian and it is unlikely to change. The quest for power cannot be reformed and winning is important	3. While competition is the basis of international relations today, the competition is negotiable and common interests can be worked out between competing states	3. Wars settle nothing in terms of the organization and distribution of world power; wars are costly and wasteful in economic and human terms
	4. Arms racing is necessary to freeze strategic conflict, as is the presence of nuclear arms. Frozen conflict is better than anarchical conflict	
	5. Military-technological development is essential to support arms racing	
	6. Because of the existence of world-wide mistrust, it is necessary to be vigilant against domestic and external enemies	
	7. Constant communication between enemies is essential to avoid an accidental war	

(continued)

Table 1.3 (continued)

Attributes of the War System	Attributes of the Cold War and Detente System	Attributes of the Peace System
4. Recurrent and constant arms racing—to mobilize and to increase military strength—usually leads to war; war preparation usually leads to use of violence to settle disputes between states	8. Brinkmanship and limited wars are tolerable militarily and politically as long as general war and system-breakdown are avoided 9. A strategy of continuous communication of military threat by the superpowers into the world environment is essential as a substitute to war-fighting, and is essential to the superpowers' management of power relations	4. A sense of world community should be developed to foster peace. Mankind, the individual, and humanitarianism ought to be the basic units of behavior in international life

Source: Compiled by the author.

16

this system is excluded by definition. So the cold war/detente system (second column) is the only real alternative. It is the logical outcome of a number of factors: two international poles of power have emerged, and these poles manage international communications; with the introduction of atomic weapons into military and diplomatic strategy, a war is no longer winable; finally, the military-industrial complex (MIC) in the United States and Soviet Union has created an organizational impact on the decisionmaking process.[4] National goal making depends on organizational interests, and subnational factors and considerations are the primary inputs in interstate relations. The MIC in different societies means that interstate relations are expressions of parallel, culture-bound, and self-serving national strategy organizations. The consequences of the core values of the two major military-industrial societies are noted in Table 1.4.

Whereas the image of superpower relations is that of unremitting hostility, the reality is that of public competitiveness and private collaboration between the superpowers. Differences do exist between the United States and the Soviet Union, but they are about details, not approach. These differences center on who gets what and why and when, and whether their code of international conduct has been broken. Both accept the necessity to satisfy each other's interests, and both claim a right to intervene abroad in defense of their interests. Each offers an elaborate doctrinal defense for its interventions.[5] Even when Soviet and U.S. definitions vary, the inseparable link between national and international security is explicit in their statements. They see themselves as being responsible for securing a system of international peace and security, but on their own terms. They are united in this attitude in relation to the lesser states.

For instance, the United States complains about Soviet military intervention and expansionism abroad. However, the United States itself is a firm believer in intervention—when it suits its purpose.[6] The methods vary but the goals are the same. The United States speaks about democracy and freedom. Yet it has a record of dealing pragmatically with, and occasionally of building up or creating, autocratic and dictatorial regimes.[7] Table 1.5 lists U.S. military allies abroad, and a majority of these are repressive regimes. The United States speaks about the importance of helping people remain free. Yet it did not lift a finger when the Soviet military overran the Baltic states and East Europe in the aftermath of World War II. It should also be noted that there is oppression in the United States itself.

TABLE 1.4

Cold War/Detente System

Public U.S. Core Values	External Behavior of U.S./USSR	Public USSR Core Values
Soviet Union is the main enemy	Defense and foreign policy are expressions of these core values. The U.S./USSR "deal" is to continue arms racing and arms control talks.	U.S. is main enemy
Communism is expansionist unless checked		Capitalism is expansionist unless checked
Capitalism is better than socialism/communism		Communism is better than capitalism
International agreements cannot depend on political trust; they must be verifiable	Continuous technological competition and higher military expenditures are constants in the policy process: that is, whether or not an agreement is reached, whether the relationship is that of cold war or detente, military technology and expenditures have grown in the United States and Soviet Union.	International agreements should rely on political trust and socialist strength
To negotiate, one needs bargaining chips; negotiations must be from a position of strength		To negotiate, one must have strength
National interest is more important than individual interest	The MICs in these countries interact with each other no matter what happens	National interest is more important than individual interest
Individualism and capitalism depend on a strong defense		Individuals express themselves through socialism and a strong national defense

18

TABLE 1.5

Bilateral and Formal U.S. Military Commitments Abroad

Region and Country	Type of Commitment	Type of Regime
Western Europe		
Multilateral:		
North Atlantic Treaty established NATO in 1949. This treaty was signed by Belgium, Britain, Canada, Denmark, France, Iceland, Italy, Luxembourg, the Netherlands, Norway, Portugal, and the U.S.A. Greece and Turkey joined in 1952. The Federal Republic of Germany joined in 1955	Members are to provide all assistance in case of "armed aggression in Europe"	Most NATO members have democratic governments. However, Portugal, Greece, and Turkey have had authoritarian or military regimes in the past
Bilateral:		
Iceland	Stationing of U.S. forces in these countries, and use of bases and/or facilities by the U.S.A.	As noted above
Italy		
Norway		
Portugal		
Turkey		

(continued)

Table 1.5 (continued)

Region and Country	Type of Commitment	Type of Regime
Spain	As noted above	Originally fascist; now a constitutional monarchy that seeks constitutional and democratic change
Middle East:		
Iran (up to 1979)	Military sales and grants.	Most regimes are authoritarian. Exceptions are Egypt and Israel and Kuwait. The political system of several countries in the region is undergoing change
Egypt	"	
Israel	"	
Jordan	"	
Kuwait	"	
Lebanon	"	
Morocco	"	
Saudi Arabia	"	
Sudan	"	
Tunisia	"	
Oman	Military aid as well as	
Bahrein	use of facilities by U.S. forces in Oman and Bahrein	
Sub-Sahara Africa:		
Ethiopia	Mutual defense and assistance agreements. Many of these were negotiated in the last two decades	Most regimes are authoritarian and furthermore, face problems of regime-instability
Ghana		
Kenya		
Liberia		

Mali
Niger
Senegal
Zaire
Somalia

and are inactive or suspended. Agreements with Kenya and Somalia are active and provide for U.S. access to local military facilities

Asia

Multilateral:
ANZUS (Australia, New Zealand, and the U.S.A.), 1951

Members agree to act "to meet the common danger" in the event of an attack on territories, armed forces, and public vessels in the Pacific

All are democracies

Manila Pact and SEATO Treaty, 1954, involved military cooperation between U.S.A., France, Australia, New Zealand, Thailand, Philippines, Pakistan, and the United Kingdom. The Pact is still in force but SEATO (the organization set up to implement it) was disbanded in 1977 and Pakistan and France have withdrawn from the Pact

The Pact calls for action to meet the danger of armed aggression, and provides for consultation in case of threat to territory, sovereignty, and political independence of any party

Of the Asian members of the Pact and SEATO, Pakistan and the Philippines are authoritarian regimes and Thailand is a benevolent monarchy with strong participation of the Thai military in political and civil affairs

(continued)

Table 1.5 (continued)

Region and Country	Type of Commitment	Type of Regime
Bilateral:		
Japan	Mutual military coopera-tion and security arrange-ment; U.S. bases rights	Democracy
Republic of Korea	Same as above	Authoritarian military regime
Philippines	Same as above	Authoritarian regime
Australia	U.S. communications facilities and access to refuelling facilities	Democracy
Thailand	Military aid	Benevolent monarchy with strong participation of Thai military in civil-political affairs
Taiwan	Mutual cooperation and security arrangements lapsed in 1980 but arms supply and production arrangements continue	Authoritarian regime
Indonesia	Military aid on credit and grant	Military regime that is authoritarian with a benevolent face
Malaysia	Military aid on credit and grant	Seeks development as a multi-racial society
Diego Garcia (1965-)	U.S./U.K. base with com-munications and air/naval support facilities	Mauritius claims Diego Garcia but the U.S. has a 50-year lease

22

South America

Multilateral:

Act of Chapultepec, 1945, was signed by Argentina, Bolivia, Brazil, Chile, Colombia, Costa Rica, Cuba, Dominican Republic, Ecuador, Guatemala, Haiti, Honduras, Mexico, Nicaragua, Panama, Paraguay, Peru, U.S.A., Uruguay, and Venezuela	In case of aggression, or threatened aggression across their boundaries the parties would consult each other to prepare a response	With some exceptions most of the regimes are authoritarian
Inter-American treaty of Reciprocal Assistance (Rio Treaty), 1947, includes all members of the Act of Chapultepec except Ecuador and Nicaragua. Cuba withdrew in 1960	Parties are constrained to seek peaceful settlement of intra-regional disputes and to seek collective self-defense against external attack	See comment above
Charter of Organization of American States (OAS), 1948, is based on the Rio Treaty and includes Barbados, El Salvador, Grenada, Jamaica, Trinidad, and Tobago. In 1962 OAS excluded Cuba but in 1975 OAS normalized relations with Cuba	An Inter-American Defence Board was formed to coordinate planning	See comment above

Table 1.5 (continued)

Region and Country	Type of Commitment	Type of Regime
Bilateral:		
The U.S.A. has numerous bilateral military sales arrangements with most countries in the region		
In 1903 the Panama Canal Zone was established. It was re-negotiated in 1977-79	40% of the former Canal Zone is to remain under U.S. control till 1999 when sovereignty will return to Panama	Panama has a military regime
Guantanamo Bay, Cuba	U.S. has had complete control since 1934	

Source: First and second columns are compiled by the author from The Military Balance 1981-82, The International Institute for Strategic Studies, London, pp. 22, 40, 47, 60, 76, and 91-92. The table does not include data on U.S. military sales and grants overseas. Third column reflects the author's judgment and not that of the IISS, London.

These characteristics of U.S. conduct lead the weak states (particularly in the third world) to make the harsh observation that the United States does not have clean hands. No super-power does.

The most significant point about the third system is neither the emergence of two competitive international power centers nor the introduction of nuclear weapons into interstate relations. Rather, the most significant change is that the cold war and detente system has emerged and has transformed the policy process. It has created a circular and mutually reinforcing relationship between military-corporate-intellectual organizations of the state (and society) and conflict management. The trans-formation of policy process and society lies in the emergence of competitive, bureaucratized, social, entrenched, growing, and internationally significant elite networks. They enjoy access to domestic and international communication channels and operate from a perspective of strategic ethnocentricism and culture-bound thinking. Because of their growing presence, domestic debates and power struggles are hard to settle. The cold war and detente system faces competition at home and abroad from constituencies that favor more social and less military expendi-tures.[8] Such see-saw battles are inconclusive. They cannot arrest the growth of the military-corporate-intellectual dimen-sions of the cold war and detente approach to foreign and domestic policy.

Cold war/detente international relations are not mainly a study of competitive interstate communications. The new phe-nomenon should be studied as competitive, foreign-linked, domestic factionalism (see Figure 1.2). These domestically based and internationally significant competitive factions control and manipulate select domestic and international communications channels; they define and redefine public issues. They are able to do so because they have a monopoly over the latest infor-mation. Through secrecy, they are able to control the flow of information to their constituents. These competitive subnational units are the basic international units, not the nation-states. The state system is merely the cover, the form, in which these real power centers function. The territorial state is the base of operation for these centers of decision and international influ-ence.

The cold war/detente system is an international system not only because moves in the United States affect policies in the Soviet Union and vice versa. It is also an international system because the pattern of relationship between military, political, industrial, and social organizations of a peacetime,

FIGURE 1.2A

The Galtung Model (Modified)

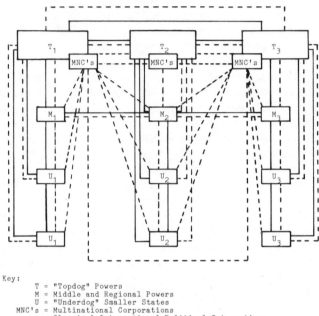

Key:

```
      T = "Topdog" Powers
      M = Middle and Regional Powers
      U = "Underdog" Smaller States
MNC's = Multinational Corporations
        = Classical International Political Interactions
------- = Transnational Interactions
```

Note: This model fails to identify the impact of competition in the post-1945 international system. Competition is horizontal (between topdog powers), vertical (between topdogs and middle/ regional powers, and between topdogs and underdogs), and finally between middle dogs and underdogs. If the impact of competition between, say, the topdogs and the middle powers is empirically examined in select case studies, it would probably demonstrate that for the topdogs, gaps are emerging between potential power, mobilized power, and applied power that yields desired outcomes.

Source: Marshall R. Singer, "The Foreign Policies of Small Developing States," in J. N. Rosenau et al., eds., World Politics (New York: Free Press, 1976), p. 275.

FIGURE 1.2B

The Structure of Imperialism

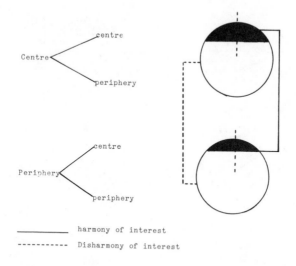

Note: Disharmony and conflict between vertical power centers is explained in the Galtung model; that is, disharmony between vertically organized Center-Periphery relations is explained.

However, Figure 1.2B fails to explore the possibility of subnationally based elite competition within the elite structures of the Center and Periphery units. In other words, intra-elite conflict points to the existence of horizontal conflict within the elite structure. Our use of the Galtung model, as modified, is represented in Figure 1.2C.

Source: Johan Galtung, "A Structural Theory of Imperialism," Journal of Peace Research 8 (1971):84.

FIGURE 1.2C

The Structure of Imperialism

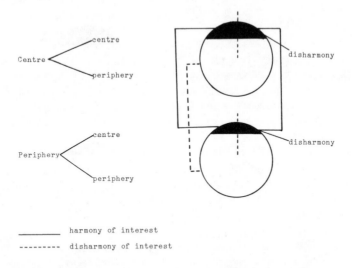

                    _____ harmony of interest
                    --------- disharmony of interest

Note: Premise of Figure 1.2C: Collaborating elites in the Center and Periphery have similar or mutually supportive interests; there is permanent intra-elite conflict in the Center and the Periphery elite structures; modern communications facilitate moves by, and into, target decision structure by competitive subnational elites; international relations is a study of competitive social elite networks and the work of these networks is facilitated by elite socialization, contact, and shared experiences; these occur through travel, correspondence, and briefings; the subnational elite structure, not the state or the nation, is the basic unit of analysis and behavior in international relations.

Figure 1.2C is a modified version of Marshall Singer's (Figure 1.2A) and Johan Galtung's (Figure 1.2B) models.

Source: Johan Galtung, "A Structural Theory of Imperialism," Journal of Peace Research 8 (1971):84.

militarized society and international conflict is now entrenched
in the domestic and international attitudes and policies of the
major powers in the post-1945 world. The pattern is now being
exported to and imported by African, Asian, and Latin American
elite structures. The superpower cold war and detente system
is becoming global.

The system is international in a third sense. Communications (telex, telephone, electronics, and computers) play an
instrumental role in globalizing the cold war/detente system.
Foreign-linked domestic factionalism should be studied as a normal, routine activity. As noted earlier, the domestic/international
elite networks, not the nation-state, are the primary and deter-
mining units of behavior in international life. In this meaning
of the cold war/detente system, global communications facilitate
the flow of information and moves within and between the international elite networks. For example, in communications from
President Carter to Andrei Sakharov on human rights, Leonid
Brezhnev may have been the obvious audience, but right-wing
hard-liners at home may have been the real audience. When
National Security Assistant Brzezinski communicated publicly
with his "like-minded" opposite number in Peking, the obvious
target was the Soviet Union, but the real target, the hidden
agenda, could be to signal President Carter to slow detente and
make the cold war colder. In such cases the purpose of international communications is not to modify enemy behavior. It is
to reinforce the behavior of the membership of one's own international elite network, and to widen that membership. International communications, or communications aired before an
international audience, are not meant to settle interstate disputes.
They are meant to reinforce the domestic and international network of one's own constituency.

In the third system of international relations, the superpowers have created a new mode of organizational behavior that
structurally links the cold war with detente. The linkage is
expressed in the creation of permanent national security systems
in the United States and the Soviet Union. The national security
system defines the threats, allocates resources, and formulates
regimes to cope with threats and uncertainties. Before 1945,
"war" and "peace" were discrete legal conditions in international
life. The new superpower-led third system substantially erodes,
if not destroys, this distinction. It has merged war and peace
into a gray zone of armed peace. This kind of peace is kept
and nourished by a policy of superpower activism that shapes
the procedures and conditions for limited conflict and crisis
diplomacy. Furthermore, the new system destroys the meaning

of national territoriality. Historically, international law and practice have emphasized territorial self-defense and it has required a respect for other states' rights. Today other states' rights to a defense is not the primary norm in the superpowers' attitudes toward lesser powers and weak states. Furthermore, national security means international security, and respecting other states' rights is no longer the primary norm for the superpowers.

In the United States and the Soviet Union, national security managers speak the language of international security and internationalism. In doing so, they are in effect seeking a mandate to extend their power into the international arena. Thus construed, for the superpowers internationalism means nationalism extended beyond the territorial frontier. It is meant to facilitate their national penetration of the international environment, not vice versa. This behavior does not reveal a willingness by superpowers to make real sacrifices of their national interests.

THE FOURTH SYSTEM

The third system partially explains the fundamental change in post-1945 international relations. To complete the picture of international change, we turn briefly to a discussion of the fourth system, which is represented by the rise of the South in the world since 1945.

The literature usually stresses the importance of multinational corporations (MNC) as new primary nonstate actors in the twentieth century.[9] However, the appearance of MNCs is only a formal change in the organization charts. It simply underlines the fact that organizations in the public and private sectors became bigger and centralized to achieve economy of scale. This is the obvious point about contemporary organizations. But the more significant point is that government bureaucracies, and particularly military bureaucracies, now organize themselves along corporate lines.[10] The military behaves like a corporation— it manages the arms trade and enhances its power position and prosperity. War fighting and threat making are its obvious but less significant functions. Organizing the production lines is its real task, the sale of U.S. AWACS to Saudi Arabia has less to do with Saudi security and more to do with the desire to organize the production line of AWACS. To increase the penetrativeness of the corporate organization (be it the government or the MNC or the military) into its strategic environment, it is necessary to centralize control and to define the issues.

Today, third parties are worth study as independents, not as collaborators of the superpowers. In a world with uneven power distribution, the superpowers still monopolize the means of coercion. They still have an enormous capacity to mobilize domestic and international resources, although they are being forced to pay a higher economic and diplomatic price. They have better means to acquire intelligence and they have continuous access to international communications. They determine the parameters of international security debates, and their doctrines and educational materials socialize the public. The emergence of third parties is significant precisely because the condition, the context, is one of unequal distribution of military, economic, and intellectual resources. Because the uneven distribution is skewed in favor of the superpowers, the loss of superpower control over international security affairs—to begin with "over" threat definition or "issue definition"—is all the more significant. Third party emergence in the contemporary international system is remarkable because of (and despite) inequality among states. Chapter 2 addresses this phenomenon and its implications for the 1980s.

NOTES

1. W. T. R. Fox, The Super-powers (New York: Harcourt, Brace, 1944); and S. J. Rosen and W. S. Jones, The Logic of International Relations, 3d ed. (Cambridge, Mass.: Winthrop, 1980), p. 237.
2. John S. Service, The Amerasia Papers (Berkeley: University of California Press, 1971).
3. J. G. Stoessinger, Nations in Darkness, 3d ed. (New York: Random House, 1978), Chapters 2-7 for an overview.
4. K. E. Boulding, ed., Peace and the War Industry, 2d ed. (New Brunswick, N.J.: Transactions Books, 1973); R. J. Barnet, Roots of War (New York: Atheneum, 1972); C. R. Beitz and T. Herman, eds., Peace and War (San Francisco: W. H. Freeman, 1973), particularly section 7; "Military Industrial Complex—Russian Style," Fortune, August 1, 1969, pp. 84-87, 122-26.
5. T. M. Franck and E. Weisband, World Politics: Verbal Strategy Among the Superpowers (New York: Oxford University Press, 1971).
6. M. Gurtov, The United States Against the Third World: Antinationalism and Intervention (New York: Praeger, 1974). For CIA's role, see in particular P. Agee, Inside the Company:

CIA Diary (London: Allen Lane, 1975), and Dirty Work: The CIA in Western Europe, ed. P. Agee and L. Wolf (Secaucus, N.Y.: Lyle Stuart, 1978); and J. Stockwell, In Search of Enemies: A CIA Story (New York: Norton, 1978).

7. For example, K. Roosevelt, Countercoup: The Struggle for the Control of Iran (New York: McGraw-Hill, 1979).

8. R. L. Sivard, World Military and Social Expenditures, annual, World Priorities, Leesburg, Virginia.

9. The literature on MNCs is extensive. For a general overview see C. Tugendhat, The Multinationals (Markham, Ontario: Penguin, 1971, 1973); Peter R. Odell, Oil and World Power (New York: Penguin, 1979).

10. This point is made in Boulding, op. cit., p. 17.

2

Middle Powers and Regional Powers in the Third World Today

The subject of middle powers is both old and new. It is old in the sense that middle powers existed in ancient international systems. For example, Evan Luard discusses bipolarity, great power struggles, balancing powers, and "middle-sized states" in Greek international relations (480-350 B.C.).[1] Hierarchy, alliances, wars, and great powers constituted the context in which middle-sized states existed. They were objects of great power attention and existed as potential participants. Given this, the questions to consider are: How widespread was the presence of middle-sized states in ancient international relations? Did size mean power or was size only one ingredient of power? Were middle-sized states upwardly mobile in ancient international systems? Did middle-sized states have influence in a bipolar system, in a system of competing alliances, in a system of great power struggle, and did the nature of bipolarity (tight, loose) make a difference to middle powers' influence? Did middle-sized states have influence because of the presence of great power competition, war, struggle, and alliances? Are these attributes of international systems the prerequisites or the preconditions for influence by middle-sized states? If a middle-sized state is able to achieve some autonomy for itself from the great powers, is the achievement of autonomy rather than possession of middle size (or possession of medium power in the scale of international hierarchy) the true essence of a middle power? According to Luard:

There was a great tendency for the weak to combine against the strong and for the most powerful state

eventually to overreach itself, usually by excessively
dominating its allies.[2]

Is this observation of generalized significance in relation to past
and present international relations? If so, does it represent
the setting in which middle-sized states can achieve influence,
and is influence something more than that of small states and
something less than that of great powers?

Whereas the "old" concept recognizes the possibility of
the presence of middle-sized states, the twentieth-century
concept reveals a hardening of categories. This hardening
reveals the development of a scholarly and policy attitude against
the middle-power concept, in the sense that it is qualitatively
different than a superpower, a great power, or a small state.
In the "new" concept, international power relations are hierarchically organized into two categories: great powers and small
states. Consider the following samples of scholarly work wherein
the view is that the great powers usually dominate and the small
states are usually subordinate.

The classic view is outlined by Harold Nicolson:

> It was assumed that the Great Powers were greater
> than the Small Powers, since they possessed a more
> extended range of interests, wider responsibilities,
> and, above all, more money and more guns. The
> Small Powers were graded in importance according
> to their military resources, their strategic position,
> their value as markets or sources of raw materials,
> and their relations to the Balance of Power.[3]

A more "modern" view is that of Michael Brecher. The
great power/small power focus is broadened to include superpowers and middle powers, but "behavior" is seen in terms of
the "power scale".

> In the contemporary international system states can
> be plotted along a continuum of capacity to influence
> the behavior of other actors and the dynamics of
> the system as a whole. There are four broad cate-
> gories: superpowers, great powers, middle powers,
> and small powers. The place of any state in the
> power scale depends on a combination of four
> components—size, populations, military capability
> and economic capability, the last two, especially
> at the point in time of status designation.

According to Brecher, the superpowers possess all four components, and this gives them a "unique veto" over the survival of the system and all its members. The great powers possess any three of the four, and so on. [4]

A small power is defined as one that is unable to pursue its interests unaided. [5]

R. L. Rothstein sees international relations as a study in great power-small state relations. According to him, small powers are not simply weaker great powers; there is a psychological as well as a material distinction between great and small powers:

> The latter earn their titles not only by being weak, but by recognizing the implications of that condition. Thus, a Small Power is a state which recognizes that it cannot obtain security primarily by use of its own capabilities, and that it must rely fundamentally on the aid of other states, institutions, processes or developments to do so. . . . the small power's belief in its ability to rely on its own means must also be recognised by the other states involved in international politics. [6]

Rothstein notes the existence of the middle power concept, but rejects its usage. A great power is defined in terms of its systemic interests and in terms of the weakness of a small state. The middle power notion is not dealt with for two interesting reasons: first, because "it would complicate an already complicated situation." The second reason is serious and merits a long quote:

> It is worth noting that the category itself is of relatively recent derivation. It did not exist before 1919, and the record since then has been ambiguous. Where such states—usually self styled—do seem to exist, it is normally the result not of their own achievements but of the weakness, disappearance, or disinterestedness of neighbouring Great Powers (e.g., note Poland's situation after 1919); or because the Great Powers use their power superiority effectively and seek the political support of the most prominent uncommitted states (e.g., India in the Cold War period). A "middle range" status implies a degree of external recognition. . . . However, tangible proof of significant difference between

> Small Powers and the middle-range Powers would
> have to rest on evidence that, when threatened,
> middle-range Powers do in fact possess a wider
> range of choice than Small Powers. That evidence
> does not yet exist. Until it does, the assumption
> that the distinction is formal and peripheral, not
> substantive and central, will prevail.[7]

The implications of these "modern" definitions and attitudes may be briefly noted.

The utility of the study of middle powers/middle-sized states is repudiated on grounds of convenience or irrelevance.

Hierarchical stratification of international power is narrowed to two categories: great powers and small states.

The relevance of hierarchy in distribution of capabilities is not assessed from point of view of issue politics or specific conflict outcomes.

Even if the stratification scheme is broadened from (a) great power/small dichotomy to (b) superpowers/great powers/ regional dominant powers/middle powers/small states stratification, the existence of an hierarchically arranged world system is assumed even in circumstances where the superpowers are helpless giants.

The power ranking in the international system further assumes rank concordance in interstate behavior. This becomes clear in works by Galtung, Marshall Singer, and M. P. Sullivan. According to this view, higher rank in one dimension of power means higher rank in other dimensions of power.

These definitions deny the prospect of, or fail to examine the possibility of, downward mobility of superpowers and great powers (for example, the United Kingdom from the 1940s to the 1950s and thereafter) and the upward mobility of lesser powers. ("Lesser powers" refers to middle powers, not small states.)

The attribution of dominance to the great powers in the international system and of subordination to the weak/lesser powers is definitional; it is not demonstrated empirically.

Generally, there is a failure to understand the constraints on the employment of power (capability) created by the possession of power. Constraints exist: because of the reactions that such power creates in the thinking and behavior of the weaker members of the international system; because of the effect of these reactions on the holders of great power; and because holders of high power make mistakes or are unwilling to take risks.

This brief review of the literature indicates that "old" thinking is supportive of the concept of middle powers but the "new" is not. This chapter argues that middle powers are of growing significance in the post-1945 era, in the context of the evolution of the international system since 1945.

The study of middle powers in the world today makes sense in the context of major changes. The meaning of power has changed because power "possessed" is not necessarily power "applied." A distinction should be made between nonusable power and power defined as a usable asset, or power that can be mobilized, and that itself can mobilize the environment. The assessment of power depends essentially on the context of world power relations, on the nature of the challenges, and on the instruments of power used to meet the specific challenges. By studying the conduct of middle powers (or regional powers, or "powers in the middle"), the emergence of a layer of middle power-superpower interactions may be fruitfully studied. This focus substantially erodes the exclusive emphasis on "superpower" and its underlying assumptions in defining the world power structure.

The point at issue is whether or not the middle powers have developed a strategy of the lesser (not small) power that successfully engages the superpower policies, and causes the superpowers to recognize the implications of constraints in the use of the "super power" they possess but that fails to make an impact through desired regime formation. The test of a middle power is that it can successfully obtain security for itself in the form of territorial defense; it can create and enforce the primary norms and institutions for regional security; and it can prevent international regime making and enforcement by the superpowers.

A middle power-superpower interaction is first and foremost a study of engagement of the stronger by the weaker. It represents an historical transformation because "engagement" is a sequel to the erstwhile one-sided "domination" of the weaker by the strong. In a sense, the engagement is between the advocacy and practices in the third and fourth systems of power politics that were outlined in Chapter 1. Whereas the third system codifies the superpower relationship and the lesser status of the South, the fourth system challenges the northern norm and policy and seeks engagement and international change through a process of militarization and nuclearization of the South accompanied by resources diplomacy. Chapter 5 discusses the meaning and methods of southern engagement of the North. Let us first review the northern assessment of the third world and middle powers.

THE NORTHERN PERSPECTIVE

Northern views usually dismiss the innovative behavior
and concepts of the South. The work of J. D. B. Miller is
being singled out here because it is typical of informed Western
thinking about the third world. Miller argued in 1966:

> The main point made in this book is that South [Third
> World] unity has neither been shown in practice nor
> is likely to reveal itself in the future. [8]

Furthermore:

> Many Third World leaders want the Third World to
> be a unit for certain purposes; the question is
> whether it ever is, and, if it is not, why not. The
> answer of this essay is that it hardly ever is, but
> that the process of trying to make it one has had
> important effects on the style and content of the
> diplomacy of Third World countries. The dominant
> element in their diplomacy in each case is, however,
> the burgeoning sense of their individual national
> interest. . . . That is, they become more and more
> like other states in their behavior. [9]

Miller dismisses anticolonialism and nonalignment as "ritual
incantation."[10] Third world regimes are unstable and inexperienced.[11] He sees "little future" for Afro-Asianism "if it is
defined as the preservation of a bond derived from common
experience of colonialism . . . it can hardly be expected to
survive the disappearance of European colonialism."[12] A distinction is made between European nationalism and third world
nationalism: European nationalism in the nineteenth century
was linguistic; Afro-Asian nationalism has been "essentially
administrative."[13]

Two major interests are postulated for a majority of third
world states in the 1970s: improvement of the economy and
maintenance of good terms with neighbors.[14] Promotion of
national defense and participation in international security
policy is downgraded: "Aid and trade seem more important than
defence; and defence, in any case, has reasserted itself as
more the basic problem of relations with one's neighbours than
that of participation in a worldwide conflict between two superpowers."[15] Two consequences are seen of the nuclear balance
and the shift from bipolarity to multipolarity. First the nuclear

balance between the United States and the Soviet Union has produced a "relatively easy international atmosphere and this gave the Third World opportunities which they might not otherwise have had."[16] Second, the shift from bipolarity to multipolarity (defined as acquisition of nuclear arms by the United Kingdom, France, and China) and the emergence of a relative balance "allows for greater emphasis upon economic relation because of less emphasis upon security."[17] The superpowers are seen as less interested in "actively coercing Third World countries":

> the idea of actively coercing Third World countries seems to have been covertly dropped by all the major powers, except perhaps China. They now prefer to exert influence in less direct ways. The threat of force was, in any case, a diminishing weapon, because of the fear that in a bipolar world the quarrel would become transferred to the two superpowers. Now that nuclear capability is more widely shared, and multipolarity steadily becomes more evident, the need for force seems to have disappeared, except where there is either a direct confrontation between major powers (in which case the threat is made only to the other power) or a confrontation at one remove, in which what is held to be a satellite of the other major power is coerced as a warning.[18]

Finally, nuclear proliferation is seen as a threat to the third world and to the nuclear balance:

> for the Third World the problem of the nuclear balance is essentially that of China. If China disturbs the balance or causes India to do so, there may be no end to the repercussions.[19]
>   If India and Egypt went nuclear, with their eyes on China and Pakistan in the one case, and Israel on the other, the potential disturbance would be great, and it could lead to a "chain reaction."[20]

TOWARD A SOUTHERN PERSPECTIVE

Miller's analysis is a misreading of third world diplomacy and security policy, as well as of the international setting in

which third world and southern international relations have
actually emerged during the 1970s, and as they are likely to
continue in the 1980s. The following is a brief review of the
major elements in the study of third world and southern international relations. The headings refer to Miller's thinking.

Third World Unity

If "unity" is defined as singleness of declaratory purpose
or as agreement, the third world has shown considerable unity
in recent decades. This is expressed by: bloc voting at the
United Nations; the common position on global negotiations by
UNCTAD states vis-à-vis the northern industrial democracies;
the unity of OPEC during the 1970s; the pressure on the superpowers by the nonalignment movement; the quest for unity by
the Islamic states; and the agreement in the United Nations in
1982 on the Law of the Sea, despite U.S. opposition and Soviet
bloc abstention.

The Third World and National Interest

As in all other states, the dominant concern of each third
world state is its own national interest. Third world states
seek industrialization like the northern states, but unlike the
superpowers, they do not seek to dominate weaker states through
military force, intervention, multinational activity, and cultural
imperialism.
Generally speaking, there are three approaches to international security and stability. The first seeks to implement
U.N. norms of collective security, limited use of force, peaceful
settlement of disputes, and arms reduction leading to eventual
disarmament. The first approach at present is mostly ideal.
The U.N. system has become an arena to communicate competing
national norms, but it has not altered the basic factors in international negotiations. The U.N.'s security role is marginal in
international relations, except peripherally in select peacekeeping
operations. (As a peacekeeper in Cyprus, for example, the
United Nations in effect froze local conflict, it did not solve it.)
Its role in the field of disarmament is mainly as producer of dis-
armament talk and as active promoter of disarmament study.
But the United Nations cannot succeed because the United
States is not interested in disarmament per se, and the Soviet
Union is interested only in talking about disarmament, not in

studying seriously the different norms and interests underlying disarmament. At best, the Soviet Union is willing to make a deal with the other superpower. This basis of negotiation means little to third parties who crave arms reduction rather than self-serving arms control for the superpowers. Both superpowers in effect take the view that disarmament means disarmament of others. In the past the United States has appeared willing to discuss disarmament issues, but this is more form than substance.

The second approach seeks international and regional security through the buildup of large military machinery, military alliances, and creation of an international military social elite network that is organized along corporate lines (neomilitarism). The central premise is that military force is required because the enemy cannot be trusted. Both superpowers feed on the image of the other as an enemy, even when they communicate daily and engage individually and collectively in crisis management. This is the main northern approach to international security of the northern world. Security means more arms; the greater the mistrust of the enemy, the greater the perceived importance of military buildup. The purpose of the buildup is to impress the enemy with one's determination or will. The relationship between usable military force and political and strategic purpose is unclear in post-1945 U.S. and Soviet military buildups, particularly those in the 1970s and early 1980s.

In comparison, in most third world states the use of force is limited by the political purpose behind the force. Force per se does not have a meaning; the military establishment does not have a life of its own as does the Pentagon or the USSR military establishment. In the North the military establishment is a big employer and a corporate manager of national material and human resources. It defines the national threats and the desired means and it is not accountable to anyone other than its own constituency. The developed military establishments can control the worldwide flow of intelligence about the threat. Third world military establishments do not have these attributes of developed northern military systems, which can manage threat definitions, the arms race, the allocation of national resources, the worldwide arms sales, and the development of a worldwide social elite network. The concept and the scope of third world military activity is constrained by limited military arms, and the military must compete with socially useful and development-oriented aims of third world societies.

The third approach to security lies in a quest for regionalism. Regionalism is measured as the development of norms and institutions that reduce the strains of superpower competition, which threatens regional stability because of possible superpower intervention in regional life. This is the approach successfully adopted by the Association for Southeast Asian Nations (ASEAN). South Asian states have tentatively started to explore this idea, as have Gulf states and South Asian states. Argentina and Brazil, two regional rivals, have begun to cooperate regionally. South/South cooperation is meant to minimize external interference and to create a setting for regional normalization by using step-by-step diplomacy and incentives. This approach is different from, if not the opposite of, coercive diplomacy. At issue is not the centrality but the definition of what constitutes "national interest." The northern approach relies heavily on the second approach for the definition of national interest. The third world and southern approach is innovative, experimental, and hopeful. It seeks to give a new meaning to "security."

Anticolonialism and Nonalignment Is Ritual Incantation

Many Western thinkers (such as Henry Kissinger and Zbigniew Brzezinski) mistakenly assume that anticolonialism has become irrelevant in the technocratic age. Nationalism is mistakenly and narrowly identified as self-determination, the implication being that nationalism is satisfied with formal independence. The dynamic utility of nationalism—as a method to mobilize subnational cleavages and competition by creating a clear public identification with unequal global power relations— is not usually stressed. Selig Harrison, a veteran Washington Post foreign correspondent, argues that

> a concept of nationalism restricted by the narrow confines of European experience is only superficially relevant to the developing countries today and is peculiarly blind to the character and power of nationalism in Asia.[21]
>
> Subnationalism, nationalism, and regionalism are all expressions of the same hunger for a reordering of world power relationships.[22]

Harrison's observations are insightful. Third world leaders define colonialism not simply in terms of the past, but in terms of contemporary neocolonialism, in terms of the impact of unequal global power relations on third world states, and in terms of the interventionist behavior and attitude of the superpowers in the North who see themselves as managers of international security.

Nonalignment is a posture that requires constant attention to the external environment; it requires the development and constant management of active communication between the South and the North. Nonalignment may also be defined as a domestic and a foreign policy compromise between capitalism and the anti-imperialism of third world states. Nonalignment may be defined as an essential doctrine that facilitates the process of nation building in a world where competitive subnationalisms and provincialism are the essence of domestic politics, and unequal power relations are the essence of world politics.

Federalism in third world countries is in essence a quest to balance centralism and statism with localism and provincialism; to develop new norms and institutions that emerge from a creative tension between centralism and localism. Federalism, as a domestic process, seeks to create active two-way communication and consciousness-raising between centralist and localist tendencies — a quest also for a normative-pragmatic balance in the ongoing two-way process.

Similarly, "internationalism" may be viewed as a quest to create, in the words of Ali A. Mazrui,[23] a "federation of cultures." The United States and Soviet Union speak of internationalism, but in essence this is a disguised superpower interest that is extended into the international sphere, where the superpowers' military strength, economic capacity, and policy norms are meant to be the guiding light of international policy. To a nonaligned country, this is colonialism or neocolonialism and domination. Nor is internationalism simply a bargain, an accommodation between the two superpowers; that would be going back to the notion of a concert of great powers and their respective spheres of influence. Internationalism means a quest for new norms that can emerge from the creative tension of norms of different societies and cultures. So defined, the quest for internationalism is the product of dissatisfaction with the present, not a yearning for the past glory of Western norms.

Just as federalism requires ambiguity to facilitate the process of norm and institution building in domestic society, the ambiguity of nonalignment is purposive and instrumental in promoting active interstate and intercultural communications. The creative tension of competitive subnationalism can produce a synthesis of nationalism; therefore, creative subnational competition can result in internal mobilization of societies, and an unfreezing of social inertia and of rigid socioeconomic structures and norms. Internal social mobilization is necessary for active reengagement of international forces. The reengagement is necessary, as is remobilization.

The engagement of traditional structures in the third world during the last three centuries by the European capitalist economy led to the development of colonialism, and to the development of center-periphery and dependency relations. Because of the past impact of Western technology and military power on eastern and southern culture and tradition, third world societies emerged with distorted socioeconomic structures and with links with the international environment. This setting created social inertia, social immobility, and frozen internal economic and social cleavages that could be managed only with the aid of an international (extra-regional) power or a patron.

To achieve a reengagement of the North by the South, a remobilization of the South is necessary. The presence of unequal global power relations and external enemies facilitates the redefinition of issues and the desired responses. Nonalignment therefore is alive insofar as it has succeeded in creating a domestic consciousness about the implications of unequal power relations (and hence the need for development). The new consciousness and development are instrumental in reengaging the North in terms that help the South. To the extent that instability creates fluidity, it creates a setting for reengagement and a reordering of existing relations. This is the new power in world politics: the power to cause rethinking and reordering of frozen power relations. The subnationalist actors in this dynamic process are cultural (such as linguistic, ethnic, and religious units in crises in the Middle East, South Asia, Southeast Asia, and Africa) and not simply administrative. The focus of their quest for change is to reorder the style of global thinking and the pattern of world power relations, including the development of regional institutions and norms concerning neighbors. To the extent that regional power relations are linked with global power relations, and to the extent that subnationalism and nationalism interact with unequal world power relations, Harrison's linkage between subnationalism, nationalism, and regionalism appears valid.

Aid and Trade Versus Defense

Most third world states see aid and trade as more important than defense, says Miller. Nonalignment stresses three themes: disarmament, improvement in terms of trade for the third world, and nonintervention.[24] The quest for disarmament is meant to reduce the attitude of reliance on military force, threats, and arms races. The advocacy of nonintervention is also intended

to reduce and eventually eliminate military intervention in interstate behavior. This advocacy is a constant element in third
world speeches in the last three decades.

In third world thinking, a fundamental reappraisal has
occurred about the role of force as both a crucial part of the
international context and as a useful instrument of state policy.
The evolution of the relationship between alignment and force
in Yugoslavia, India, and Egypt is illustrative. Yugoslavia
never renounced the use of military force as an instrument of
individual self-defense. It is sensitive to the role of force in
the international environment, primarily in the context of its
relations with the Soviet Union. India downplayed the role of
force up to 1962. Thereafter, the presence of Indian military
force has been a precondition for Indian nonalignment. In
part, force has been employed by India in wars with its neighbors (Pakistan in 1948, 1965, and 1971, and China in 1962).
But since South Asian crises have always involved the superpowers (directly or indirectly), the crises were not merely
quarrels between neighbors. Egypt under Sadat also recognized
the utility of initiating force in 1973.

These examples can be augmented by data about the militarization of the third world. According to UNESCO data, since
the 1960s one-third of the world's arms trade involved developing
countries, one-third involved oil-producing states (particularly
in the Middle East), and one-third involved the industrialized
world. Of course, the main arms suppliers are in the North.[25]
The theme of third world militarization can be augmented further
by data about the growing incidence of global conflict in the
South—and a shift away from the North. Table 2.1 provides an
overview. If information about the gradual nuclearization of
the third world—in India, Pakistan, Iraq, Egypt, Israel, South
Africa, Brazil, and Argentina—is taken into account, the indicators point to the growth of the military and security constituencies in the South. These constituencies react not simply to
fear of neighbors, but also to unequal global power relations.
The concerns are vertical, not simply horizontal.

A hallmark of third world diplomacy is attentiveness to the
implications of superpowers' behavior. In the post-1945 world,
superpower behavior fell into two phases. The first phase was
that of bipolarity, cold war, mistrust, misunderstanding, and
crises. This lasted until the early 1950s. After Stalin's death,
bipolarity became bipolar cooperation; cold war became detente.
Mistrust between the United States and the Soviet Union continued, but then all foreign policy and security policy is based
on secrecy and mistrust (this is a normal attribute of bureau-

TABLE 2.1

Incidence of Conflicts in the South (List of Wars, 1945-1976)

Site	Period	Type	Foreign Participation*
Greece	1944-45	A/1	DC
Algeria	1945	A/1	DC
Indonesia	1945-49	A/1	DC
Spain	1945-48	A/2	
Indochina	1946-54	A/1	DC
Greece	1946-49	A/1	DC
India (religious)	1946-47	B/2	
Philippines	1946-54	A/1	DC
China	1946-49	A/2	
Iran	1946	B/2	
Paraguay	1947	A/1	DC
Madagascar	1947-48	A/1	DC
India (Hyderabad, Telangana)	1947-48	A/2	
India—Pakistan (Kashmir)	1947-48	C/1	DC
Yemen	1948	B/2	
Costa Rica	1948	A/2	
Burma	1948-	A/2	
Colombia	1948-53	A/2	
Israel-Arab countries	1948-49	C/1	DC
Malaysia	1948-59	A/1	DC
Bolivia	1949	A/2	
Korea	1950-53	C/1	DC, S, TW
Puerto Rico	1950	A/1	DC
Egypt	1951-52	A/1	DC
Tunisia	1952-54	A/1	DC
Bolivia	1952	A/2	
Kenya	1952-56	A/1	DC
Morocco	1952-56	A/1	DC
Guatemala	1954	A/1	DC
Colombia	1954-57	A/2	
Algeria	1954-62	A/1	DC
China (Islands)	1955	B/1	DC
Costa Rica—Nicaragua	1955	C/1	DC
Cyprus	1955-59	A/1	DC
Cameroon	1955-63	A/1	DC

Site	Period	Type	Foreign Participation*
South Vietnam	1955-75	A/1	DC, TW
Oman	1955-63	A/1	DC
India (Nagas)	1956-64	B/2	
Hungary	1956	A/1	S
Israel—Egypt (Suez)	1956	C/1	DC
Cuba	1956-59	A/2	
Aden, Yemen	1956-58	B/1	DC
Indonesia	1957-58	B-1	DC
Honduras—Nicaragua	1957	C/2	
Spanish Morocco	1957-58	A/1	DC, TW
Lebanon	1958	A/1	DC
Jordan	1958	A/1	DC
China (Quemoy)	1958	B/1	DC
Nyasaland	1959	A/1	DC
China (Tibet)	1959	B/2	
Laos	1959-62	A/1	DC, S
Dominican Republic	1959	A/2	
Paraguay	1959-60	A/2	
Zaire (Congo K)	1960-64	A/1	DC
Angola	1961-74	A/1	DC
Nepal	1961-62	A/2	
Cuba	1961	A/1	DC
Tunisia	1961	A/1	DC
Ethiopia (Eritrea)	1961-	B/2	
Iraq (Kurds)	1961-64	B/2	
Venezuela	1961-70	A/2	
India (Goa)	1961	B/1	DC
Indonesia (W. Irian)	1962	B/1	DC
Guatemala	1962-72	A/1	DC
Colombia	1962	A/1	DC
Yemen	1962-70	A/1	DC, TW
India—China	1962	C/2	
Brunei	1962	A/1	DC

(continued)

Table 2.1 (continued)

Site	Period	Type	Foreign Participation*
Guinea (Bissau)	1963-74	A/1	DC
Malaysia ('Confrontation')	1963-66	A/1	DC, TW
Algeria—Morocco	1963	C/2	
South Yemen	1963-67	A/1	DC
Dominican Republic	1963	A/2	
Somalia—Ethiopia	1963-64	C/2	
Zaire	1963-69	A/1	DC
Cyprus	1963-64	B/1	DC
Rwanda	1963-64	B/2	
Kenya--Somalia	1963-67	C/2	
Laos	1964-73	A/1	DC, S, TW
Colombia	1964-72	A/1	DC
North Vietnam	1964-68	A/1	DC
Mozambique	1964-74	A/1	DC
Iraq (Kurds)	1965-70	B/1	TW
India—Pakistan	1965	C/2	
Dominican Republic	1965	A/1	DC
Peru	1965	A/1	DC
Oman (Dhofar)	1965-	A/1	DC, TW
Sudan	1965-72	B/2	
India—Pakistan	1965	C/2	
Thailand	1965-	A/1	DC
India (Mizos)	1966-67	B/2	
Bolivia	1967	A/1	DC
Israel—Arab countries	1967	C/2	
Zaire	1967	B/1	DC
Nigeria (Biafra)	1967-70	B/2	
Zimbabwe (Rhodesia)	1967-	A/1	TW
South Yemen	1968	A/1	TW
Chad	1968-72	A/1	DC
El Salvador—Honduras	1969	C/2	
South Yemen—Saudi Arabia	1969	C/2	
Gr. Britain (N. Ireland)	1969-	B/2	
Cambodia	1970-75	A/1	DC, S, TW
Sudan	1970	A/2	

(continued)

Site	Period	Type	Foreign Participation*
Philippines	1970-76	B/2	
Jordan	1970	B/2	
Guinea	1970	A/1	DC
Pakistan (Bangla Desh)	1971	B/1	TW
Sri Lanka	1971	A/2	
Jordan	1971	B/2	
North Vietnam	1972-73	A/1	DC
Burundi	1972	B/2	
Uganda—Tanzania	1972	C/2	
Yemen—South Yemen	1972	C/2	
Israel--Arab countries	1973	C/1	TW
Iraq (Kurds)	1974-75	B/2	
Cyprus	1974	B/1	DC
Lebanon	1975-76	B/1	TW
East Timor	1975-	A/1	TW
Angola	1975-76	A/1	S, TW
West Sahara	1975-	A/1	TW

*DC = Developed capitalist country/countries; S = socialist country/countries; TW = third world country/countries.

Source: I. Kende, "Wars of Ten Years (1967-1976)," Journal of Peace Research, No. 3, 15 (1978):239-41.

cratic behavior). Finally, crises become crisis management.
In the second phase—the phase since the late 1950s to the
present—despite the ups and downs of detente, the cold war
relationship has become a cooperative relationship in which the
two superpowers know that neither side can pursue its interests
unaided. Despite many overt disputes between the superpowers,
such as over Afghanistan, they stand united over one major
point: there are but two principals in international relations,
and they have more interests that unite them than divide them
in relation to third party challenges from the European states,
China, and Japan. Their public competitiveness is posturing
that is meant to manage hidden internal enemies rather than
external public enemies.

Bipolarity of the latter phase of superpower relations created
a sense of change because it created the danger of a superpower
concert against third parties. When the superpowers share
common interests, such as over regional conflict management in
the Middle East and South and Southeast Asia, in nuclear proliferation control, in the Law of the Sea and in assuming a
primary responsibility for maintaining their position in the high
seas, then the "easy atmosphere" of the superpower detente is
actually a danger to the lesser powers.

There is no real shift from bipolarity to multipolarity. The
image of multipolarity is superficial; it rests on the formal status
of five nuclear weapon states. But this image is misleading because, politically and strategically, the world power relations
are bipolar and nuclear weapons are frozen assets. The point
is that superpowers have nuclear weapons and not that all
holders of nuclear weapons are superpowers.

MIDDLE POWERS AND REGIONAL POWERS

Major third world states are secondary international powers
(or middle powers) and primary regional powers. These states
claim an ability to influence the formulation of norms and institutions for regional and international order, and an ability to
challenge and disrupt the existing regional and international
order. The international powers cannot act in isolation of the
middle and regional powers in developing viable international
regimes and in pursuing their own vital interests. Whether
international relations is defined as "exchange" or as "intervention," the cooperation of middle and regional powers is necessary
in the superpowers' strategy. Without a strategy and political
purpose that can generate common interest and obligations among

allies, the dispropriate possession of power by the superpowers will fail to yield influence—defined as "movement" in a strategic situation—in the right direction for the superpower concerned.

The claim of the middle or regional power rests on the existence of impact in the aforesaid ways. Middle powers are also regional powers in the third world, but conceptually the definitions of influence proceed from two different angles. A middle power has influence in relation to the primary international powers. A regional power, on the other hand, has influence first, in relation to a definable geographical and political security sphere; and second, in terms of the relationship between that regional sphere or "regional subsystem" and the international system. Both definitions beg a question about the definition of "international power" and about the limits of the influence of the superpowers insofar as there are barriers—self-inflicted or inflicted by others—against the free flow of the power of the superpowers.

The issue emerges clearly when the constraints in the use of certain kinds of power are discussed—as is the case with massive nuclear power. It is an image builder and a threat only as long as the enemy chooses to be frightened by it. Asian, African, and South American international relations are hardly ever responsive to the fear of Soviet and U.S. nuclear arms. The role of nuclear arms in shaping or controlling the different parameters of international and regional power relations should therefore be cut to size and discounted in the daily communications among competitive states and cultures.

The issue also emerges clearly when a relationship between security and cultural policy is seen as an essential element in regional international relations. Crises in Africa, Southwest Asia, South Asia, the Middle East, and Southeast Asia have all included a heavy focus on ethnicity and culture in strategic disputes. On the one hand, regional, ethnic, racial, cultural, and religious disputes have divided neighbors (such as India and Pakistan, Israel and Arab states, Iraq and Iran, Ethiopia and Somalia); but on the other hand, they have also created a consciousness about the encounter between Western technology and market economy and third world culture and nationalism. The Western impact created a sense of humiliation in third world social psychology.[26] As such, the relationship between strategy and culture has emerged in the study and practice of politics in the southern world today. The recent revolution in Iran is a cultural reaction to Westernization in the third world.

In the abstract, a great power or superpower is obviously stronger than a middle or a regional power, and there is no room for confusion between the two types of powers. However, when the attributes of the two powers are assessed in relation to world politics in the 1970s and the likely pattern of power in the 1980s, the significance of the obvious differences became unclear and open to debate. The following section will conceptualize the differences and indicate why ambiguity exists in terms of: the overall relationships between a superpower and the international system; the relationships between a middle or a regional power and the international system; and the relationships between middle powers and superpowers. This will be presented in terms of relationships and not in terms of a mechanical view of the distribution of military (particularly nuclear) and economic capabilities.

Martin Wight's discussion is a useful starting point because he provides an historical overview of the meanings and patterns of powers, and he is also sympathetic to the concept of a middle power. His views are, however, not free of flaws. Table 2.2 provides Wight's definitions of the two types of powers.

Overall, says Wight:

> Two kinds of minor power achieve an eminence
> which distinguishes them from the common run;
> regional great powers, and middle powers. Political
> pressures do not operate uniformly throughout the
> states-system, and in certain regions which are cul-
> turally united but politically divided, a subordinate
> international society comes into being, with a states-
> system reproducing in miniature the features of the
> general states-system. Italy and Germany before
> they were unified are examples in Europe; the Arab
> world and South America are examples in the wider
> world. In such sub-systems as these, there will be
> some states with general interests relative to the
> limited region and a capacity to act alone, which
> gives them the appearance of local great powers.
> Egypt, Iraq and perhaps Saudi Arabia have been
> great powers in the Arab world; Argentina and Brazil
> have played a similar role in South America. Simi-
> larly, South Africa may be regarded as a great power
> relative to Black Africa. Such regional great powers
> will probably be candidates, in the states-system at
> large, for the rank of middle power.
>   The grading of powers, as distinct from the
> older questions of precedence, first became a sub-
> ject of diplomatic discussion at the peace settlement

TABLE 2.2

Martin Wight's Views on Politics

Great Powers	Middle Powers
General interests worldwide	Has limited interests; has regional interests
Its destruction requires a coalition of powers	Greater gulf between great and middle powers than between middle and minor powers
Internationally recognized	Recognized in 1815
Has distinct superiority over its neighbors	Disputes with neighbors
Has greater resources	Fewer resources than a great power
Possesses main responsibility to settle international conflict	Possesses limited or no responsibility to settle international conflict
Its strength can be tested ultimately in war; it is able to fight	Limited ability to fight
Usually conceived in violence	May be a declining great power
	Is an intermediate grade of power; role is a consequence of size
	Has sufficient strength and authority to perfect itself and stand on its own without external help

Source: M. Wight, Power Politics (New York: Penguin, 1979), pp. 43, 45, 46, 47, 52, 63, 65, 295, 299, and 300.

of 1815. It was then that a class of middle powers
was first formally recognized, among the states of
Germany.[27]

The study of the emergence of middle powers and regional
powers benefits from two other observations by Wight. First,
he notes a decrease in the number and an increase in the size
of great powers.[28] Table 2.3 provides an overview. The
pattern from the nineteenth to the twentieth century is one of
concentration of powers into fewer hands, but there is no single
world power or universal empire. Second, Wight notes that:

> Middle powers appear when the qualifications for
> great-power status are being revised. The number
> of middle powers varies inversely with the number
> of great. In the nineteenth century, when the great
> powers were a stable and relatively numerous group,
> there were no recognized middle powers. (But in
> the German Confederation between 1815 and 1866,
> as we have seen, there were two great powers—
> Austria and Prussia, nine recognized as middle
> states, and twenty-eight small states). Claimants
> to middle-power status reappeared in 1919, when
> the aristocracy of the great powers had been gravely
> shaken. The most obvious middle powers today are

TABLE 2.3

The Number/Size Ratio of Great Powers in Historical Perspective

Year	Great Powers
1500	There were a number of great powers, including Venice and Portugal
1815	Five great powers
1914	Eight great powers
1939	Seven great powers
1945	Five nominal great powers, but really two superpowers

Source: M. Wight, Power Politics (New York: Penguin,
1979), p. 54.

the powers which have lost the status of great power as a result of the two World Wars: Britain, France, Germany and Japan.[29]

This begs two alternative questions. First, is there an inverse relationship between decrease in influence (but not military and economic capabilities) of great powers, and increase in influence (but not necessarily military and economic capabilities in relation to the great powers) of middle powers and regional powers, as is suggested by Wight? Second, could it be that in the post-1945 international system there has been a parallel growth in the military and economic capabilities of great powers and middle/regional powers, and a growth in middle powers-great powers interactions, which has increased the uncertainties in superpower strategies (and hence its international influence)? Is this true, given Wight's view that power politics organize the struggle for power, manage the process of great power expansion, and recognize the politics of force or threat whether power is an end or an instrument?[30]

Great powers monopolize the ability to create the norms and institutions of the international market and of international force. If great powers must seek the support of middle powers, and if middle powers can inflict costs that make great power intervention cost-ineffective, then the big gulf in the distribution of capabilities between great powers and middle powers is not the central issue.[31] If middle powers and regional powers cannot only absorb superpower punishment but also survive and project their power and influence against their neighbors and beyond, then the crucial process is that of middle power-superpower interactions in the 1980s.

NOTES

1. E. Luard, Conflict and Peace in the Modern International System (Boston: Little, Brown, 1968), pp. 4-5.

2. Ibid., p. 6.

3. H. Nicolson, The Evolution of Diplomatic Method (London: Constable, 1954), pp. 73-74.

4. M. Brecher et al., "A Framework for Research on Foreign Policy Behavior," Journal of Conflict Resolution 13 (1969):90.

5. D. Vital, The Inequality of States (Oxford: Clarendon Press, 1967), pp. 55, 87.

6. R. L. Rothstein, Alliances and Small Powers (New York: Columbia University Press, 1968), p. 29.

7. Ibid., pp. 6-7.

8. J. D. B. Miller, The Politics of the Third World, RIIA study (London: Oxford University Press, 1967), p. XII.

9. Ibid., pp. XII-XIV.

10. Ibid., pp. 14, 154.

11. Ibid., p. 15.

12. Ibid., pp. 38, 79.

13. Ibid., p. 4.

14. Ibid., pp. 88-89, 111.

15. Ibid., p. 68.

16. Ibid., p. 111.

17. Ibid., p. 8.

18. Ibid., pp. 62-63, 110.

19. Ibid., p. 119.

20. Ibid., p. 115.

21. S. S. Harrison, The Widening Gulf: Asian Nationalism and American Policy (New York: Free Press, 1978), p. 4.

22. Ibid., p. 5.

23. A. A. Mazrui, A World Federation of Cultures (New York: Free Press, 1976).

24. L. V. Radovanovic, The Non-Alignment Policy Today (Belgrade, 1966).

25. The UNESCO Courier, April 1974, p. 8.

26. A. A. Mazrui, The African Condition (London: Cambridge University Press, 1980).

27. M. Wight, Power Politics (New York: Penguin, 1979), p. 63.

28. Ibid., p. 54.

29. Ibid., p. 65.

30. Ibid., pp. 23, 29.

31. Ibid., p. 65.

3

The American Approach to
World Power Relations:
The Cold War Experience and
Its Implications

[NATO] was not exclusively or even primarily to
deter an impending or threatened Soviet military
attack. [John J. McCloy, The Atlantic Alliance:
Its Origins and Its Future (New York, 1969),
pp. 22-25.]

World power relations are concerned with power politics.
Power politics is not merely a continuous, organized, and predictable relationship between independent powers in a world
of sovereign states without a single central authority.[1] Power
politics is also the use or threatened use of force and intervention to shape international order. Power political relations are
coercive relations—relations derived by coercive diplomacy.[2]
Power politics means a continuous struggle whether power is
used as an end or an instrument. Its primary concern is not
with justice or right.[3] In power politics the great powers
monopolize the right to create and manage international (and
regional) conflict.[4] Traditionally, power politics has meant a
policy of expansion of power. The implication is that expansion
is sought indefinitely and occurs until another force checks the
expanding power.[5] In the pre-1945 world expansion meant
expansion of territory, military strength, and control. Today
the method of expansion and dominance is neomilitary, commercial, cultural, and intellectual.
    Conceptually, power politics may be divided into two notions:
the balance of power and the pattern of power (although the two
may overlap). Balance of power, according to Martin Wight,
might lead to military and economic weight,[6] whereas the pattern
of power leads to a consideration of strategy and tactics. The
distinction is a crucial one because in practice it is possible to
have massive military power in nuclear and conventional terms,

but: its use may be circumscribed because of absence or failure of strategy or political purpose; the weak could combine against the strong and check them; or the strong power could overreach itself by excessively dominating its allies and thus create resistance to its power and strategy.

In post-1945 literature and policy statements, a distinction is usually made between traditional (or conservative great or superpowers) and revolutionary powers. In the policy context, the United States is usually described as the former: it seeks either the status quo or stability; the Soviet Union is usually described as the latter: it seeks revolutionary change, instability, and upheaval to enable it to fish in troubled waters. The latter is associated with violent change (both internal and external), fanaticism, and ideological rigidity.[7] Wight asserts that

> The balance of power, the Concert of Europe, the
> Monroe Doctrine and the opening of the world by
> western capitalism seemed together to form a system
> of international relations that combined stability
> with elasticity, security with progress. [8]

He approvingly quotes Professor H. A. Smith

> that the deepest significance of the Bolshevik
> revolution will in future be found, not in the
> changes which it introduced in Russia or else-
> where, but in its successful repudiation of the
> rule of law among the nations. [9]

In seeking "to transform international society by force," revolutionary doctrines "blur the distinction between domestic and foreign policy; they transform diplomacy; and they transform war."[10] Table 3.1 shows the differences.

This distinction between traditional and revolutionary international relations is formal, not real. In a sense, all superpower foreign policy is revolutionary by Wight's definitions, although Wight himself casts only the Soviet Union as a revolutionary state. Consider the following.

United States foreign policy, especially in the cold war era, maintained that the Bolshevik regime was temporary and unrepresentative.[11] Government-sponsored activities (such as Radio Free Europe) aimed at Soviet and East European audiences tried to manipulate the loyalties against the Soviet Union and satellite regimes. This was particularly so during the era of

TABLE 3.1

Traditional and Revolutionary Approaches Contrasted

Traditional Approach	Revolutionary Approach
International relations are normally between governments that represent their people	It is assumed that governments do not represent their people and will furthermore try to manipulate the potential stratification of loyalties within other countries
International relations are conducted by diplomacy— by adjusting conflicting interests, negotiation, and compromise	The aim is to transform and convert rather than to compromise. The focus is on spying, subversion, and propaganda rather than on information, negotiation, and communication
It sees a difference between peace and war as discrete phenomenon in interstate relations	It is morally and psychologically at war with its neighbors at all times, even in peacetime
In traditional politics, state behavior favors the status quo and stability, not imperialism	Revolutionary politics usually gives in to national interest but it can continue to fuel the imperialism of a great power, as is the case with Soviet imperialism (which is tsarist imperialism "writ large and with a new impulse," according to Wight)

Source: M. Wight, Power Politics (New York: Penguin, 1978), Chap. 7.

John Foster Dulles, when the call to "roll back" communism was prominent in U.S. rhetoric. A similar view existed about the unrepresentative nature of the early years of Mao's regime.[12] Salvador Allende gained power in Chile through a free election, although Henry Kissinger argued that he did not represent Chilean interests and that Chileans did not know what was good for Chile.[13] Again, when Sheikh Mujibir Rahman won an open election in Pakistan and eventually came to power (1972-75), he was destabilized. The United States utilized the dissatisfied elements in Bangladesh against Rahman.[14]

The hypothesis that may be drawn from these examples is that an international power that claims and seeks stability may in fact have two faces of power: it may seek horizontal stability vis-à-vis its equal international enemy; but at the same time, it seeks vertical destabilization vis-à-vis the weak states in the third world. Superpowers are practitioners of the revolutionary approach because they usually seek to codify horizontal world power relations between equals. This is done through horizontal crisis management, summitry, and predictable arms races that do not or cannot alter the distribution of power, even if they do foster the image of competition. Arms races between equals are competitive, not distributive; that is, they cannot alter the existing distribution of power if both sides seek to preserve their position vis-à-vis each other in the international hierarchy. But to achieve stable horizontal relations, it is necessary to reduce conflict between two strong powers. This requires the development of "buffer zones" or "power vacuums" that justify the diversion of a great power conflict to secondary zones of international conflict. This protects the primary zones of international interaction between the great powers.

According to Wight:

A buffer state is a weak power between two or more stronger ones, maintained or even created with the purpose of reducing conflict between them. A buffer zone is a region occupied by one or more weaker powers between two or more stronger powers; it is sometimes described as a 'power vacuum'. Each stronger power will generally have a vital interest in preventing the other from controlling the buffer zone, and will pursue this interest in one of two ways, according to its strength. It will seek either to maintain the buffer zone, as neutral and independent, or to establish its own control, which may lead in the long run to its annexing the buffer zone

and converting it into a frontier province. Buffer
states may therefore be roughly divided into trimmers, neutrals and satellites. Trimmers are states
whose policy is prudently to play off their mighty
neighbours against one another; the most famous
of European trimmers was the Duchy of Savoy, which
earned thereby first a kingdom and then the hegemony of United Italy; the neutralist states today are
of their number. Neutrals are states without an
active foreign policy at all; their hope is to lie low
and escape notice. Satellites are states whose foreign policy is controlled by another power.[15]

Great power conflict management therefore requires buffers.
Since 1945 the superpower naval competition indicates that the
sea is a buffer zone, as are secondary regions in the Middle
East, South, Southeast, and Southwest Asia, and Southern
Africa.

Buffers absorb and divert conflict and competition and
stabilize great power relations with respect to their primary
interests. In arguing the notion of a structural and psychological relationship between great power competition in periphery
buffer zones, and stability with respect to each power's primary
strategic and material interests, one must take into account the
view expressed by the veteran U.S. diplomat that the Soviet
Union "has been a major source of pre-occupation not only to
the U.S. government but also to every government on the face
of the earth, even including some of the satellite Soviet regimes
in Eastern Europe.[16] Bohlen gives four reasons for the primacy
of the Soviet threat. First, its size and population give the
Soviet Union the potential to make a modern industrial state.
Second, it is organized along totalitarian lines. According to
Bohlen:

Nazi Germany, despite the total dictatorship exercised by the Nazi party, despite its extreme brutal-
ity, nevertheless was not, in one sense of the word,
a "totalitarian" state. There were entities in Germany
which had been there before Hitler—banks, business
institutions, publishing houses, press, all the media
of the modern society; these were under the total
control of Nazi Germany but were not changed. In
the Soviet Union these same institutions, which
existed before 1917, were dissolved, and indeed
atomized by the Soviet government, which replaced

any vestige of ownership with total ownership by
the Soviet government. The government, in turn,
was controlled by the Communist Party of the Soviet
Union. Therefore, in a sense, the Soviet Union is
the first totalitarian state the modern world has ever
seen.[17]

Third, the Soviet Union has grown stronger militarily:

The Soviet Union at no time since its inception in
1917 has ever relaxed its attention to its military
posture or its military establishment. The rise of
Soviet military power has been in one straight line
from 1917 up to the present date.[18]

Finally, Soviet ideology contains a fixed premise "that anything
that is not Soviet is ipso facto inherently an enemy. The Soviet
Union has never really departed from that."[19] Because of these
features, U.S. foreign policy has been a response, and solely
so, to Soviet behavior. It has nothing to do with U.S. material
interests, ambitions, or desires, says Bohlen.[20]

Such views are shared by many Americans. However,
revisionist U.S. scholars have probed their country's cold war
behavior from 1944 to 1946 and have concluded that its strategic
behavior did or could have partly instigated the cold war.[21]
Conceptually, the arguments divide along the following four
lines.

First, the U.S.-USSR relationship is primarily, if not
exclusively, one of competition and conflict instigated by the
Soviet Union and responded to by the United States. Here
action-reaction is Soviet induced. The conflict and competition
is of overriding importance in U.S. foreign policy. A majority
of U.S. policy statements and scholarly analyses fit this framework of "communication" (not necessarily of "thinking" because
the communications rest on untested but policy relevant premises
about the Soviet Union's behavior and intentions).

Second, superpower competition in northern international
relations is obvious but actually is insignificant. It is insignificant because the development of buffers or power vacuums in
the third world permit deflection and management of superpower
conflict in the northern strategic cores. Furthermore, the conflict is manageable and predictable, and hence is not critically
significant.

Third, the image of superpower competition is more important than the competition itself. The utility of third world

buffers and power vacuums in stabilizing superpower relations
is usually not studied publicly in U.S. writings, although it
clearly merits inquiry. Just as the European balance of power
from 1860 to 1914 benefited from overseas European empires
and power struggles, the superpower balance benefits from its
"informal empires" and power struggles in peripheries of world
power relations. Third world crises absorb superpower tensions,
thus serving a stabilizing function. Foreign policy and defense
policy are normally based on mutual suspicion, which is to be
expected between two superpowers. The significance of superpower "conflict" lies elsewhere; it rests in the necessity and
utility of the image of an international public enemy. With this,
intra-elite competition can be managed (settled or frozen) by
creating a clear public identification against the external enemy.
Implicit is the notion that it is easier to create an identification
against an external enemy that against internal enemies. Furthermore, a public enemy is required to transform or develop foreign
policy and security policy. Elite accommodation and domestic
mobilization require an external focal point (the enemy). The
enemy is the catalyst for internal mobilization. The aim of foreign
policy is not to accommodate overseas interests by interstate
agreement. The image of competition with a hostile international
environment must be preserved and nourished, even if the enemy
is weak and nonexpansionist.

Fourth, today the notion of superpower competition is
relevant mainly to the buffer zones or the secondary zones of
international politics. But even here the competition is guided
by rules. For instance: neither superpower is to seek an exclusive sphere of influence in the buffers, and in regional
politics they are supposed to permit the involvement of several
external powers on a nonexclusive basis; [22] the superpowers
cannot control the origin of regional crises but they ought to
manage (and they do—in the 1973 Middle East crisis, for example)
the outcomes to prevent the escalation of regional crises into a
superpower confrontation; and superpowers' involvement in
regional affairs may be competitive (such as the Indian Ocean
naval rivalry), but there is informal restraint in the distribution
of military power in the third world regions—for example, through
control over arms transfers and in the management of the ratios
of military power between the superpowers and between regional
enemies.

Of these four views, the first is clearly oversimplified.
The public literature—including revisionist cold war writings,
declassified U.S. foreign policy documents, and the history of
detente, arms control, and crisis management—yield a number

of points. First, U.S. foreign policy is influenced by a desire to keep foreign markets strong and open to U.S. industry (for example, the material self-interest in the Marshal Plan).[23] The notion that U.S. "policy is not rooted in any national material interest . . . as most foreign policies in other countries in the past have been"[24] is misleading, given the relationship between military power and economic activity in the U.S. Constitution and in its post-1945 behavior.[25] Second, the U.S. self-image that it "cannot avoid the responsibilities—except at its peril—which history has placed on its shoulders as the strongest power on earth" is self-serving. It induces the United States to act unilaterally and self-righteously in a collective and revolutionary way rather than in a democratic fashion.[26] Third, according to Bohlen:

> Even now there is really no conflict of interest be-
> tween the United States as a country and the Soviet
> Union as a country. The tension between us is,
> in my opinion, caused by the ideological factor.[27]

The existence of detente and arms control indicates that the superpowers can find common strategic interests and the ideological factor can be downgraded at will by their leaders. The ability to act and intervene internationally since 1945 indicates that the concern about Soviet intervention is overstated and that U.S. culpability since 1945 is understated.

The second interpretation merits a study of the role of buffers as safety valves to release the pressures of superpower tension. It yields the notion that the availability of areas other than vital areas (Europe, North Atlantic, North and Central America, East Europe, the Soviet Union, China, and Northeast Asia) is essential. Just as the Europeans from 1800 to 1914 were able to safeguard the central balance by exploring the third world, the superpowers have been able to do the same. Strategic interest is the basis of this approach. This pattern of behavior is the common mode of equally strong states. Furthermore, it is the nature of industrial states in the north—as respective allies of the superpowers—to participate in the management of third world buffers. Thus, German investment and aid in recent years to Turkey, Afghanistan, and Pakistan, and East Germany's help in Africa and the Middle East, may be studied as northern efforts to manage the third world buffers, along with the pursuit of their own political economic interests.

The third interpretation is important as a study of the role of image in foreign and defense policymaking. One starting point is that, as Bohlen points out, "In truth there is no such thing as a permanent solution in international affairs. There are only tolerable adjustments."[28] This insight requires development—from the point of view of the study of interstate relations and the relationship between domestic politics and foreign policy. Bohlen's comment points to the incremental, ad hoc nature of change in decisionmaking and in interstate relations, but it neglects the diversionary use of military strategy and image building about the enemy to promote the material interests of the United States.

Bohlen's contrast between "permanent solutions" and "tolerable adjustments" is relevant for an understanding of U.S. foreign relations since 1945. American foreign policy was transformed in 1945 only in the sense that the United States emerged as a superpower in a bipolar world. The change lay in a different global context because of the fall of the European empires and the end of Japanese power. The center of gravity in world politics shifted away from Europe and toward two continental powers: the United States and the Soviet Union. The changed global power context also meant that a limit emerged against the application or expansion of U.S. power. Whereas its self-image was that of unlimited power, the rise of Soviet military power meant the United States had to deal with an alien military and political force. Bipolarity, therefore, entailed pessimism for U.S. elites who before 1945 had sought and acquired "open doors" at will. Before 1945 the U.S. diplomatic experience did not prepare the leadership for a process of continuous engagement.[29] The United States emerged in 1945 as a great power with a viable economy and military strength without having had to engage or test its power with an equal; now it had to share power with an alien international force. (It had entered World War II after Great Britain and the Soviet Union had broken the back of Hitler's armies.)

Before 1945, U.S. foreign policy could function with a divorce between strategic purpose and military force. War and peace were regarded as mutually exclusive: war was abnormal and peace was the normal condition of man. The context in 1945 was the thinking of the 1800s, when

> Europe stood for war, poverty, and exploitation;
> America for peace, opportunity, and democracy.
> Nonentanglement was therefore the logical policy
> by which Americans could quarantine themselves
> from Europe's hierarchical social structures and
> immoral international habits. At the same time,

by confusing the results of geography and international politics with the supposed consequences
of democracy, Americans could smugly enjoy a self-
conferred moral superiority.[30]

Because of internal strength, the blessings of geography
and British naval power in the Atlantic, and the attitude against
entangling alliances, the United States did not have to choose
between isolation or political globalism, between moral and power
politics. Above all, it did not have to find a lasting and evolving
relationship between military power and its strategic and political
purposes. The original link in the U.S. Constitution was between power—for continental peace and order (against the
Indians)—and commerce—for America's well-being. This union
was expressed in the economic development of continental America
in the 1800s, in the defeat of the native Indians, and in the
development of U.S. commerce in the Americas and the Pacific.
Table 3.2 describes the definition of the national interest in
the 1800s.

After 1945 the United States adopted a new posture and a
new rationalization: from isolation to an active global power;
from an abhorrence of European power politics in the 1800s to
a decision to participate in a bipolar world; from nonengagement
to engagement after 1945 on its own terms. The posture it chose
was to contain the evil communists. Containment was not simply
bravado against the communists, or a military buildup against
the Soviets, or an ideological crusade for democracy. Funda-
mentally, it represented a shift in attitude: a recognition, for
the first time in U.S. diplomatic history, that the future material
and political well-being of the United States required abandon-
ment of isolationism; that the world was divided into two major
international forces; that there was no escape from the necessity
of horizontal engagement; and that international engagement
required a remobilization of domestic nationalism to rebuild the
military machine in peacetime. Although the United States could
have chosen between accommodation and confrontation with Soviet
power from 1944 to 1946, it chose confrontation to refashion a
domestic and foreign policy consensus.

The U.S. instigation of the cold war after the death of
President Franklin Roosevelt may be viewed as a search for a
new domestic and foreign policy strategy—a consensus of sorts—
whose purpose was to engage a domestic audience into foreign
affairs. The mobilization of internal military strength was necessary to promote confrontation politics, and confrontation politics
was necessary to fashion a new domestic consensus to support

TABLE 3.2

Pattern of U.S. External Behavior in the 1800s

Method	Opportunity	Implications for Foreign Policy
Brute force (or war to win)	Interventions in South America in 1800s, World War I, World War II	Avoids entangling policies; war is an abnormal interruption of peace
Commerce (to exploit the peace)	Growth of South American regionalism under U.S. umbrella; promotion of open door policy in the East	Military power should support goal of peaceful commerce at home and abroad

Source: Compiled by the author.

overseas commitments. Overseas commitments were necessary because the United States could no longer pursue its constant quest for foreign markets and raw materials unaided.

The United States was not ready in 1945 to assume global responsibilities. It was not willing to shape a strategy based on common interests and mutual obligations that entail sacrifices with other states. This was not the result of inexperience in world diplomacy; it reflected an attitude that "what is mine is mine, but what is yours is negotiable." To regard U.S. foreign policy mainly or merely as an exercise to project power internationally and to defend order, peace, and democracy, is to misunderstand the nature of the U.S. attitude to foreign affairs. One should not assume that U.S. foreign policy is mistaken because of its failure to develop a meaningful relationship between military power and strategic purpose. The relationship between military power and strategic purpose has not been explained by the United States convincingly because the issue is not about peace, order, or justice, it is about how to renegotiate the terms of international trade and resource transfer. It may be argued that by 1945 the United States was already a

seasoned practitioner of open door diplomacy and that this was
the constant element in U.S. diplomacy. The control of force
and revolution or the promotion of democracy was secondary
to the quest for open doors. In 1945 the challenge to the United
States was to balance the quest for open doors with a world of
two power centers. As one scholar points out:

> After the Second World War, American statesmen
> were confident of America's strength and Russia's
> weakness (although later they and their apologists
> found it convenient to argue that the contrary had
> been the case). Furthermore, they believed that
> "we cannot have full employment and prosperity in
> the United States without foreign markets," as
> Dean Acheson told a special Congressional committee
> on postwar economic policy and planning in Novem-
> ber 1944. These considerations led to the conclusion,
> as President Truman put it in April 1945, that the
> United States should "take the lead in running the
> world in the way that the world ought to be run";
> or more specifically, in the words of Foreign Eco-
> nomic Administrator Leo Crowley, that "if you
> create good governments in foreign countries,
> automatically you will have better markets for our-
> selves." Accordingly, the United States pressed
> for the "open door" in Eastern Europe and else-
> where. [31]

President Truman put this approach succinctly:

> The objectives of peace and freedom . . . are
> bound up completely in a third objective—
> reestablishment of world trade. In fact, the
> three—peace, freedom, and world trade—are
> inseparable. [32]

In short, the operative perceptions from 1944 to 1946 were
as follows: the Soviet Union was weak and in need of U.S.
financial help; it had reached the limits of its power in East
Europe and West Europe was not in danger. The public image
fostered by U.S. leaders advocating an anti-USSR stance was
the exact opposite of the private assessment of Soviet economic
and political weaknesses. The public theme was that of Soviet
expansionism, which implied the threat of its ideology and a
fear that its military power would expand. Yet, the concept

of Soviet expansionism has never been convincingly explained publicly in economic, cultural, and strategic terms.

The relationship between military power and strategic purpose is not the primary one in U.S. foreign policy. Rather, the real issues concern the relationship between commerce and military power, the use of an international public enemy to justify domestic elite coalition building, and the building of a public identification against the enemy. In 1945 the domestic setting in the United States revealed ideological and policy diversity (that is, between isolationists and internationalists) with radically opposite implications for policy and resource allocation. The issue is not the nature of the public international enemy, but the domestic implications—in terms of resource allocation and distribution of domestic economic and political power—once a public identification against the enemy has been organized. Excessive discussion about the nature of the enemy is a necessary diversion from a close inspection of the implication of the presumed enemy. Threat definition is purposive. At issue is not if it is an accurate description of reality, but if it is policy relevant. The U.S. instigation of the cold war was successful insofar as it defeated the advocates of accommodation between the United States and the Soviet Union, and insofar as it ratified the position of the universalists, who saw that peace, freedom, world trade, and military power were inseparable as domestic and foreign policy.

THE U.S. DEBATE FROM 1944 TO 1946: FOREIGN POLICY AS REDEFINITION, RENEGOTIATION, AND CONFRONTATION POLITICS

United States foreign policy may be conceptualized not as a quest for accommodation of interests between states, but as a search for issues that shape an image of confrontation. The strategy is to polarize international and domestic power relations, and then work toward a redefinition and renegotiation of issues. The key concept in the U.S. approach is to constantly churn up new issues because it is by constant redefinition and renegotiation that the upward and downward mobility of actors in the U.S. domestic power structure can be organized. The framework of action is U.S.-centric in attitude and purpose. The aim of foreign policy is to keep the world open to U.S. economic and military mobilization. International developments provide the issues and threats that nourish domestic perceptions and debates. Foreign policy is the medium of communication that projects U.S. norms and power on the world.

United States norms about international power relations are such that by definition they do not lend themselves to conflict resolution. The debates and norms build domestic constituencies that inevitably favor a strong consensus toward U.S. commerce and military power. These norms and constituencies create vetoes against accommodation of foreign interests. U.S. foreign policy is a quest to get something for nothing; in President Truman's words, "to get 85% of the bargain"; and in the words of John J. McCloy, "We ought to have our cake and eat it too."[33]

U.S. cold war decisionmaking from 1944 to 1946 is revealing. It created the framework of U.S. foreign policy thinking in the post-1945 era. Over time the formal issues and the actors have changed, but the premises or the approach to the world remains unchanged. The basic thesis about the U.S. approach to foreign affairs may be characterized as follows:

U.S. National Objectives	Untested U.S. Policy Premises
Ensure the United States physical survival	Soviet Union is motivated to be a dominant world power; it is expansionist
Protect the U.S. way of life	In another war the United States will quickly become the target for mass destruction
Ensure economic well-being of the United States	"World peace" means war avoidance between superpowers
Prevent spread of international communism	Containment of communism takes precedence over world peace; freedom is more important than peace
Prevent another world war	World War II created power vacuums that are tempting for Soviet expansionism
	United States tried appeals, financial inducements, and tough talk from 1944 to 1946 to avoid Soviet expansionism, but nothing worked to contain the Soviets from 1946 to 1948. The United States is the only countervailing power to check Soviet expansionism
	Communist advances would critically undermine the non-communist world and the global balance [34]

Brown argues that the U.S. debate from the 1950s to the 1970s has been over "means, not objectives."[35] The untested premises reflect the cold war stance of the U.S. "establishment". Despite variations in detail, these irreducible norms and perceptions have become integrated into U.S. social psychology about foreign affairs. These fundamental premises about the U.S. self-image and the external world have not changed since 1945. In that sense, the cold war approach has not altered; only the means change from time to time.

The emergence of policy-relevant but untested premises from 1944 to 1946 may be characterized as a fundamental transformation in U.S. elite behavior and the underlying U.S. social psychology. With this transformation it is probably correct to say that there could be no permanent solution, only temporary adjustments in this world view.

The faulty threat perception and definition of the U.S. establishment has been criticized by cold war revisionist historians. Brown classifies them into three categories:

We had been taking for granted that the Soviets and Chinese Communists had unrequited appetites for expansion. Did the record of the past two decades support this proposition? A serious body of "revisionist" history of the Cold War period had emerged during the middle 1960s supportive of alternative propositions. The more extreme revisionists were arguing that the United States was more clearly the expansionist power since the Second World War, arrogantly attempting to reshape the world in the image of its ideological preconceptions and that the Soviets and Chinese were only reacting defensively to this "encirclement." Moderate revisionists stressed the likelihood that both sides have been victims of tragic misperceptions of the other's real intentions, which were to assure themselves substantial, but limited, spheres of influence for legitimate reasons of economic and military security. Others, more agnostic with respect to the intentions of the Communists, nonetheless claimed that Russian and foreign actions as distinct from their rhetoric tended to be prudent if not conservative, that the Communist nations, like the Western countries, had difficult resource allocation problems and unmet domestic needs which placed weighty constraints on their inclinations for foreign adventure.[36]

To regard U.S. foreign policy as "American expansionism," as "tragic misperception," as a "mistake," or to emphasize Soviet conservatism and downgrade the Soviet threat, is to miss the point about the self-serving nature of U.S. diplomacy. It is to ignore the "loner" or insular basis of the U.S. approach to world affairs.

Martin Herz, a U.S. diplomat, argues that "in 1945 Soviet policy was not inexorably prescribed and expansionist" and that U.S. mistakes prevented compromise and accommodation. Anatol Rappaport regrets the loss of opportunity to make a deal with Stalin.[37] This author's view is quite different. Precisely because the Soviet Union was weak and nonexpansionist, the United States made deliberate "mistakes". They were intended to prevent accommodation, to enable President Truman and his successors to acquire an "85% bargain," or at worst to have their cake and eat it too—to make an offer they knew would be refused, and to mobilize the economy and the military to ensure U.S. preponderance. It is an old bureaucratic maneuver to make an offer to court a negative response (such as the Marshall Plan offer to the Soviet Union and East Europe) and then to use the negative response as evidence of threat, aggression, and bad faith. It may be argued that U.S. foreign policy since 1946 has not been fashioned to create a balance of power and a pattern of power, to engage in power politics (defined as a quest for constant relations involving both force and accommodation). Rather, it was intended to create an external enemy and to use the image of this enemy as the basis to mobilize domestic elite and public communications and resources. American foreign policy may thus be conceptualized as a quest for internal elite accommodation and internal balance of power, and also, as an instrument to mobilize (or remobilize) internal and international resources for economic and military growth. Rationalizing U.S. military and economic expansion and intervention, not inducing Soviet restraint, is the name of the game. The cold war debate was won by universalists who did not see "containment" as simply a short-term arrangement toward a long-term "sensible arrangement" with the Soviets. To them, world peace was indivisible politically and militarily, as L. C. Gardner points out in his review of J. J. McCloy's writings.[38] According to McCloy, West Europe was economically and politically prostrate, it could not revive itself alone, and it was open to Soviet influence. The Western security system was fostered by the United States to give West Europe a sense of direction. Furthermore, a link existed between the U.S. approach to Latin America and to Europe:

As American policies evolved in the immediate postwar period, at least two assumptions were applicable to both Latin America and Western Europe: First, in order to deal with fascism or militant socialism in either place, the key was to isolate outbreaks of radicalism (either local or national) within a larger community of nations. Nonvirulent fascism such as Franco's Spain could be tolerated and even turned to good purpose so long as the area's "security system" leaned in the proper direction. And that was the second assumption: If the "security system" leaned properly, the policy would succeed.

There was no need for a Latin-American Marshall Plan: private enterprise could do the job. But it was essential to establish a United States Government monopoly over arms sales to Latin-American countries. As in Europe, these countries needed the "concentrated direction" of a security system. Besides enabling their governments to keep order at home, participation in an international military partnership would divert unwanted nationalistic passions into safe outlets. Their pride satisfied by the acquisition of nearly up-to-date weapons systems, the generals could be counted on to support Washington's policy aims. Intra-American squabbles and territorial conflicts would not lead to the misuse of United States military aid in local wars for the same reason that West Germany could later be trusted to work in harness with the multi-national NATO force.

The analogy is far from perfect, of course, but even including such other uses of NATO as a "trip-wire" to bring into action American air power, the comparison is helpful as a reminder that Washington's Cold War policies did not come into being willy-nilly in response to the Soviet menace.[39]

In other words, universalism meant indivisibility between political and military objectives and between Europe, Latin America, and the Far East, the strategic cores in U.S. foreign policy.

In summary, containment of the Soviet Union was a new U.S. strategy to serve old aims, namely, the assertion of the indivisibility of peace, freedom, world trade, and military power in the northern strategic cores. Containment means confrontation politics with the Soviets. Confrontation means an unwillingness to assume common obligations, an unwillingness to sacrifice universalist aims of expanding American commercial and military security systems under U.S. leadership in different regions. Confrontation was not the same thing as territorial conquest; conquest led to war and nationalism. Commercial expansion, arms transfers, and military training and advice aided war avoidance. This neocolonial "peaceful" system was a prescription to retain U.S. leadership.

From 1944 to 1946, confrontation with the Soviets on an international basis helped shape the direction and leadership of security systems in Latin America, Western Europe, the Middle East, and Japan according to U.S. norms and interests. The economic interests of the United States were submerged by the cold war rhetoric, which stressed the ideology of peace, freedom, and the security of arms.

The opportunity for the creation of confrontation politics came from the change in leadership from Roosevelt to Truman, in the acquisition of the atomic bomb by the United States in 1945, in the new sense of power, and above all by Stalin's conduct in East Europe. But the strategy was to fashion world power relationships with regional security systems which rested on the indivisibility of peace, freedom, and bilateral and regional commercial and military ties—where the United States controlled the agenda and the 85 percent bargains.

OVERVIEW

The study of the cold war discloses a pattern of rationalization about the international environment, and offers the background to the new cold war that allegedly began in 1975. In discussing the old and the new cold war, it is necessary to address a number of perspectives. These offer insights and possible explanations about the U.S. approach to the communist world (particularly the Soviet world) and the third world. Nine perspectives are summarized below.

First, the new cold war (1975 to the present) is a continuation of the old cold war. Both operate on the theme of anti-Russianism. [40]

Second, public rationalization in the United States about the cold war was and is the expression of a "winning" domestic coalition that emerged after World War II around the theme of national security. [41] The development of a domestic organizational and conceptual focus on national security during peacetime was an innovation in U.S. foreign affairs. Its purpose was to alter the image of neoisolationism of the past and to establish a stable balance of power within the U.S. elite structure.

National security organizations come into being as a reaction to disorganized domestic struggles. National security constituencies establish a network of communications within a state and society. They are created by polarizing domestic politics, by responding to a need to develop us-versus-them groups within a country, and by consolidating subnational groups that can later expand.[42] The national security network is established within a country to gain access to and to manage the national power structure. The structure becomes powerful by its control over secrecy, the agenda, the allocation of national resources, and the distribution of rewards in the system. It is the ideal instrument to create an ideological and organizational constituency for these purposes as it gives shape to an external threat image.

The reader should bear in mind that when the United States decided to engage the Soviet Union in a cold war containment and conflict relationship, it was actually an international military, economic, and political power, and the Soviet Union was only a regional great power in military terms and its economy and social structures were devasted and insecure. Zbigniew Brzezinski's overview of superpower relations from 1945 to 1974 demonstrates that by and large the United States enjoyed an advantage over the Soviets in various dimensions of international power, including international standing, military power, economic power, and domestic policy base.[43] As such, it may be hypothesized that: innovative elite structures try to shape the domestic consensus before an external threat actually emerges; foreign policy is not simply a reaction to an external threat, but a reaction to a possible external threat; the possibility of a threat is enough to create a clear public identification against an external enemy; and the possibility is utilized by innovative elites to polarize the domestic policy audience and to build a domestic policy based on polarization. The desired outcome is to consolidate a domestic policy base rather than to engage in conflict resolution or accommodation with the international public enemy.

Third, if the ideological split between capitalism and communism is sincerely intended as the basis of U.S. foreign relations, then it is arguable that the utilization of ideology as the basis of foreign policy is a sign of American ignorance and naivete about foreign affairs. It reflects inexperience with world affairs and a lack of understanding of the value of negotiation and diplomacy. On the other hand, it may be plausibly argued that ideology is a rationalization rather than a factor in the U.S. decisionmaking process. It is an instrument to show the external division between "us" and "them". Publicly organized and demonstrated ideological divisions polarize world power relations. Ideological divisions help alliance formation and activity, and they can be used to revise and strengthen the domestic policy base. In short, the exaggerated use of ideology as a policy instrument is functional in alliance building in world and domestic relations. It helps to develop the international and domestic policy base, as well as the image of internal and international societal support for the proposed policy. As ideology is a powerful instrument to tap symbols and emotions, ideological polarization facilitates communications with attentive audiences.

Fourth, United States' cold war communications have conjured up the norm of "peaceful and friendly relations with the USSR." Peace and friendship are seen as measures of good relations. This norm is irrelevant as the basis of any interstate relationship. State relations require common interests, a willingness to assume obligations and to make sacrifices to form a pattern and a balance of international and regional power. Peace and friendship are not bases to shape world power relations. It is natural to base foreign policy and military policy on mutual suspicion and mistrust. For instance, among European practitioners of balance of power in the 1800s, there was mistrust in policy relations even though the social background of the elite groups was similar.

However, the introduction of irrelevant criteria like "peace and friendship" has its policy use. It touches basic human emotions and creates a public identification with the goodness of those who advocate peace and friendship. It serves as a basis to reject the peace and friendship of the enemy because, by definition, short of surrendering its sovereignty by opening itself to U.S. military inspection and economic dependency, there is nothing the Soviet Union could do that would remove U.S. mistrust. Moreover, there is no human or technical instrument to verify peaceful intentions. When the demander is militarily and economically powerful, it can help itself in the security field by its own means and it does not require the cooperation of the enemy. Yet the onus of good behavior is placed on the weaker side and the criteria of good behavior are formulated by the stronger state. Ordinarily, according to diplomatic norm, the demander should pay a price. In U.S. cold war behavior, the demander seeks a price from the other side—a price for U.S. cooperation, a price for ensuring that the United States will not raise the ante and change the criteria of good behavior, a price for satisfying U.S. interests—defined as American preeminence in the security and economic fields.

Fifth, the cold war and containment policy may be defined as a ploy by a world power against a regional great power in the mid 1940s. The ploy was to put the regional power in its place by drawing ideological, economic, military, and diplomatic lines against it. The operative premise of this approach was set out by George Kennan:

> My objection to the Truman Doctrine message revolved
> largely around its failure to draw a distinction be-
> tween various geographic areas. Repeatedly at that
> time and in ensuing years, I expressed in talks
> and lectures the view that there were only five
> regions in the world—the United States, the United
> Kingdom, the Rhine valley with adjacent industrial
> areas, the Soviet Union, and Japan where the sinews
> of modern strength could be produced in quantity;
> I pointed out that only one of these was under Com-
> munist control; and I defined the main task of con-
> tainment, accordingly, as one of seeing to it that
> none of the remaining ones fell under such control. [44]

As such, the cold war and containment policy may be assessed as an attempt to freeze the territorial and political status quo. The primary method was to use military power to transmit a threat—a continuous threat—to deter a change of the territorial status quo. [45]

Sixth, the cold war and containment policy may be viewed as a strategy to permanently escape the isolationist impulse in U.S. history (and the consequent image in American thinking). Instead, the cold war developed a commitment to international relations. It created the necessity of a permanent peacetime military establishment against a permanent foreign threat and a hostile world environment.

Seventh, the cold war and containment doctrine may be studied as a massive diversion from the necessity to deal with a diversified international world after 1945. United States' decisionmakers apparently feared the emergence of multiple centers of power such as China, the third world nationalism, European communism, and so on. Even when evidence of inde-pendence in the Soviet bloc came to light—for instance, in requests by Mao of China and Ho Chi Minh of Vietnam to establish relations with the United States—the Soviet bloc was still per-ceived as a monolith. [46] By projecting U.S. hostility against all communists, the ideological polarization forced loyalty to the Soviet Union; potential moderates were radicalized by U.S. behavior. The general significance is that the kaleidoscope of diverse international and regional or local forces can be changed and threats may be utilized to polarize the environment and to induce alliance formation. Military alliances require a hierarchical structure of decision making. In alliances, the decision structure is responsive to the norm that he who has the greater power has the greater weight in the decision structure. Alliance activity helps transform the military weight of a strong state into weight or right in decisionmaking.

This approach is relevant for the United States because it has no international experience in dealing with other countries as equals. The U.S. diplomatic experience prior to 1945 was essentially in terms of the Monroe Doctrine and the open door policy of expansion. [47] Hierarchy and alliances are predictable and controllable. They are desirable because quantified power generates greater political mileage in the decision structure. The quest for greater control and predictability in the U.S. temperament points to the utility of alliance formation; and alliance formation requires polarization. As such, the cold war diplomacy of the United States may be studied as a quest for alliances that offer an escape from the messiness of dealing with a diversified international environment. The cold war may be studied as an intolerance of ambiguity and diversity in the international environment, as a strategy that diverts attention to a higher, bigger, and permanent threat, whereby lesser threats are subordinated in the domestic and international policy debates.

Eighth, the cold war and containment approach may be seen as an elaboration of an old theme. Since the late 1800s, U.S. foreign policy has been built on the theme of overseas expansion. This was perceived as a necessity to preserve U.S. economic and political well-being. Before 1945 the United States intervened militarily to promote overseas expansion, and reiterate its primacy in inter-American affairs, and promote its economic claims overseas. Since the late 1800s, a link existed between external military intervention and U.S. economic purposes. [48] The economic interest was the cause, the military intervention was the effect. The U.S. military and naval power was a major tool of a peacetime and expansionist economy before 1945. The relationship between the use of a military threat and its underlying economic purpose became an American norm before the Bolshevik revolution. The image of American isolationism and noninterventionism before the two world wars is bogus and diversionary; it masks U.S. involvement in world affairs since the late 1800s. After 1945 a publicly explicit linkage emerged between U.S. military power and the Soviet threat. Thereafter, the peacetime militarization of the U.S. economy became significant in the sense that it altered the image of U.S. isolationism or neoisolationism.

At the same time, it is significant that the direct employment of U.S. military force after 1945 was both continued and modified in comparison to its use before 1945. The link between economic purpose and military force continued in U.S.-third world relations, but with one major difference. The interventions in the Middle East, Latin America, Asia, and Africa (such as Lebanon in 1958, Iran in 1953, Cuba in 1961, Indochina in the 1960s, and Angola in 1974 and 1975) involved a number of instruments: overt and covert aid and the use of existing center-periphery relations or patron-client relations. The military was no longer the primary instrument to enforce American will.

In summary, the cold war and containment strategies partly express and partly elaborate the pre-1945 approach in the following ways. The induced polarization of the international environment along East-West lines after 1945 obscures the continuous quest for overseas markets for U.S. products, as well as the need for U.S. access to raw materials from overseas, particularly from the third world. Kolko provides data about the United States' growing dependency on overseas resources.[49] Overseas expansion is essential to maintain the U.S. system of check and balances because, without prosperity and expansion, this system tends to become paralyzed. International polarization is required so that the United States can foster its image as the defender of free world security. In return, it can demand the commitment of the free world toward the economic well-being of the leader of the free world. In other words, the cold war is useful because it is politically cheap (the Soviets do not have a constituency in the United States) and it is profitable (international polarization keeps the world insecure and dependent on U.S. military protection).

The relationship between military force and economic purpose has, however, been modified in one way. Direct U.S. military intervention is economically, politically, and militarily costly because of the incompetence of the U.S. military professionals (they cannot win wars), and the availability of Soviet support for weak third world states that are facing the U.S. threat. The availability of Soviet support for weak members of the international system increases the costs and risks of military intervention. It is no wonder that the United States tries very hard to codify a rule with the Soviet Union: namely, the superpowers ought to avoid the use of force in proxy wars. This is the U.S. definition of peace: war avoidance and Soviet control of third world nationalistic wars. It is self-serving. It means that if only the Soviets promise not to help nationalist movements in the third world who want to alter economic relations (and the consequent power relations), then the United States could peacefully continue to pursue and expand unequal exchange through center-periphery or patron-client relations. (Note that the term "client" is quite openly used in American rhetoric. It was frequently used by Nixon and Kissinger to admonish the Soviets to keep their clients in line. Soviet officials do not use this term, probably because they know that aid does not create reliable clients.)

The rising costs of direct military intervention have not prevented U.S. interventions (for example, Korea and Vietnam), but the costs account for a greater reliance on the communication of threat and self-advertising of the United States' global military reach. Such threats are communicated by statements like "we are the greatest power on earth," by the size of the military budget, by showing the flag on naval missions, by creation of new commands like the rapid deployment force, and by demonstration of overseas military power in the form of military bases. As an American scholarly work points out, the fear of war is an instrument of U.S. foreign policy.[50]

Ninth, U.S. cold war experience hides a profound domestic struggle that concerns ideology and intergroup power politics. The first group in this struggle may be broadly described as the advocates of confrontation politics with the Soviets and the third world. The intent is to polarize the international environment, to secure center-periphery or patron-client relations, and to ensure a North Atlantic military alliance. All of these are presumably based on fear and U.S. leadership. The premise is that there are five strategic cores in the world (as described by Kennan earlier). The method in foreign policy and defense policy is to achieve international polarization with a view to securing desirable alliance activity. The purpose is to continue the international economic expansion of the United States in both the industrial and the developing worlds.

The second group seeks accommodation with both the Soviets and the third world. It tries to work with nationalism, not against it. It sees nationalism as a viable cultural force that has not been, and possibly cannot be, overtaken by modern technology and organization norms. The focus of the second group is to develop an approach that is different from, if not the opposite of, confrontation politics. The second group recog-

nizes third world and Soviet nationalism and nationalization as
products of the revolutionary impulse. After all, did not revolutionary America once confiscate British property and proclaim
its independence? This group argues that confrontation politics
radicalizes the moderates, and so it seeks to limit the role of
military force and subversion overseas as instruments of policy.
It further argues that overseas commitments ought to be tailored
to U.S. needs and capabilities,[51] and that foreign policy should
address itself to the essentials of world power relations.[52] In
relation to the Soviet Union, the second group would accept a
spheres-of-influence policy. As Henry Wallace pointed out:

> The real peace treaty we now need is between the
> United States and Russia. On our part we should
> recognize that we have no more business in the
> political affairs of Eastern Europe than Russia has
> in the political affairs of Latin America, Western
> Europe and the United States. We cannot permit
> the door to be closed to our trade in Eastern Europe
> any more than we can in China. But at the same
> time we have to recognize that the Balkans are
> closer to Russia than to us—and that Russia cannot
> permit either England or the United States to domi-
> nate the politics of that area.[53]

A variation of the second group may be noted. This group
refers to the irrelevance of "major" U.S. foreign policy actions.[54]

Both groups have won inconclusive victories. The shaping
of the military-industrial complex as a civilian policy—as described
by Gabriel Kolko and by Richard Barnet—reveals the strength
of the first group.[55] The acceptance of the European status
quo in the Helsinki agreement in 1975 was a victory for the
advocates of spheres of influence and territorial status quo
in the second group. But it is wrong to suggest that the
second group has the upper hand. The debate about detente
during the 1970s reveals the fragility of the advocacy of the
second group. Yet the debate continues.

From the 1940s to the 1970s, the direction of U.S. foreign
policy was determined by civilian strategists in the White House
and other branches of government. They were not really accountable to anyone other than establishment and corporate interests.
In the 1980s the debate may be determined by the necessity to
trim the defense budget and to balance the budget—to reduce
the costs of security by military means. As such, the budget
director seems to be in competition with the advocates of con-

frontation politics and bigger defense forces and expenditures.
As budgetary limits to defense spending take shape, strategic
priorities will have to be thought through in relation to the
growing disutility of confrontation politics (which radicalize
the moderates) and the utility of accommodation politics (which
brings Soviet expansionism in conflict with third world nationalism
and permits an altered economic exchange between the Western
North and the South).

The advocacy of the second group is presently defensive,
but in the long run it is "winnable" because this group is sensitive to the real triangle in the 1980s. The first side of this
triangle is the extension, renegotiation, and institutionalization
of North/South capitalistic relations. The second side is the
recognition of the North's dependence on the South's economic
resources, and the need to promote the North's economic well-
being in exchange for the North's willingness to respect third
world nationalism—expressed by, say, a neutralized Palestinian
state on the Austrian model and by movement toward the dis-
mantling of apartheid in South Africa. The third side is limiting
the Soviet military presence outside the Soviet bloc by reducing
superpowers' military rivalry in the third world regions. The
Soviet Union is not a role model of social and economic development for a majority of third world states. It is, nevertheless,
useful as the second-best helper of third world states. If
moderates can be kept moderate and radicals can be tamed into
behaving like moderates (like Mugabe in Zimbabwe), third world
nationalism, not U.S. intervention, will be a major barrier to
the institutionalization of the Soviet military presence in the
Indian Ocean world.

NOTES

1. M. Wight in Power Politics, eds. H. Bull and C. Holbraad (New York: Penguin, 1978), p. 23.
2. T. C. Schelling, Arms and Influence (New Haven:
Yale University Press, 1966).
3. Wight, op. cit., p. 29.
4. Ibid., pp. 42-43.
5. Ibid., p. 144.
6. Ibid., p. 168.
7. Ibid., pp. 81, 83.
8. Ibid., p. 85.
9. Ibid., pp. 85-86.
10. Ibid., pp. 86, 88.

11. See for instance G. F. Kennan's famous "X Article" in Foreign Affairs (1947) on "The Sources of Soviet Conduct," particularly the discussion about the "circumstances of power."

12. Thus, President Truman told British Prime Minister Atlee that "the Chinese Communists were Russian satellites." See Harry Truman, Memoirs, Vol. 2 (New York: Doubleday, 1956), p. 399.

13. "I don't see why we have to let a country go Marxist," Kissinger reportedly told a 40 Committee meeting about Chile on June 27, 1970, "just because its people are irresponsible." Cited by Roger Morris, Kissinger's former NSC assistant, in Uncertain Greatness (New York: Harper & Row, 1977), p. 241.

14. L. Lifschultz, Bangladesh: The Unfinished Revolution (London: Zed Press, 1979).

15. Wight, op. cit., p. 160.

16. Charles E. Bohlen, The Transformation of American Foreign Policy (New York: Norton, 1969), p. 110.

17. Ibid., p. 111.

18. Ibid., p. 112.

19. Ibid., p. 113.

20. Ibid., p. 124.

21. The literature is extensive. For some revisionist views see Walter La Feber, America, Russia and the Cold War, 1945-1980, 4th ed. (New York: Wiley, 1980); Gar Alperovitz, Atomic Diplomacy: Hiroshima and Potsdam (New York: Simon & Schuster, 1965) and Cold War Essays (New York: Doubleday, 1970).

22. M. D. Shulman, "Beyond Containment," in C. Gati, ed., Caging the Bear: Containment and the Cold War (New York: Bobbs-Merrill, 1974), ch. 10.

23. Thus, a major U.S. document dated May 23, 1947 notes that "In the first place, the United States people have a very real economic interest in Europe. This stems from Europe's role in the past as a market and as a major source of supply for a variety of products and services." See the text in T. H. Etzold and J. L. Gaddis, eds., Containment: Documents on American Policy and Strategy, 1945-50 (New York: Columbia University Press, 1978), pp. 108-09.

24. Bohlen, op. cit., pp. 95-96.

25. W. W. Wilcox, "The Foreign Policy of the United States," in J. N. Rosenau et al., eds., World Politics (New York: Free Press, 1976), p. 37; and R. J. Barnet, The Roots of War (New York: Atheneum, 1972); and note 23.

26. Bohlen, op. cit., p. 124. George F. Kennan, "The Ideology of Containment: The X Article," in Gati, op. cit., p. 24.

27. Bohlen, op. cit., p. 51.

28. Ibid., p. 97.

29. L. J. Halle, The Cold War As History (New York: Harper Torchbooks, 1967).

30. J. Spanier, American Foreign Policy, rev. ed., 1962, p. 6.

31. Alperovitz, Cold War Essays, op. cit., pp. 11-12.

32. Cited in ibid., pp. 87-88.

33. Cited in S. E. Ambrose, Rise to Globalism: American Foreign Policy 1938-1976, rev. ed. (New York: Penguin, 1976), pp. 113, 116.

34. S. Brown, The Faces of Power (New York: Columbia University Press, 1968), ch. 1.

35. Ibid., p. 14.

36. Ibid., pp. 376-77.

37. The Herz quote is from Alperovitz, Cold War Essays, op. cit., pp. 36-37. A. Rappoportt, The Big Two (New York: Pegasus, 1971), p. 83.

38. L. C. Gardner, "Truman Era Foreign Policy: Recent Historical Trends," in R. S. Kirkendall, ed., The Truman Period As a Research Field: A Reappraisal, 1972 (Columbia: University of Missouri Press, 1974), p. 55.

39. Ibid., p. 57.

40. Le Feber, op. cit.

41. Barnet, The Roots of War, op. cit.

42. L. R. Beres and H. R. Targ, Constructing Alternative World Futures (Cambridge, Mass.: Schenkman, 1977), ch. 2, particularly pp. 26-28. This work is not directly concerned with national security policymaking, but it provides a useful discussion of the impact of cool, analytical, specialist, "in-here" groups vis-à-vis the "out-theres".

43. See Brzezinski, "The Competitive Relationship," in Gati, op. cit., ch. 9, particularly Appendix B.

44. Cited in ibid., p. 88.

45. J. L. Payne, The American Threat (Chicago: Markham, 1970).

46. J. W. Fullbright, "Truman Doctrine Reconsidered," in Gati, op. cit., pp. 65-74.

47. R. Klien, The Idea of Equality in International Politics (University of Geneva, Thesis No. 166, 1966).

48. W. A. Williams, The Tragedy of American Diplomacy (New York: Dell, revised and enlarged edition, 1962).

49. G. Kolko, The Roots of American Foreign Policy (Boston: Beacon, 1969), ch. 3.

50. Payne, op. cit.

51. S. E. Ambrose outlines Walter Lippmann's position on this point in his book, op. cit., p. 168. See also Walter Lipp-

mann, U.S. Foreign Policy: Shield of the Republic (Boston: Little, Brown, 1943), p. 7, for the emphasis on the relationship between means and ends.

52. G. F. Kennan, Realities of American Foreign Policy (New York: Norton, 1966).

53. H. A. Wallace speech, Sept. 12, 1946, and letter to President Truman, July 23, 1946, cited in H. A. Wallace, Toward World Peace (New York: Reynal and Hitchcock, 1948), pp. 9-10.

54. Morris, Uncertain Greatness, op. cit., prologue.

55. Barnet, op. cit.

4

The Soviet Approach to
World Power Relations:
Domestic and International Constraints

The Russians have always been aware of their weakness and their danger; the Americans have, since
an early date, been aware of their strength and
their safety. The Russians have achieved success
by way of repeated failure; the Americans believe
that they have never lost a war. The Russians
have regarded the outside world with awe, and
have felt their own points of inferiority; the Americans have regarded the outside world without
respect, and have gloried in their superior way
of life.

    Neither the Russians nor the Americans have
found it easy to establish rewarding relationships
with the world outside their borders. [L. J. Halle,
The Cold War as History (New York, Harper Torchbook edition, 1975), p. 20.

    Conceptualizing the Soviet approach to world power relations
is not easy. To some, Soviet foreign policy is heavily shaped
by ideology and it has a grand plan for world revolution and
aggressive expansion. Foreign policy is seen as an extension
of the totalitarian nature of a Stalinist political system.[1] Others
see the Soviet Union as a bureaucratic state with inherent tensions and pulls between competing bureaucratized political forces,
where the right hand may not know what the left hand is doing
on the wide stage of world politics.[2] Some see the Soviet Union
as a world power that has transformed itself from a prewar middle
power.[3] Others recognize the obvious growth of the USSR's
"presence," but debate the meaning of its "influence".[4] Yet
others question the entire range of U.S. policy assumptions about
post-1945 USSR foreign policy, implying that there is a funda-

87

mental problem in the way Western analysts approach the subject of the Soviet Union.[5]

It is not our intention to describe the literature. But in coping with the utter confusion in U.S. writings on the subject, a framework is needed. We will pick and choose elements scattered in the available literature and try to formulate a composite picture of how to study the Soviet Union generally, and how to study it specifically with regard to the third world and the Indian Ocean regions. The following questions will be addressed: What is the ideological setting in which USSR foreign policy is formulated? What is the impact of domestic policy in the foreign policymaking process? What is the interplay between the Soviet Union as a great or superpower, as a socialist state, and as head of the international socialist movement? What is the impact of the international environment on Soviet external behavior? What are the implications of Soviet aid and trade flows into the third world since the 1950s? What are the lessons of Soviet crisis behavior since the 1950s—in Korea, Vietnam, South Asia, the Middle East, and Africa—in terms of horizontal superpower relations and with respect to Soviet interests? What kind of insights does Soviet behavior reveal with regard to the old theories about geopolitics?

IDEOLOGICAL SETTING: THE U.S. VIEW OF SOVIET IDEOLOGY

A number of points may be noted as elements in the U.S. view of the role of ideology in Soviet foreign policy.

Although great power conflict can usually be explained in historical terms as a natural and inevitable consequence and function of the system of states, the post-1945 superpower conflict is unique because the Soviet Union seeks world domination in pursuit of the Marxist (and Trotskyist) conception of world revolution. According to B. Wolfe, "It should be clear then that the men who make policy in the Soviet Union think and act differently from the Tsars, and that we neglect their ideology to our peril."[6] The emphasis on Soviet ideology comes from an analysis of the ideological and authoritarian make-up of the Soviet political system and its elite. In other words, Soviet foreign policy is ideological because the Soviet system is ideological.

Even though Soviet totalitarianism of the Stalin period has been transformed into authoritarianism under Khrushchev and Brezhnev, the ideas of Marx, Lenin, and Stalin shape the Soviet perceptions of the outside world. To the extent that perceptions determine decisions, USSR foreign policy is still ideologically affected.

The Soviet Union operates with a world view of two opposite international social and economic systems: capitalism and socialism. As Khrushchev pointed out, it sees that there can be no ideological coexistence between the two. Peaceful coexistence is only between states. The Soviet Union must continue to support national liberation movements as it has done in Vietnam, Cuba, Angola, Ethiopia, Mozambique, and Afghanistan. "Class struggle" and opposition to anti-imperialist forces is the essence of the Soviet approach to the world. Soviet intervention and crisis behavior during the 1960s and 1970s point to its expansion in the third world, and this expansionism points to an unfolding of the revolutionary process under Soviet direction.

As a self-styled leader of the world communist movement, the Soviet Union must act in ideological terms. It must do this to maintain itself against the challenge from China and to guard its position in the satellite states of Eastern Europe.

According to Nogee, "It is widely agreed that the current group of Soviet leaders is the least ideologically inclined of all those who have exercised power since the revolution." If this is true, ask Nogee and Donaldson, does ideology matter? The answer is that it does, "but it is difficult to establish a simple and direct connection between ideology and Soviet behavior." But on the other hand, neither is it "totally and always irrelevant to Soviet decision-making." Soviet power, policy, and ideology interact with each other. According to them, "The ideological conflict between the United States and the Soviet Union may not have been the cause of the Cold War but it has certainly impeded the search by both sides for a modus vivendi." Nogee concludes that ideology is important in the Soviet Union because it legitimizes the exercise of power by the USSR elite; neither elections nor military power confers legitimacy without ideology.[7]

Ideology may be defined as a cognitive belief system where images or perceptions of reality represent inputs into the decision-making process. It may also be defined as a system of values that is unchanging over time and that cannot be corrected by any input from reality. In the former instance, there is a prospect of "learning" from "reality" by a decisionmaker. Even if there is a time lag, there is the prospect of change in the image of a decisionmaker. In the latter, the image is fixed and not open to transformation as a result of the impact of the "reality" of the external environment. In the former, ideology is a prism that colors the perspective but is itself open to change by the international environment. In the latter, ideology is the fixed instrument that guides the implementation of policy.

Figures 4.1 through 4.4 outline the shifting focus in the concerns and ideological formulations of Marx and Soviet leaders. When compared to each other, these figures make clear that there is no permanent system of ideas in the ideological expressions of the Soviet leaders. Ideological pronouncements may be defined as a system or channel of communications to domestic and international audiences—the targets of ideological shift. As such, ideological communications are policy communications that are meant to be instrumental and purposive. The primary role of ideology in this case is neither to explain the inner values of decisionmakers nor to predict outcomes. Rather, it is to prescribe policy in relation to the perceived balance of domestic or international forces. Ideology so defined is an

FIGURE 4.1

Marx's Focus

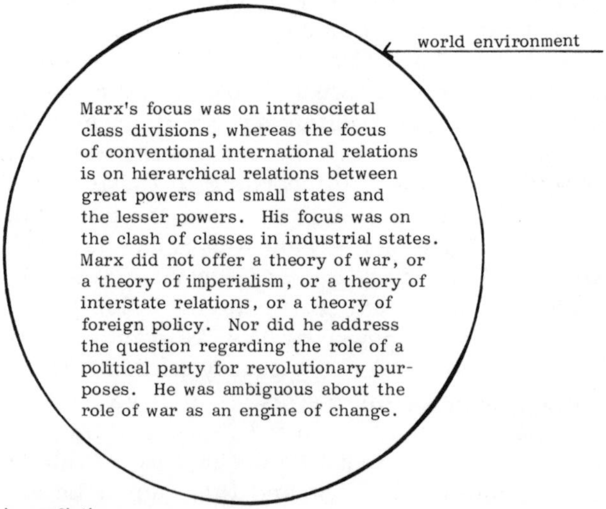

world environment

Marx's focus was on intrasocietal class divisions, whereas the focus of conventional international relations is on hierarchical relations between great powers and small states and the lesser powers. His focus was on the clash of classes in industrial states. Marx did not offer a theory of war, or a theory of imperialism, or a theory of interstate relations, or a theory of foreign policy. Nor did he address the question regarding the role of a political party for revolutionary purposes. He was ambiguous about the role of war as an engine of change.

Marx's predictions

1. Revolution would occur in advanced capitalist society.

2. The state would wither away as an institution after the demise of capitalism.

Source: Figure adapted from J. L. Nogee and R. H. Donaldson, Soviet Foreign Policy Since World War II (New York: Pergamon, 1981), pp. 15-17.

FIGURE 4.2

Lenin's Focus

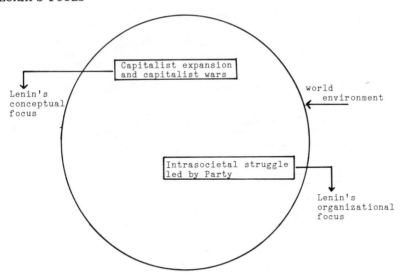

Lenin's approach. In contrast with Marx, Lenin's primary
focus with respect to intrasocietal and intrastate relations was to
stress the importance of the role of the party as the vanguard
of the revolution; he was distrustful of spontaneous uprisings
and about trade union consciousness. This approach was expressed in his What is to be Done? (1902). In Imperialism, the
Highest Stage of Capitalism (1917), the focus was on monopoly
capitalism's quest for maximum profits—which led to export of
capital to less developed countries (where capital was scarce and
materials and labor were cheap)—which led to division of the
world by capitalist powers—which led to conflict among capitalists—
and eventually to capitalist wars.

Lenin did not discuss interstate relationships between capitalist and socialist states and between socialist states. He did
not discuss the nature of war in feudal, monarchical, and early
capitalist states or societies. Lenin raised the possibility of
peaceful coexistence, but at the same time predicted East-West
struggle (Selected Works, volume II, part 2, p. 750). He moved
away from Marx's prediction that revolution would occur in an
advanced capitalist society. Lenin predicted a revolution anywhere in the world, and his writings were intended to appeal to
oppressed third world nations.

Source: Figure adapted from J. L. Nogee and R. H. Donaldson, Soviet Foreign Policy Since World War II (New York: Pergamon, 1981), pp. 18-22.

FIGURE 4.3

Stalin's Focus

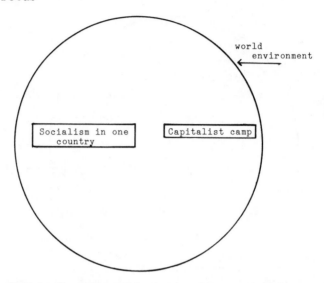

By 1925 Stalin hypothesized that the world had become
bipolarized. Two camps were in existence and neither could
destroy the other; temporary equilibrium had been established.
This laid the foundation for peaceful coexistence based on re-
ciprocity. Zhadhnov's 1947 speech reflected this thinking; war
with the capitalists was inevitable, according to Stalin, but it
was not imminent.

By 1952, however, Stalin revived the old Leninist line that
wars between capitalists were inevitable. The implication was
that war between capitalists and socialists was less likely. See
Stalin's Economic Problems of Socialism in the USSR.

Source: Figure adapted from J. L. Nogee and R. H. Donaldson, Soviet Foreign Policy Since World War II (New York: Pergamon, 1981), pp. 24-26.

FIGURE 4.4

Khrushchev's Focus

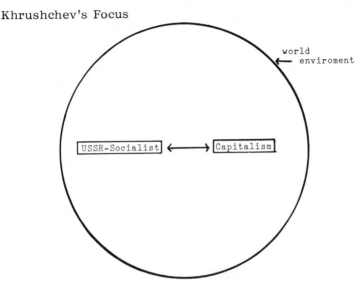

Khrushchev highlighted peaceful coexistence in his 1956 speech. He stated that: nuclear weapons had altered the character of war; wars between capitalists and socialists and between capitalists were no longer inevitable; the next stage was to develop communism by parliamentary means; and the military power of socialism would prevent capitalist aggression.

Source: Figure adapted from J. L. Nogee and R. H. Donaldson, Soviet Foreign Policy Since World War II (New York: Pergamon, 1981), p. 29.

expression of the balance of forces and a rationalization to enable the decisionmaker to relate and mobilize the international and domestic audience. It is not a factor that underlines the decision; it is a vehicle to convey the decision. An ideology is meant to create a clear public identification with an issue. It is by defining issues and prescribing policies that decisionmakers stay in power. The role of ideology in fulfilling the necessity of communication and mobilization of domestic support merits attention in the Soviet case.

The study of Soviet ideology is useful in another way. As an incomplete and changing set of norms and prescriptions, it precedes or anticipates interstate outcomes. It also precedes changes in interstate tendencies. Consider the following estimate of the predictive quality of Soviet ideology in Table 4.1. The

TABLE 4.1

The Changing Focus and Implications of Soviet Ideology

Ideology	Focus of Analysis	Domestic and Foreign Policy Relevance
Lenin (1917)	Advanced capitalism and phenomenon of war between capitalist states	Expressed theme of third world exploitation; aroused nationalism in third world and USSR Implied East-West struggle; the change is far away
	Peaceful coexistence is possible	Conciliatory to West
Stalin	1925: Two camp theory; neither can destroy the other because two camps create temporary equilibrium. This underlines peaceful coexistence	Requires reciprocity by West
	War with capitalism is inevitable	Requires military preparation and industrialization by USSR
	1952: War between capitalist states was inevitable (Lenin thesis revived)	War is less likely between capitalism and socialism
Khrushchev	Inevitability of war thesis is rejected because nuclear weapons change the nature of war Peaceful coexistence is necessary Socialism is strong enough to stop capitalist aggression	Optimism is portrayed internationally, with emphasis on the peaceful nature of communism

Source: Compiled by the author.

94

record is a mixed one, but it progressively gets better with
successive Soviet leaders. This suggests a capacity for growth
or change, a capacity to improve the coincidence between perception and reality.

THE DOMESTIC SETTING OF SOVIET
FOREIGN POLICY

The role and meaning of Soviet ideology depends on the
balance and distribution of political power in the Soviet elite
structure. Soviet ideology is significant as a method to communicate and mobilize elite and public support precisely because
there is a continuous and unsettled elite power struggle. Two
consequences of the bureaucratic revolution in the world today
are the proliferation of competing bureaucracies and the institutionalization of bureaucratic or intrasystemic (actually sub-
systemic) interests in modern industrial states. Given these
two, the task of strong leadership is to mediate competing
interests and, if possible, to formulate an overarching synthesis
to mobilize these interests within state and society. However,
if leadership is weak it will try instead to accommodate itself to
the winning coalition within the state apparatus. In either case,
it is necessary to understand the notion of balance of power
within the state apparatus as a crucial determinant in decisionmaking. Foreign policy communications in this perspective are
intended for mobilizing or rearranging the domestic balance of
power.
        The work of A. Yanov merits serious study. He was born
and trained in the Soviet Union. After 20 years experience as
a journalist and analyst of the Soviet system, he is now working
in the United States. His analysis shows that: there is an ongoing debate in the Soviet Union about foreign policy; detente
figures prominently in this debate; the debate also has much
to do with elites' privileges; and Brezhnev's regime faces a
danger from the Soviet right—the military-industrial complex
(MIC).
        Figure 4.5 provides an overview of the structure of elite
relations within the Soviet Union. Note that the top elite structure is divided and power must be shared between the two sides
at the top—the cosmopolitan officials and MIC managers, with
Brezhnev and the centrists acting as the head of a shaky coalition.
MIC managers seek order in the Soviet bloc and a policy of
imperial-isolationism. The imperial-isolationist strategy[8] is the
preferred norm compared to: world domination; rational state

FIGURE 4.5

Model of Soviet Elite Relationships

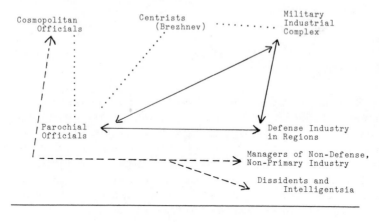

....	Unstable conflict relationship	
_____	Strong relationship/alliance (Group B)	
--------	Potential alliance that could lead to economic reform and true detente with West (inter-dependence) (Group A)	

Common Beliefs/Values:

1. All elites seek security against mass disorder. They fear Pushkin's "mad and merciless Russian uprising."

2. The elites seek privileged access to West for travel and luxury goods.

Source: Compiled by the author.

construction or decentralization of political power (which allows for managerial initiative and maximization of economic production and requires structural economic reform); real improvement in East-West relations (real, detente) that allows real arms reduction; and a world war. These alternatives are not acceptable to the USSR's MIC managers. World domination is not possible. World war is likely to be mutually destructive. Real structural reform is a threat to the alliance between MIC managers, managers of heavy industry, and the parochial party organs in the republics. Detente creates ambiguity for the role of the MIC and weakens public identification with the enemy, thereby weakening the rationale for MIC's industrial and military buildup. The MIC's strategy is to continue the Stalinist system to control and exploit the Soviet and East European economy—that is, to maintain military and political control over economic and cultural life and over the allocation of resources. The MIC's current strategy is to justify further military buildup.[9]

In Figure 4.5 the dissidents are officially personae non gratae. They are not presently allied with the cosmopolitan elite, but the dissidents, being the USSR's intelligentsia, are a potential ally who could help regenerate the USSR's economic and social/political life.[10] An alliance between the intelligentsia/ dissidents, the managers at the local/republic level, and the cosmopolitan officials at the top is potentially a check to the growth of the MIC-parochial party officials at the local level.

In Figure 4.5 the centrists preside over a faction-ridden Soviet establishment in which the interests of competing groups are at stake. So the question of stability and legitimacy is a constant one for the Brezhnev regime.[11] The position and advocacy of the Brezhnev-type centrist regime should be examined in the context of the legacy of the Stalinist system.

The Stalinist system is a security system built on the principle of spheres of influence or orbits in relation to a strong center—that is, the Soviet Union. As Yanov points out, Stalin's goal was not national state construction (as advocated by Bukharin), nor world revolution (as advocated by Trotsky), nor even solely the building of socialism in one country (as advocated by Kirov). It included Kirov's aim, but it also sought a circle of states with the Soviet Union as the center; the Union Republic as the first orbit; the East European states as the second orbit; Yugoslavia (and now Rumania) as the third orbit; and so on.[12]

Stalin's circle of states reflected a crucial reality that was different from his preferred norm. In his conversations with the allied powers during the war, Stalin had argued that he who controls a region has the right to impose his social system.[13] But the failure to annex East Europe despite the existence of Soviet military preeminence revealed the strength of local nationalism in East Europe. Here was local nationalism winning over proletarian internationalism.[14]

Stalin's internal political organization is outlined in Figure 4.6. Its economic management had a single center. The primary instrument to organize economic and cultural life was fear of state power. Stalin has been described as the father of industrialization and mobilization of the working class, as the son of Soviet nationalism and the Holy Spirit of the constitution.[15] But he was also the center of command who presided over a responsive bureaucracy; he was not a center who presided over competing bureaucracies and mediated factional disputes. To achieve and maintain political control, the Stalinist scheme of economic management required economic scarcity, not abundance. The mobilization of Soviet nationalism required "capitalist encirclement" and the "inevitability of war." Encirclement and

FIGURE 4.6

Stalin's Political Organization

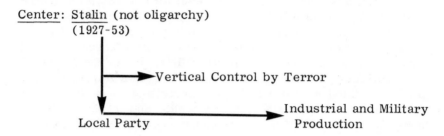

Center: Stalin (not oligarchy)
(1927-53)

Vertical Control by Terror

Local Party

Industrial and Military Production

Source: Compiled by the author.

war danger required nationalism to increase industrial and military preparation. Industrial and military priority led to the distortion of rational economic planning—"rational" defined as resource allocation for socially productive expenditures rather than wasteful military expenditures. Finally, to preserve the primacy of the center, it was essential to practice the politics of scarcity. Without scarcity the political boss loses the opportunity to control the allocation of resources and to manage the political process.[16] In Stalin's time the political and economic process was stable not in the sense that it fulfilled popular needs for consumer goods, but because there was no competition between heavy industry and light industry. Therefore, there was no interference in the flow of communications from the top. When "power" is the ability to communicate and to mobilize resources, intrasystemic resistance and inertia are barriers to the flow of power.

The post-Stalinist system continues the Stalinist system, but there are subtle and fundamental differences. The system of economic management follows the Stalinist shape.[17] The politics of scarcity continue, but the center now is an oligarchy and terror has been replaced by vertical and horizontal arbitrariness. Vertical arbitrariness is reflected in the setting up of production quotas without providing managers with the means to fulfill these without seeking resort to political mediation by local party bosses. Furthermore, consumerism exists at the top—as a quest for personal privilege and luxury goods, and as advocacy of light industry for the Soviet people. But unlike in Stalin's time, there are now parallel and competing lines of horizontal communications and interest articulation, as indicated in Figure 4.5. These interfere with the traditional lines of vertical control and communication. Furthermore, horizontal centers of thinking and policy advocacy imply an upward flow of interference in the administrative process of implementing "decisions" from the top.

FOREIGN POLICY IMPACT OF DOMESTIC FACTIONALISM

The foregoing discussion reveals an interface between the domestic and foreign policy interests of competing groups, A and B. The continuation of precarious (but not collapsing) economic performance strengthens the hands of the right-wing MIC (group B). Their "red line"—the arena for safe operation, or their margin of safety—has these parameters: no real detente because that would lead to interdependence, mass production or mass consumption, and a loss of opportunity to manipulate the politics of scarcity; no mass uprising at home because that could lead to system breakdown; and no cultural and ideological cosmopolitanism in elite and mass thinking because that could destroy the MIC-parochial party alliance.

Group B cannot win because group A is also entrenched in the political system. Group A's norms are to favor structural economic reform by accommodating the managerial elite and its norms. The Centrists have failed to align with the economic reformers,[18] yet it has resisted group B. The Soviet military is under civilian command, and the direct access of Soviet marshals to the Politburo has apparently been blocked. The Brezhnev leadership has repeatedly sought arms control and disarmament.[19] Overall, neither group is dominant. Elite relations now are, vertically and horizontally, bargaining relations. The related question is whether Soviet international—interstate and intrasocialist—relations have also become bargaining relations, and whether domestic international linkages have come into being in the USSR's decision structure.

The impact of a fragmented domestic elite structure is inevitably reflected in Soviet foreign policy decisionmaking. A pessimistic view of Soviet foreign policy may be warranted in terms of its ability to engage in a successful struggle to achieve Pax Communa, if that is the Soviet aim. The Soviet Union's public posture concerning the issue of war and peace is not of paramount importance in Soviet decisionmaking as it has been for the West. Peace, as it is defined in the West, is not the desired norm. In Soviet diplomacy, "peace" is a part of the struggle. In the Soviet approach, war and peace are only two different instruments of class struggle or of an international struggle wherein civil wars are meant to be transformed into revolutionary wars. In other words, "peace" is not the opposite of war; it is an instrumentality and not an end itself.[20]

Accordingly war/peace are instruments and not ends of the struggle between two opposing international systems (capitalism and socialism). Similarly, detente and peaceful coexistence should be viewed as instrumentalities, not as ends. Soviet scholarly works fail to make such a distinction. George Arbatov's The War of Ideas in Contemporary International Relations (1973) reveals the focus of Soviet thinking:

There is "a debate over the basic issue of present-day international relations—the question whether the contradictions between socialism and capitalism will be resolved by war or peacefully—only began in 1917. Subsequent history had to provide an answer."[21]

On this question there is an internal debate in socialist states and communist parties, and the "Leninist political line" has to struggle against both "Left and Right opportunist distortions."[22]

The thesis of "revolutionary war" was the line of the "Left" communists and the Trotskyites. These elements were ideologically defeated during Lenin's lifetime, but the "leftist-opportunistic" ideology is still preached today (including China).[23]

A basic tenet of Marxism-Leninism is that a socialist revolution should not be imposed on the people by force. It is, however, the right and durty of socialist countries to prevent the capitalist countries from "exporting counter-revolution."[24]

Lenin put forward in 1919 the principle of peaceful coexistence (or cohabitation) as the foundation of the Soviet Union's relations with capitalist countries.[25]

"The Cold War is not an ideological conflict between the two opposing systems but a state of acute tension in international relations witnessing a ceaseless arms race and political, economic and frequently, military clashes precipitated by imperialism's policies."[26]

Peaceful coexistence "is the only possible alternative not only to a world war but also to the Cold War." But peaceful coexistence also requires ideological struggle. Peaceful coexistence is not pacifism.[27]

N. I. Lebedev's A New Stage in International Relations (1976) provides a useful Soviet analysis of the "World Balance of Power," the "Bourgeois Concepts of Detente," peaceful co-existence and disarmament.

"The main factor that determined the switch from confrontation and cold war to detente and the world-wide assertion of the principles of peaceful co-existence was the shift in the balance of power in the world in favour of socialism," says Lebedev. The Cuban missile crisis "gave eloquent proof that the balance of power had changed in favour of socialism."[28] Now "no important question in world affairs can be settled without the Soviet Union. As for the place of Soviet-American relations in the modern world, it is determined by the decisive role played by the two great powers by virtue of their tremendous industrial and military potentials for the prevention of a world nuclear war."[29]

In the socialist community "there are no dominant and subordinate countries and no commanding and subordinate parties. But on account of its vast inner political and international experience, the CPSU has become the most authoritative of the communist parties of socialist countries."[30]

Despite the "significant successes" of socialism, relapse into "cold war and military ventures" was still possible, but "the process of social change in the world" cannot be halted by force. In the new situation it is necessary "to agree to restructure international relations on the basis of the two systems' peaceful co-existence."[31]

Political and military detente is the "only alternative to war."[32]

According to Brezhnev, international relations are now at a crossroad. One route leads to trust, cooperation, and lasting peace (eventually); the other leads to mutual fear, arms race, and brinkmanship. The arms race must be halted.[33]

The activity of new (ex-colonial) states is made possible because the socialist world has restructured international relations, and the winning of independence by the third world "is integrally connected with the struggle between the two social systems in the world arena."[34]

There is an anti-imperialist alliance between the socialist world and the developing countries.[35]

"It could not be clearer that the multiplicity of international relations, the complexities of the alignment of forces, cannot be reduced to a bi-polar system, to a contention between two powers—the United States and the Soviet Union. The present international situation is keynoted by a multiplicity of forces, each furthering its own interests. But the invigoration of

polycentric tendencies—the emergence of new centres of power
and imperialist rivalry, and the greater involvement of medium
and small states—does not abolish the fundamental contradiction
of the modern world, its division into two systems, and their
historical confrontation. It is this confrontation that determines
the most profound, objective foundation of the alignment of
world forces, despite all the twists and turns in international
development."36

These samples of Soviet scholarship point to an incomplete
set of "theory"—if theory is defined as a set of ideas that explain
and predict. There is a problem in Soviet writings. The relationship between the ideas themselves is not precise: for instance,
what is the relationship between "war" and "peace," between
"peace" and "armed struggle against counterrevolution," between
detente and peaceful coexistence on the one hand and "revolutionary war" on the other? What is the intended role of Soviet
force against counterrevolution in socialist countries in Eastern
Europe, and in third world countries, such as Angola and Afghanistan? (Is there a distinction between the roles in the two
situations?) Lenin emphasized that mass action had to be accompanied by secrecy in decisionmaking; if this norm has not
changed, then can Soviet pronouncements be taken at face
value?
The absence of clear analytical relationships in Soviet foreign
policy ideas may be explained as deception, or that Soviet International Relations theory is in the making. This implies that
Soviet thinkers have not yet thought through the implications
of their norms, or that each norm refers to a category of situation, but a general theory cannot be formulated because Soviet
theory is not meant to be a guide to its decisionmaking. Rather,
it is meant to explain ex post facto the decisions taken. To
fulfill this function, "Soviet theory" must be ambiguous. In
other words, ambiguity in theory is a consequence of ambiguity
in the norms of the decision structure. The problem then is
not that a difference exists between Soviet theory and behavior,
but that Soviet behavior itself has different faces because the
Soviet decision structure has different and competing voices
(as described in the review of Yanov's analysis). The incomplete-
ness in the Soviet system of foreign policy ideas is a consequence
of competing voices in the Soviet establishment. Soviet ideology
with regard to its external relations is fragmented.
It is easy to dismiss the notion that Soviet International
Relations theory is in the making because the essential ideas
in contemporary Soviet scholarly works can conveniently be

traced back. Peaceful coexistence goes back to Lenin—in 1919.
The notion of two competing international systems was expressed
in 1925 in Stalin's view of a "temporary equilibrium" between
capitalism and socialism before American scholars discovered
bipolarity. Khrushchev's commitment to national liberation
struggles and wars can be traced to Lenin's focus on revolutionary wars. The focus on disarmament in Soviet writings goes
back to the tzar's proposal on the subject at the Hague Conference in 1899.

The richness in the study of Soviet foreign policy lies in
the examination of the interplay between norm and decisionmaking
in Soviet external relations in East Europe, the socialist world,
the third world, and in great power relations. The richness
lies in an examination of the domestic and international context
of detente and peaceful coexistence between the two superpowers.
It lies in the interplay between detente and revolutionary wars
from 1975 to 1980. It lies in the vulnerability of the Soviet
policy of detente because of the impact of Afghanistan and
Poland. If the Soviet Union's forays into Africa, Southwest
and Southeast Asia, and the Middle East were successful—and
this is open to debate—events in Poland during 1980 and 1981
reveal Soviet vulnerability. Surely, if the Soviet Union "gains"
Afghanistan and the Horn, and "loses" Poland, the two cancel
out each other. The net result is one of activity and movement—
both forward and backward. If power is the ability to control
the flow of military, material, and cultural-psychological communications in the world, if power is an ability to enforce one's
own social system in areas one controls physically, then the
expansion of Soviet military power is not necessarily one-sided.
The Soviet Union itself seems to be open to counterpressure
and countermovement when it projects its power beyond its
territorial frontier. It is hard to measure exactly the counter-
flows, but their existence is undeniable.

The changing composition of the Soviet circle of states
merits attention in this regard. The defections of Yugoslavia
and China from the Soviet circle of states in the late 1940s and
mid-1950s are signs of Soviet insecurity. The shift of Rumania
from the second circle to the third circle in the 1960s is another
example of the changing composition of the circle. Finally, the
Czech and Polish desire to shift from the first circle to the second
is a matter for the future, as is the potential quest of Ukrainian
and Georgian nationalists to move from the USSR "sun" into the
first circle. In other words, when power is the ability to achieve
the territorial, material, and cultural integration of a group,
the changing composition of a circle of states is a sign of weakness of the center.

OVERVIEW

In assessing the elements of the Soviet Union's international presence and impact, it is essential to note the domestic sources and constraints and the external opportunities and constraints. The elements in Table 4.2 may be utilized in assessing the evolution of the Soviet international position from a regional great power in East Europe in the late 1940s into a superpower in the 1960s. The measure of the change lies in three indicators. First, the Soviet Union is a recognized strategic power. It has the capacity to project its military power beyond its territorial frontier and into Southeast Asia, the Indian Ocean, Angola, Afghanistan, and Cuba. Second, the Soviet Union has established its diplomatic presence almost worldwide. As such, it is an active, and in many regions, a primary participant in the political strategic process, achieving a seat at the table through its military and economic aid diplomacy. Third, the Soviet Union discloses a self-image that no problem in the world can be solved without its participation.

However, in noting the growth of the Soviet international presence, the existence of influence cannot necessarily be assumed. "Influence" may be defined as: the ability to alter the other side's behavior; the ability to reinforce one's own behavior, or to reinforce an enemy's past behavior (that is, to induce a reinforcement of existing norms); the ability to induce a change in the other side's attitudes; and the ability to reinforce one's own attitudes. By these definitions (individually or collectively), the Soviet Union (or the United States) does not appear entirely successful in the previous three decades. It has established itself as a key player in the international system, but so what? The Soviet circle of states has shrunk from the 1940s to the present. There is divisiveness in the world communist movement. The USSR's ability to project its military power has grown, as is evident by its military deployments since the mid 1970s into areas hitherto inaccessible to it.

But its behavior has also mobilized both international opinion and third world nationalism against it. The Soviet Union is not viewed as a model world citizen after its brutal invasion of Afghanistan in December 1979. Continued instability in the third world has meant the Soviet Union has had opportunities to exploit and expand its activities, but in transforming itself from a regional great power into a world power, it has had to pay a price. There has been a strain on its economic productivity and the growth of its consumer activity because of the diversion of vital economic and human resources to materially and socially

TABLE 4.2

Major Elements in Assessing the USSR's Presence and Impact

Domestic sources of power and constraints	External opportunities and constraints in international environment in facilitating and limiting USSR's power projection

Economy
Military power
Elite consensus, including
  role of ideology
	USSR's quest for international
	  legitimacy
	Superpowers' arms race
	Divisiveness in the Soviet bloc,
	  including relations with China
	Third world nationalism

Source: Compiled by the author.

nonproductive uses. The Soviet Union has sought international legitimacy by promoting a detente relationship with the United States; only another superpower can confer legitimacy to the USSR's desire to be viewed as the other principal in world politics. But at the same time, the Soviet Union has been involved in proxy wars or in revolutionary wars in Asia and Africa. This has aroused the ire of the anti-Soviet constituency in the United States. For the Soviet elite the choice is unpleasant: detente with the United States or military involvement in the third world. This range of choices points to the impact of the international environment on intrasystemic struggles between Soviet economic reformers who seek superpower detente, and the neo-Stalinists and the imperial-isolationists who seek military power and an anti-West posture.

The detente-versus-intervention choice points to a difficult situation. On the one hand, there is a desire to achieve legitimacy and predictability in horizontal superpower ties. On the other hand, the Soviet Union seeks expansion of its international position by intervening in third world crises. It is by continued demonstration of its international interventionist capability that the Soviet Union can justify its military expenditures, the need to be militarily prepared against "imperialist intrigues," and, above all, to create a "bargaining chip" with the United States. Moreover, the claim that military power is needed to bargain has to be repeatedly made to convince critics in the Soviet establishment. In other words, the Soviet Union's basic strategic choice today—between "horizontal" engagement of the United States and "vertical" intervention in third world crises—suggests a linkage between the two strategies, and a built-in contradiction that cannot be resolved. To prove that it is indispensable as the United States' international partner, the Soviet Union must make itself a voice in international and regional security issues.

The Soviet Union seems to be in a no-win situation. If it presses for closer economic ties with the United States, it reveals its economic and managerial weaknesses. The fear of becoming interdependent (or dependent) on the capitalist world clashes with that stream of Soviet political and social thought that is anti-West and antiforeign. On the other hand, Soviet military interventions in regional crises strengthen the anti-Soviet advocacy in the U.S. establishment. Furthermore, the fear of superpower conflict and its likely impact on third world interests strengthens third world nationalism against the expansion of both superpowers—an identification the Soviet Union prefers not to have. In short, the Soviet Union would like to be seen as a reliable partner by the United States. To achieve this distinction, it must be recognized as a military, economic, and cultural equal of the United States, but it would prefer not to be seen as yet another "bad" superpower by the third world. It must guard its image in the third world because it knows how quick third world nationalism is in reacting against it (namely, its defeats in Egypt, Sudan, and Somalia during the 1970s, and in the first elections in Zimbabwe in 1979).

The Soviet Union cannot win a regional crisis militarily because a win would dilute, if not delete, U.S. involvement in the area, and for this reason it will be resisted by the United States and its allies. Furthermore, a Soviet "win" would be seen by many in the third world as an invitation to Soviet domination, and as a loss of opportunity to play both sides to the advantage of the third world states. Thus, in effect, the Soviet Union denies victory to the United States, and vice versa. Third world states prefer this outcome compared to one where the superpowers either act in concert or where one of them wins decisively. A no-win superpower involvement in regional crises is the preferred outcome of many third world states because a world of limited superpower competition is ideal to extract material assistance and political support by a diplomatically sophisticated weaker third world state. From this perspective, the "Angolas" and "Afghanistans" are good because these crises imply continued divisiveness in superpower relations.

The foregoing analysis adds up to a picture of paralysis in the range of strategic choices for the Soviet Union. It is not a case of deception. Deception becomes an issue if a state is mobilizing the international environment to its own advantage. The picture of the results of the Soviet Union's international experiences is hardly one of one-sided gain. Soviet foreign policy is not evolutionary. Rather, an interplay of competing organizational or group interests in the Soviet establishment, and of strategies and outcomes, is indicated. It appears that the nature of success in policy process in the Soviet Union and elsewhere is that the key domestic and international players should continue to be involved in a decisionmaking apparatus in which no one wins. Just as the notion of military victory has lost its meaning in the post-1945 world, "political victory" seems to have no relevance for the study of decisionmaking politics. Continued involvement, not decisive influence, is the name of the game. The improbability of a particular side or group "winning" makes "winning" an insignificant term in the study of Soviet foreign policy.

NOTES

1. For example see Merle Fainsod, How Russia is Ruled (Cambridge, Mass.: Harvard University Press, 1967), rev. ed.; and Robert Conquest, Present Danger (Oxford: Blackwell, 1979).

2. J. F. Triska and D. A. Finley, Soviet Foreign Policy (New York: Macmillan, 1968), Chapter 3; J. L. Schwartz and W. R. Keech, "Group Influence and the Policy Process in the Soviet Union," in J. L. Nogee, ed., Man, State and Society (New York: Praeger, 1972); and M. Schwartz, The Foreign Policy of the USSR: Domestic Factors (Belmont, Calif.: Dickenson, 1975), particularly Chapter 6.

3. J. L. Nogee and R. H. Donaldson, Soviet Foreign Policy Since World War II (New York: Pergamon, 1981), p. 1.

4. See R. H. Donaldson, ed., The Soviet Union in the Third World: Successes and Failures (Boulder, Colo.: Westview Press, 1981), particularly the comments by D. E. Albright.

5. See former Senator J. W. Fullbright's essay in C. Gati, ed., Caging the Bear (New York: Bobbs-Merrill, 1974).

6. Quoted in Nogee and Donaldson, op. cit., p. 3.

7. Ibid., pp. 37-39.

8. A. Yanov, Detente After Brezhnev: The Domestic Roots of Soviet Foreign Policy (Berkeley: Institute of International Studies, University of California, 1977), pp. 63-67.

9. Ibid.

10. Ibid., p. 15.

11. Ibid., pp. 74, 77.

12. Ibid., p. 61.

13. For Stalin's belief in a Soviet sphere of influence where a USSR-controlled regime manages the material and cultural relations of a society, see I. Deutscher, Stalin (London: Oxford University Press, 1967), particularly Chapters 13 and 14 and pp. 411-13.

14. Yanov, op. cit., p. 62.

15. Ibid., p. 57.

16. Ibid., p. 27.

17. Ibid., p. 28.

18. Ibid., p. 20.

19. Ibid., p. 19.

20. T. A. Taracouzio, War and Peace in Soviet Diplomacy (New York: Macmillan, 1940), Chapter 2.

21. G. Arbatov, The War of Ideas in Contemporary International Relations (Moscow, Progress, 1973), p. 255.

22. Ibid., p. 256.

23. Ibid., pp. 256-57.

24. Ibid., p. 257.

25. Ibid., p. 258.

26. Ibid., p. 270.

27. Ibid., pp. 273-74, 277.

28. N. I. Lebedev, A New Stage in International Relations (Oxford: Pergamon, 1976), pp. 35, 44.

29. Ibid., p. 222.

30. Ibid., pp. 39-40.

31. Ibid., p. 46.

32. Ibid., p. 99.

33. Ibid., pp. 114-15.

34. Ibid., pp. 149-50, 153, 154.

35. Ibid., p. 156.

36. Ibid., p. 235.

Nonalignment and
National Security in
the 1980s:
The Changing Context of
World Power and the Tendencies
toward International Change

INTRODUCTION

The nonalignment movement coincided with three international developments: the emergence of two bloc structures at
the end of World War II that polarized East-West relations; the
introduction of atomic energy, which nuclearized military strategy
and created fear of global disaster in social psychology; and
the development of the United Nations system, which strengthened
the hope for a democratic international life and recognized, in
the organization of the Security Council, that the principle of
balance of power should continue.

In its declaratory aims, nonalignment was a reaction to
the cold war and the threat of a hot war. It reflected opposition
to polarization of international relations on an East-West basis,
as well as on the basis of a world with but two international
principals. Its original aims were mainly political: antiwar,
prodisarmament, anticolonialism, proU.N., and so on. In the
thinking of its founding fathers (Tito, Nehru, and Nasser),
the focus of the third world's international policy ought to move
toward denuclearization and demilitarization of military bloc
structures. Their national policies stressed economic and social
development and, to a lesser extent, national security through
military defense. These leaders did not face the paradox of
the 1960s and the 1970s: the quest for northern denuclearization,
arms reduction, and disarmament on the one hand, and the
South's own militarization and nuclearization. Neither did they
have to face issues that confront the nonaligned states today,
namely, development, not disarmament, is now the main concern
of nonaligned states; the growing incidence of conflict in the
South as a consequence of internal and external sources of
conflict, which requires more arms than before; and yet if

military force can hold off military conflict, it is not a solution
to endemic domestic social and economic conflict (the domestic
conflict requires meaningful economic and social change and
development).

The international setting for the development of nonalignment has changed since 1945. As an international idea, as a
sign of national policy development, and as an international
social movement, nonalignment should be studied as a dynamic
force that grows and adapts to external and internal change.
It has grown into a large group (over 80 states) and its members
occupy a major part of the South. This could be a sign of a
belief that international relations ought to be something more
than a world of competing military blocs, a world of two international principals who share an interest to preserve their
primacy. However, the superpowers have never liked nonalignment and have sown the seeds of dissent in the movement through
their proxies: Cuba for the Soviet Union, Pakistan and Singapore
for the United States.

The ideological diversity of the movement in the 1970s
suggests that nonalignment has lost its original innocence, its
exclusivity, its purity as an expression of peoples' aspirations
for peace and accommodation among states. There is, however,
also the view that ideological diversity is the basis of international
consensus making, value formation, and attitude change. It is
an alternative approach to the one that speaks of deterrence
and behavior modification through use of force and threats. In
this sense the present paralysis of the movement could be defined
as a phase of hibernation and adaptation to international change.
As such, the paralysis of the "nonaligned weak" may be studied
in the context of the paralysis of the strong powers in the North,
and generally in the context of major tendencies of international
change since 1945.

INTERNATIONAL CHANGES

Since 1945 international relations have turned in a number
ways. These may be summarized as follows.

With the rise of two superpowers with equal or almost equal
military weight, "military victory" is now irrelevant. At the
same time, the distinction between war and peace as legal and
psychological conditions in public thinking is no longer meaningful. Modern states exist in varying degrees of armed peace.

By and large, industrial societies prefer not to engage in
open military warfare. Instead, they prefer to prepare for war

and to engage in international arms trade, which is a component of global commerce. It is significant that historically the incidence of war has shifted from the North to the South.

International politics since 1945 is a product of the "organization revolution." The concern is with production and efficiency, not with intuition, culture, and happiness (unless money equals happiness). This revolution creates technocracy, which requires mastery over nature and science and which makes physical conquest unnecessary. Yet the organizational revolution offers all the benefits of colonial conquest in the sense that it provides unequal exchange in center-periphery relations (that is, access to resources and markets, and control over decisionmaking relating to the mobilization of resources and world power).

Nuclear weaponry is not the primary factor in the mobilization and organization of global power. Nuclear arms reinforce the powers, but they do not create power. Nuclear arms freeze strategic conflict among the powers. Access to nuclear power does not alter the economic, social, and political status of a state; it does not alter a state's capacity or incapacity to mobilize usable nonnuclear instruments of power. Nuclear power and nuclear diplomacy reinforce the utility of coercive diplomacy, but it does not create the imperative toward coercive diplomacy.

Decolonialism after 1945 was a consequence of the failure of European powers against third world nationalisms. More important, it was also a consequence of the failure of European powers to match the rise of U.S. and Soviet power since the 1800s. The emergence of decolonialism occurred simultaneously with U.S. and Soviet power development. In particular, it occurred in the context of the pattern of development of U.S. power: first, with the expansion of American power within the continental United States; then the expansion abroad in the form of Monroe Doctrine; then the development of open door policy in the Pacific and the Far East; and finally, the expansion of the open door policy in Europe, the Middle East, and Africa after 1945.

Since 1945 the third world has adopted statism and industrialism as its primary methods for economic, social, and political development. Today there are about 150 states and the globalization of the states' system is an accomplished fact. The concept of a world system of sovereign and politically independent states is northern in origin. The North successfully exported to the South the norms of statism and industrialism after the North had successfully penetrated southern societies during the colonial era (that is, after the southern societies had failed to retain their traditional social, political, and economic structures in the

encounters between southern culture and Western technology
during the 1800s). It was in a setting of failure of the South
against the North that the notion of political independence and
nationalism was transmitted by the North and to the South. In
most cases in the third world, statehood came after the traditional
structure of social stability and political authority had been disrupted by the colonial experience.

The transfer of the norms of statism and industrialism to
the South generated an intellectual and strategic impasse in
third world development. Starting with fragile social, economic,
and political structures at the time of independence, the nationalistic but fragmented societies faced a dilemma. If rapid economic
modernization was sought through industrialism and state intervention, the sources of traditional identity in its society had to
be threatened and weakened further. But rapid economic change
and social disruption, without appropriate nation building, could
lead to social disorder and revolution. On the other hand, if a
developing state tried to preserve its social order along traditional
lines, it risked failure in satisfying its public's needs. This
dilemma may be described as the trauma of transitionalism. A
transitional society is the worst of two worlds: the stability of
traditional society has been destroyed, and development has
been retarded so that a mass consumption society has not been
achieved. By and large, state and social structure in the South
is that of retarded development, of social and economic transitionalism. This is the setting for neocolonialism or unequal
exchange in a world of North-South or center-periphery relations.
Neocolonialism is both cause (the impact of the colonial past)
and consequence of (after neocolonial relations are established)
transitionalism. Transitionalism implies the existence of rhetorical
political nationalism and subnational or local elite competition.
Such competition is not likely to be settled unless attitude or
cultural reformation occurs. This is difficult. When power is
divided in a transitional state and society, social interaction
usually becomes an exercise in continuous talk and propaganda
among competing elites. The third world states have formulated
neither a framework to accommodate the need for mass consumption
society (through technocracy) nor a developed national culture
(which offers a sense of identity). The North prefers the South
not to find a formula for such accommodation because it could
threaten relations.

The patterns of global relations are changing with regard
to the nature of power, the nature of intraregional and interregional communications (flows of norms and influence), and
with respect to the relationship between the superpowers (the

dominant powers in traditional analyses) and the lesser powers (states with regional and interregional influence). In post-1945 history (specifically applied to assessment of superpowers' influence) a fundamental paradox is noteworthy. The superpowers' presence has increased globally since 1945, if presence is measured by: increases in diplomatic representation; military (and specifically nuclear) capability; aid flows by both superpowers; ability of superpowers to communicate threats to each other and to lesser powers; their ability to increase the flow of propaganda internationally; and so on. If "presence" is defined as activity or effort, the superpowers clearly have international presence. However, superpower influence seems to have declined internationally. It has declined if "influence" is defined as outcomes, as consequences of applied power that are significant in the following ways: the superior power is able to modify the behavior of opposing powers; the superior power is able to reinforce existing behavior of actors in international regimes that serve its interests; the superior power is able to modify the attitude of opposing powers; and finally, the superior power is able to reinforce existing attitudes that serve its interests. Behavior modification or reinforcement may be a consequence of fear; hence, it does not necessarily mean that voluntary participation of the international constituencies exists in favor of superpower policies. As such, attitude modification or reinforcement merits separate treatment.

The superpowers, particularly since the 1970s, have been frustrated in their attitudes and policies by evidence of growing interregional relations (such as political, trade, and cultural ties between West European and South American states; between South American states and Africa; between Latin America and Middle Eastern states, and so on). Furthermore, the superpowers have failed as role models for third world development. They remain useful as sources of foreign aid and technology transfer, but for major third world states (Brazil, Argentina, Nigeria, India, and so on), their range of choices has increased. This is so because of a number of reasons: growth in their internal weight and regional/international influence in select matters; growth of their military capacity to resist foreign threats and to escape superpower-enforced military intervention and diplomatic isolation; growth of their diplomatic experience and intelligence, which enables them to seek out opportunities and to make better cost-effectiveness calculations and bargains; growth of tendencies in many regions to shape intraregional and interregional cooperation and, in doing so, to cut across traditional ideological, political, and cultural barriers.

The United States and the Soviet Union are superpowers in terms of their military power, particularly because of the fear that they could destroy the world. But they are no longer poles of attraction for the third world. The United States is still more attractive compared to the Soviet Union—if attraction is measured in terms of migration for economic and political reasons. But they are not attractive as long-term ideological and political partners for third world states. The superpower impact on the third world is a story of temporary "presence" or impact in different parts of the world (for example, the Soviet Union—first involved in Somalia, then shifted to Ethiopia; the United States—first "in" Vietnam, then "out"; first "in" Iran, then "out"; and so on). These presences come into being as superpowers' reactions to perceived crisis situations. In a sense, once the production lines are established for the military industry, the quest is to move on, to think of relating to new crisis situations. The superpowers' foreign policy is not simply crisis management; it is also the quest for crisis involvement. This is logical for competing bureaucracies in search of a mission that achieves a clear public identification. To the extent that the superpowers have reduced ability to control the origin and outcome of crises, their influence shrinks in third world perceptions.

In traditional writings, it has been assumed that superpowers manage the dominant international system; that is, they are the central powers and their relationship constitutes the central balance in the world. According to this view, secondary powers or middle powers have influence in their own regional system or the "subordinate system," and they could at best influence select developments in interregional issues. Presumably, the superpowers could manage international relations horizontally (in relation to superpowers and great powers) and vertically (in relation to secondary or middle powers, and obviously with small states and colonies). Presumably, according to the traditional view, the secondary or middle powers could only generate interregional influence and vertical influence in relation to smaller states; they could not alter (vertically) the behavior and attitudes of the superpowers.

This traditional view is now doubtful. It may be argued that superpowers, by competing against each other, have to an extent cancelled their influence against each other. Furthermore, secondary or middle powers have broken the flow of superpowers' influence into regional affairs. Consequently, the world may be seen as a number of pockets of regional autonomy, and of (established or emerging) interregional links in the middle and southern parts of the globe. Moreover, a study of crisis behavior shows that secondary or middle powers can initiate crises and, in select cases (such as Indira Gandhi in 1971 and Anwar Sadat in 1973), they can influence or control the outcome. The ability to initiate and control the outcome is power and influence in the sense that regional crises attract the attention of superpowers and significantly involve the utilization of their diplomatic and military capabilities. When a regional crisis gets on the superpowers' agenda (usually the agenda consists of a new crisis every day, or a continuing crisis that reappears on the agenda) that is influence. In other words, when regional crises—created and managed by the secondary or middle powers—impact on superpowers' perceptions and policies and drag them into regional conflict, then the power in the "subordinate system" not only achieves regional and interregional influence, but it can also manipulate, intrude into, and influence the decision process of the so-called dominant, central, or international powers.

For most third world states, national security is usually a quest to achieve military security; a quest to find the military power to check external threats; and a quest to escape from external military intervention and diplomatic isolation. The context of national security for many third world states is somewhat as follows. For newly independent states, foreign policy and military policy flow from domestic problems and politics. Initially, it is a question of establishing a viable central elite power structure—a strong center that can accommodate competing regional and subnational pressures and articulate, aggregate, and synthesize the conflicting interests into national norms or postures. These norms or postures are not policies or specific decisions. They convey attitudes, values, and beliefs that create a framework for specific policies and programs. Thus, the upward flow of communications by competing subnational groups and regions becomes crystallized into deliberately vague or ambiguous declarations by a center. The downward flows are filtered, debated, negotiated, and translated into policies and programs by the administrative and party structures of a state and society. A "national" policy, therefore, is a synthesis of decisions taken by the center as a consequence of upward flows, and the decisions taken by the administrative and party structures as a consequence of bureaucratic interventions that occur in the process of implementing the norms of the center. Because the center itself is an arena for horizontal bargaining among competing factors, there is a linkage between horizontal (cabinet decisions) and vertical (administrative implementation) bargaining processes. This process reveals dynamic vertical-horizontal-vertical flows of intranational communications in developing states, which are trying to cope with fluid domestic and international environments.

In essence, the task of decisionmaking is to <u>satisfy</u> those who are "in-here" and to <u>manage</u> those who are "out-there". The northern industrialized societies, the centers of the world, follow this pattern of behavior. In peripheral and neocolonial (center-periphery ties) societies, however, this pattern of behavior is reversed: the system manages those who ought to be in-here (nationals) and satisfies and accommodates those who ought to be out-there (foreigners). To satisfy the in-heres, the process of political, economic, and social change should be distributive—or more distributive and less competitive. By this norm, internal policies of economic, social, and political change should constantly aim toward improved distribution and reduced domestic competition. Furthermore, competitiveness ought to be externalized, not internalized, the enemies should be out-there, not in-here. In fact, in many developing societies the real enemies tend to be in-here rather than out-there, although state propaganda and interstate communications usually stress, in diversionary fashion, the presence of enemies out-there. The challenge before these societies is to transform their basic attitudes and processes. Instead of being competitive and not distributive with constituents in-here—as is the case with many third world states at present (with exceptions)—and instead of being accommodative or "open to persuasion" to distributions or redistributions of power and resources among collaborating elites in the international environment, the pattern of behavior should facilitate an internalized distributive norm and an externalized competitive norm.

In states that accommodate the out-theres, nationalism is externalized but it is also phony and diversionary because the real behavior is to accommodate and seek distribution of power and resources between domestic and foreign collaborating elites, and there is continued domestic competition, struggle, and poverty. The posture of external competition is a bargaining chip—a step in the quest for accommodation and a share in the pie. The national security mechanism creates a pose of external competition and threat, when external policies are naturally intended to be accommodating and distributive. In states that accommodate the in-heres, nationalism is internalized in the quest for more production and better distribution for mass well-being. These states strive for a measure of intranational satisfaction through equitable distribution. Externalized competition is meant to protect domestic gains against real foreign enemies. Here the national security mechanism is truly that of external defense. In the first system, national security is defined in terms of regional cold wars and regional military balances, and threat definitions and management have a significant input from the international environment. In the second system, national security is found in the growth of the country's internal economic and military weight. The distributive policies of a country account for the satisfaction, strength, and domestic social base of external relations.

When the aim of the political system and elite behavior is to manage the in-heres or to accommodate the out-theres, then the buildup of the national security mechanism for external defense and crisis management has three purposes: first, it is primarily intended to divert systematic public scrutiny from the linkage between domestic factional activity and external elite interests; second, although threat perceptions are exaggerated (and deliberately so), the image of a dehumanized foreign enemy is functional to the extent that it promotes domestic and foreign elite collaboration; finally, the image of a foreign enemy is functional because it facilitates domestic polarization and coalition building in response to the threat perceptions that enjoy a clear public identification. A cold war[1] (defined as manageable and prolonged international tensions) facilitates and consolidates the image-building process concerning a foreign enemy. The longer the cold war goes on—be it an international or a regional cold war—the greater is the likelihood that there will be both a domestic social base of support for the threat perception and a development and institutionalization of bureaucratic power in response to threat perceptions. Finally, once bureaucratic interests emerge and coalesce against foreign enemies, then the longer the cold war goes on and the greater is the role of inertia as a barrier against the change of the threat perception. Inertia could itself become an instrument of social control. Extended cold wars tend to freeze images of foreign enemies. The elites' privileged access to national and international communications facilitates image building and achievement of a clear public identification in support of the desired image. Under these circumstances, images and their supporting elements assume a life of their own.

The primary factor in the national security policymaking process is to divert public attention to foreign enemies and to shape a clear public identification against both foreign enemies and those at home who disagree with the dominant elites' threat perception. The development of the image of a foreign enemy polarizes the external and domestic environments. In this view of politics, moderation of the enemy image is not a desired value. If moderation could lead to accommodation and agreement, a contrary strategy is desirable. When the primary concern is to manage the in-heres (the hidden domestic enemies and competitors in domestic power struggles), the proper strategy is to polarize the international and domestic environments by exaggerating and dehumanizing the enemy. In this process, the moderate elements in the enemy's decision structure are likely to become radicalized. Radicalizing the moderates is a deliberate strategy of the cold war. Once the radicalization occurs, it is then possible to use this as confirmation of the original threat perception. Given the need to manage the hidden domestic enemies, the strategy is to introduce the threat perception of the foreign enemy into domestic politics. This usually is a catalyst that loosens the lines of intranational and international communications. In other words, if the domestic elite structure is divided and a section of it seeks more power for itself and its constituency, it is necessary to establish a threat perception of a foreign enemy so that a new united front at home can be shaped. The national security mechanism reacts to the threat perception of the enemy, and not necessarily to the reality of what the enemy is doing or is capable of doing in the future. In the latter sense, national security may be anti-empirical with respect to assessing signals of the foreign enemy's moderate behavior. Anti-empiricism is necessary because signals of enemy moderation could raise doubts about one's own threat perception and create psychological discomfort in one's constituency.

The purpose of the cold war is to ensure that conflict does not become an unmanageable hot war, and that it remains a manageable and extended cold war so that the threat perception can be used against those who might be unpatriotic enough to make a deal with the enemy. Even when a cold war situation leads to interstate agreement, it is of marginal significance. The hidden agenda of items that were excluded from negotiation because of the existence of domestic bureaucratic vetoes ought to be the topic for this study, not the agenda that yields agreement. The hidden agenda concerns the interplay of intra-elite competition at home. The overt cold war is a product of the covert and significant intranational elite struggles, and these are about who gets the capacity and the right to intervene and secure compensation (or to organize the exchange or the unequal exchange relationships) in domestic and international relations.

The view of contemporary international relations is clouded by a preoccupation with superpower relations and the old and

new cold wars. Cold wars are usually studied as a contest between two ideological and economic international systems, between
the forces of democracy and authoritarianism. The nuclear arms
race is a symbol of this competition, as is the frequent exchange
of propaganda between Moscow and Washington and the division
of the world into two competing military alliances (NATO and
Warsaw Pact). The ability of the superpowers to blow up the
world many times over is seen as evidence of their international
power.

Writing in the New York Times on November 1, 1981, the
noted American analyst I. F. Stone suggests that the cold war
should be viewed differently: as a war of two communist blocs,
led by Moscow and Washington. The Moscow-led communist bloc
includes most Eastern European states, Cuba, and other Soviet
allies (about one-half billion people). The membership of the
Washington-led communist bloc is bigger: it contains about one
billion people comprised mainly of Yugoslavia, China, Cambodia,
Poland, Somalia, and now possibly Zimbabwe. Foreign policy
and strategic interests define membership in each bloc—not the
internal structure or ideology of the countries concerned.

In his conversations about world affairs with allied leaders,
Stalin said that he who has military control has the right and
the power to organize the social, political, and economic relations
of the territory controlled. This formula of power no longer
appears to be relevant in the study of the Soviet Union. If
power is visualized as a circle with Moscow in the center, the
power relations in the late 1940s would indicate complete Soviet
control over bloc relations. Generally speaking, in the late
1940s one could hypothesize two circles in the definition of Soviet
power: the inner circle contained the various Soviet republics,
the outer circle contained Eastern European countries that even
Stalin could not incorporate. (China, which emerged in 1949
as a communist state, would be included in the outer circle.)

In 1948 the Stalin-Tito split created a third circle containing
Yugoslavia. This functioned in the context of the Soviet-U.S.
split, thereby making Yugoslavia and the United States tacit
strategic partners in relation to the Soviet Union and Eastern
Europe. The riots in Hungary and Poland in the mid 1950s
revealed social dissatisfaction in the Eastern communist system.
The brutal crushing of Hungary by Soviet tanks revealed the
validity of the old Stalinist axioms: power grew out of the barrel
of the gun and social obedience could be obtained by force; a
domestic social base of regime support could be acquired by
fear; and political authority flowed from military power and its
perception. Subsequently, however, Hungary developed its

consumer and market-oriented economic system and capitalism
grew roots despite the presence of Soviet power. In this sense
even Hungary partly moved away from the second circle into
the third, or halfway between the two. In foreign policy and
military relations Rumania also moved away from its position in
the second circle, even though internally it remains Stalinist.
Poland today seeks economic and political reform as well as movement into the third circle. Finally, if nationalism in select USSR
republics represents a social movement, and Soviet muslims have
local nationalistic aspirations, even the possibility of movement
from the inner USSR circle to the second Eastern European circle
may not be excluded in the future. The existence of voluntary
participation, or of a submissive social base for policy, may no
longer be assumed as a given, even when superior military force
is present. Moscow is still an international military power center,
but it is not necessarily the prime controller or manager of economic, social, and political relations in the second and third
circles of the Soviet-managed international power structure.

The erosion of postwar, superpower-led, international
power relations is significant. The territorial map of Europe,
indeed of the entire globe, is mostly defined and frozen in the
sense that there is worldwide resistance against revision of
territorial frontiers. In Europe, the Helsinki agreement has
ratified the territorial status quo. The distribution of military
force between NATO and Warsaw Pact countries is stable and
predictable.

The arms race between the superpowers points to interaction
among military technology, internal politics, external threat
perceptions, and strategic doctrines. Generally, the arms race
can be studied as a consequence of the controlled competition
among major powers in the world and/or as a consequence of
the expansive internal structure of state systems. The worldwide distribution of force may be conceived as one of establishment of concentrated pockets of military force—distribution in
the North Atlantic, Europe, the Soviet Union, China, and East
Asia—which are the primary strategic spheres of world politics
since 1945. The flow of conventional arms to the third world
and the gradual nuclearization of the South in the last two
decades is noteworthy and will be discussed later. Suffice it
to note here that the primary concentration of military power
is still in the North. The global military map has remained
constant and stable in the sense that the distribution of world
military and industrial power is still skewed toward northern
targets and strategic cores. In particular, military relations
in Europe are stable and predictable in the sense that the accept-

ance of the territorial status quo by European and Soviet authorities creates incentives for regulation and controlled competition in interstate relations rather than an incentive to redistribute the ratio of military force in the strategic cores of the North. Without territorial dissatisfaction or revisionism, the incentive to possess military force is limited to deterrence and territorial defense.

If global territorial and military maps are generally predictable and stable, political, cultural, and subnational maps are dynamic in the sense that political, sociocultural, and economic relations are no longer tied to erstwhile bloc loyalties. The movement is toward cultural interaction (even if this is conflict-prone) and economic exchange among peoples of diverse backgrounds and political loyalties. Beneath the stable territorial and military maps, new political-psychological-economic maps are being redrawn. Hungary seeks economic and social satisfaction through consumerism; Poland finds it necessary to depend on Western finance; Yugoslavia has developed a system of decentralized economic management (but the future of this system is problematic); and the Soviet Union is studying the various economic reform movements in Eastern Europe (particularly Hungary's). It appears that Western capitalism has emerged as a pole of attraction for communist members of the international system as well as for many of the revolutionaries in the third world (such as Angola and Zimbabwe). As I. F. Stone points out, communists can join the U.S. camp without renouncing communism. In the 1970s political and economic realignment occurred without realigning formal territorial and military structures, and under the umbrella of frozen territorial and military alignments. Thus, China became the sixteenth member of NATO and is welcomed to the alliance as an honorary member without assuming the formal obligations of alliance relations.

Under these circumstances, two hypotheses are noteworthy. First, arms races and arms do not always create security and influence for those who seek more arms because changing economic, political, cultural, and subnational relations have already eroded the structure of international authority of the superpowers. More arms could lead to greater insecurity because more arms create economic and social dissatisfaction in industrialized and industrializing societies. Second, the phenomenon of international change and the challenge for the future lies in the shaping of the cultural, military, and economic alignments in the world within and between the following dyads: East/West; North/South; South/South; West/West; and East/East. In particular, culture motivates strategy in North/South and South/

North relations, and power politics is basically a cultural and not merely a scientific and military activity.

In a world of competing cultures and strategies, the two superpowers tried and failed to establish their regimes beyond the NATO and Warsaw Pact areas. The world beyond that of alliances is that of nonalignment—also loosely called the South. At present the North/South relationship is unequal—in economic, military, and political terms—but it is under attack and subject to change in the coming decades. In the North/South dyad, power lies in the relationship between culture, strategy, and material means. Its negative purposes are to deny to the superpowers truly global influence; to increase the diplomatic and financial costs of their policies; to increase their uncertainties about the international environment; and to increase their frustration and reduce their will to shape international security. Generally, its purpose is to demonstrate that the stronger states can be, and are, weaker strategically (in the long run) and the weaker states can be influential in select circumstances. Their influence lies in part in an ability to release cultural forces that change the relationship among the military, economic, and cultural maps that comprise the system of power politics.

THE CHANGING NORTH/SOUTH RELATIONSHIP

In a sense, the North/South relationship is not new. International relations developed a North/South focus with the establishment of overseas trade and colonialism by the Europeans in the 1600s, and particularly in the nineteenth century. European colonialism in Asia, Africa, and Latin America was North/South; center-periphery ties between the United States and the Americas (past and present) are also North/South. In this context, the phenomenon of East/West confrontation is comparatively recent. In the old sense, North/South meant the emergence of unequal exchange relations that produced "conflicted" societies in the South (a term borrowed from T. Geiger), which led to uneven and retarded development, and in several instances created conditions for a society becoming underdeveloped. The new North/South focus is a consequence of the 1960s. It reflects the consciousness-raising work of Paul Prebisch and is reflected in the diplomacy of the Group of 77 and United Nations Conference on Trade and Development (UNCTAD). The demand for a better economic deal is a product of third world nationalism; of a desire to restructure the international economic order on a basis of long-term mutual interest between select parts of the

North and the South; and of the awareness of the negative consequences of the North/South encounter and of the impact elite
behavior has on the in-heres in developing societies. The current
indicators of world economic distribution tell the story (see
Table 5.1).

To change the present economic distribution the South
(according to the New York Times, August 2, 1981) seeks the
following:

Increased economic cooperation; 0.7 percent of GNP is
sought as aid by 1985 and 1 percent by 2000. United States
aid was 0.60 percent in 1961 and 0.27 percent of GNP by 1980.
At present, only Sweden, Norway, and the Netherlands offer
1 percent of GNP as aid;

Improved trade conditions, because of the decline in the
third world's share of international trade in the past 30 years;

Food; between 40 and 500 million people suffer from hunger
in Africa and Asia. The South seeks a system of food reserves
and facilities for food imports;

Energy; the third world seeks alternatives to the oil economy
and conservation of oil resources by industrialized nations that
presently consume 75 percent of world energy;

Monetary relief; at present the South's external debt is
about $500 billion, of which $44 billion (1979) is for debt servic-
ing. The Brandt Commission recommends a $50 to $60 billion
per year transfer by 1985 to help the South.

TABLE 5.1

Selected Key Indicators of Developing and Developed Countries

Item	Developing Countries (%)	Developed Countries (%)
Population	75	25
GNP	21	79
Export earnings	25	75
Military expenditures	23	77
Weapons imports	81	19
Energy consumption	23	77

Source: New York Times, October 25, 1981.

The quest for an altered economic order is part of a wider resurgence of southern diplomatic, military, and cultural activities to transform the North/South relationship. Specific economic issues should be studied in their cultural context because, in a sense, the demands for order and stability by the North and the demands for change and redistribution by the South stem from different notions of power politics[2] and cultures.[3] The superpower theory is that there are but two principals in international relations. It implies both an unwillingness to dilute the position of the United States and the Soviet Union in the world power structure and a resistance to upward mobility by secondary states. To the extent that the primacy of the superpowers stems from their sense of their historical missions, power politics has a cultural base. The diplomatic and military strategy of the superpowers is cultural in the sense that it freezes the distribution of world power as it is presently organized and propagates norms of stability and order that serve their interests and those of their allies. The quest for upward mobility by secondary states in the international system is also cultural. It is based on the notion that proud and potentially strong societies ought not to exempt themselves from the opportunities and obligations of power politics and that they ought to induce a rethinking of the cultural bases of political, military, and economic relations.

The encounter between the material power, advanced technology, and superior organizational skills of the West and traditional third world cultures has had far-reaching cultural consequences. The sense of humiliation and racialism released by this encounter is now a major factor in third world thinking, particularly in Africa and Asia.

Many third world societies have experienced a changing relationship between domestic culture(s), their material power development, and their external strategy. China's transformation is an example. Before the eighteenth century, China was seen by itself and others as being culturally superior to the West and materially adequate. In the mid 1800s, Western power confronted China and Chinese culture lost against Western firepower. The Treaty of Nanking reflected the role reversal. In its self-image the West emerged materially and culturally superior and China appeared inferior on both counts. China was humiliated and confused, but it learned a major lesson several decades later. Power required culture, material means, and strategy (C+m+S) to engage external powers. Today China is an international actor precisely because it has developed some sort of balance in its "C+m+S".[4]

The example of India is also relevant. It has tried to transform its own "C+m+S" so as to balance its position vis-à-vis the external environment. If power politics is an ability to pursue strategies that exempt a country from forcible international intervention and diplomatic isolationism, and if the test is to be able to project power outside the country's frontier and to engate the outside world, then China and India have been successful in their efforts. So far India and China have been high in their "C+S" and comparatively low on the "m". But it is noteworthy that the contribution of "m" to the formula is changing gradually. The purpose of the formula is to increase the internal weight of the country concerned by developing "m" in relation to "C+S," and to balance the country's capabilities in relation to a world of competing and divided powers. The consequences of the formula may be noted. If "m" is big but "S" is weak, it results in a capability that becomes a frozen asset. Without an effective "S" there is no effective policy or purpose to create movement or impact on the world or regional power situation. Here the strong become weak. Second, if "C+S" are strong but "m" is weak, some influence exists in relation to the external environment; influence comes from weaker members engaging stronger members in the international environment.

NONALIGNMENT AND NATIONAL SECURITY

Nonalignment is national security in the sense that it seems to engage the world power structure.[5] The structure is dominated by the superpowers and it is based on the norms of industrialism and military power (rather than the norms of the United Nations General Assembly or of regional cooperation among third world states). Here the engagement is that of the stronger members of the international system by the weaker ones. The weaker members are located in the South, that is, beyond the spheres of operation of the NATO/WTO alliances. The weaker states are in varying degrees of economic, social, political, and military development. Generally speaking, it is possible to hypothesize the methods and purposes in the evolving process of engagement of the North by the South, as shown in Table 5.2.

The nonaligned movement has grown since the 1950s. It now has over 80 members and covers most of the south of the globe. Its members are significantly outside alliance relationships and in areas that have not been incorporated into the U.S. and Soviet spheres of influence. The nonaligned world is the object of superpowers' rivalry but its status, since the 1950s, is that

TABLE 5.2

Methods and Purposes of Nonaligned Strategies

Method	Purpose
Verbal political diplomacy, e.g., the demand for a new international economic order, arms reduction, and disarmament	Increase the attentiveness of the North to the interests and needs of weaker southern states
Military diplomacy, particularly regional crisis management by major third world states, e.g., Indian and Egyptian crisis behavior in 1971 and 1973 crises in South Asia and the Middle East, respectively	Enable weaker states to bargain in economic, military, and political relations with the stronger states Enable weaker states to achieve payoffs in terms of their interests Enable weaker states to deny payoffs to the stronger states
Economic diplomacy, e.g., OPEC's resources diplomacy	Increase the strategic, economic, and political uncertainties of the stronger states
Militarization and nuclearization of the southern environment, e.g., the absorption of modern arms and the acquisition of ambiguous nuclear options by secondary powers in the South	Prevent the stronger states from establishing or perpetuating international regimes that make the stronger states the principals in international relations

Source: Compiled by the author.

of zones of conflict, buffer zones, power vacuums, or peripheries. Functionally, the buffers are essential to the stability of superpower relations. Since 1945 they have absorbed superpowers' conflicts and have enabled them to play out or export their rivalries into the secondary conflict zones, thereby protecting the primary conflict zones in the North (North America, Europe, China, the Soviet Union, and Northeast Asia). Conflict in the primary zones could lead to system breakdown because of the even distribution of military power and the lack of room to alter the territorial and political frontiers. In the sense that the superpowers need secondary conflict zones to export their surplus tensions to and to preserve the stability of the North, there is a structural relationship between the primary and secondary conflict zones. Overall, the involvement of the North in the South is essential to enlarge the international economic base for the domestic well-being of the northern states and to provide outlets for the strategic and cultural tendencies of the northern competitors.

Nonalignment becomes national security when it achieves the purposes shown in Table 5.2. In the narrow sense, national security is achieved when a weaker member of the international system escapes diplomatic isolation and military intervention by stronger states (particularly by superpowers) in an international crisis. In a broader sense, national security is the ability to create and export surplus military, economic, and diplomatic influence and interference beyond the national territorial frontier of the weaker states and into the decisionmaking apparatus of the stronger state (particularly that of the superpowers). Nonalignment is working in both the narrower and the broader senses, particularly in those buffer zones of secondary conflict where the superpowers have had vital interests since 1945 (the Middle East, South and Southeast Asia, North Africa, and Southern Africa).

The growing or continuing involvement of the superpowers has been accompanied by a parallel development of the capacities of the secondary powers in terms of the purposes shown in Table 5.2. In short, nonalignment is successful national security policy when the erstwhile objects of Western colonialism and the clients of the superpowers emerge as participants in the processes of international and regional change. It is when the superpowers, the self-appointed guardians of world order, are unable to enforce the peace according to their interests and norms, and when the regional middle powers are able to promote new rules of conduct in regional and interregional (horizontal) and select international (vertical) issues, that nonalignment may be deemed to be successful. In a sense, nonalignment is national security when it refers to the rise of regional middle powers as third parties in secondary zones of conflict where superpowers and perhaps other extraregional (northern) powers are involved.

THE MEANING AND SIGNIFICANCE OF NONALIGNMENT

There is no agreement in the literature about the meaning and significance of nonalignment. It had been described as a

global social movement, a concept, an ideology, an expression
of morality, a quest for peace, a sentiment against war and arms
races, and an approach against power politics and superhegemony.
It has been viewed as a product of the cold war. Many see it
as a study in anticolonial and anti-imperialist rhetoric. To the
extent that nonalignment was preceived as an anticolonial movement, it is said to have lost its relevance with the independence
of third world states and the breakup of colonial structures.
Finally, it is seen as a reaction to world (particularly U.S.)
capitalism.[6] In this light, it is an attempt to transform the
system of unequal exchange.

A related claim is that nonalignment has benefitted from
the Bolshevik revolution, the first serious challenge to capitalism and socialism.[7] In other ways, nonalignment is seen as
a reaction to the cold war, bipolarity, the atom bomb. It is
asserted that as a product of the cold war and associated phenomena, nonalignment seeks to oppose unnecessary involvement
of nations in superpowers' conflicts.

Taking these diverse sources of nonalignment into account,
the norms of nonalignment may be listed as follows:

The world should be free of threats and pressures;
The world should be free of colonialism, neocolonialism,
and racism;
All nations must be involved in decisionmaking in all matters;
Nonalignment seeks aid without strings;
There should be interdependence between industrial and
developing states;
In a world of nuclear powers, the world system should
become a peace system;
Nonalignment is antidetente if detente means the status
quo and spheres of interests come into being without the consent
of the nations concerned;
Nonalignment seeks to keep aloof of the power politics of
competing blocs that have aligned themselves against each other;
Nonalignment seeks to restructure the world economic
system on which the structure of world political relations depends;
Nonalignment is not merely distancing from the blocs, but
is also an active policy to oppose monopoly in solving international
problems and to promote international economic and social cooperation.

These norms represent the conventional wisdom about nonalignment. It is a mistake to regard nonalignment as a reaction
to either capitalism, the cold war, or the atom bomb. It is noteworthy that many nonaligned states are capitalist or have adopted

mixed economic structures. Table 5.3 lists the economic policy of nonaligned states. When the desire is to alter the condition of unequal exchange, it is necessary to have a material development of a society, which requires capitalism (such as in revolutionary Angola and Zimbabwe in recent years). It could be argued that revolutionary violence in the post-1945 period has been followed by the adoption of capitalism by the revolutionaries (if capitalism is defined as the structuring of societal relations on material incentives to increase productivity).

Nonalignment benefits from the existence of two ideological and economic blocs. However, it is not simply a product of bloc relations. It seeks both to benefit from interbloc rivalries and to prevent the irrevocable extension of bloc (or blocs) influences into third world buffers. The aim is to preserve the buffers as trimmers and not as neutrals or satellites. (A trimmer exploits bloc rivalry; it is a participant located in the periphery that uses the center for its own benefit.) In this sense, a nonaligned state does not seek to stay clear of bloc rivalries. It remains highly attentive to the existence of such rivalries because they create opportunities for exploitation in material and diplomatic terms. Therefore, the existence of bloc power politics is an essential precondition for successful nonalignment. Finally, nonalignment is not actually against nuclear bombs, war, or conventional arms. The disarmament advocacy of nonaligned states is not an accurate measure of nonaligned policy. Talk is cheap, and all evidence of nonaligned states' behavior points in the direction of gradual militarization and nuclearization of the southern environment.

Simply stated, the main purpose of nonalignment is to project noncoercive norms into the international environment, while weaker members pursue the path of material, cultural, and strategic development of state policy that will help them to engage the world power structure. Noncoercive norms are intended to induce rethinking about the purpose and methods used by states to achieve national security. The traditional approach stresses the utility of coercive norms as expressed by arms races and military alliances. Here, arms equal security and security is military in character. Nonalignment seeks to downgrade both the utility of military alliances and the excessive dependence on arms to achieve security. By giving security a military, economic, and social content and balance, the nonaligned states endeavor to broaden the meaning of the term "national security".

In a fundamental sense, nonalignment is antigreat power rather than antipower because it is by acquiring limited power

TABLE 5.3

Nonaligned Countries Categorized According to Their Economy

Socialist

Afghanistan	People's Republic	Saudi Arabia
Algeria	of Korea	Seychelles
Angola	Kuwait	Singapore
Bangladesh	Lao People's	Somalia
Botswana	Republic	Swaziland
Burma	Lebanon	Syria
Central African	Lesotho	Tanzania
Republic	Liberia	Trinidad & Tobago
Congo	Libya	Tunisia
Cuba	Madagascar	Uganda
Cyprus	Maldives	United Arab Emirates
Egypt	Malta	Vietnam
Ethiopia	Morocco	Yemen Arab Republic
Guayana	Mozambique	South (Republic of)
Iraq	Oman	Yemen
Jordan	Panama	Yugoslavia
Democratic	Peru	Zaire
Kampuchea	Qatar	Zambia
Kenya	Rwanda	

Capitalist

Argentina
Bahrain

Mixed

Benin	Ghana	Nepal
Bhutan	Guinea	Niger
Burundi	Guinea-Bissau	Nigeria
Cameroon	India	Sao Tome & Principe
Cape Verde	Indonesia	Senegal
Chad	Ivory Coast	Sierra Leone
Comoros	Jamaica	Sri Lanka
Equatorial Guinea	Mali	Sudan
Gabon	Mauritania	Upper Volta
Gambia	Mauritius	Pakistan

Source: Compiled by the author.

that the nonaligned state is able to assume an antigreat power orientation. In its external behavior, nonalignment is deliberately ambiguous because this keeps the enemy guessing. Ambiguity, not specificity, is necessary when the aim is to release international communications to foster dialogue by a process of creative hostility or confrontation. In shifting the basis of international life from the coercive norms of military alliances and bloc hostility to the noncoercive norms of the U.N. General Assembly, nonalignment seeks to connect strategy to culture and to achieve the connection both vertically and horizontally within and between states. Ambiguity is functional in the sense that it helps to accommodate and absorb cultural and strategic diversity in intrastate and interstate relations. The alternative to accommodation is an international civil war with frozen political, military, and social alignments—with interbloc rivalries meant to penetrate and freeze local conflicts.

The international system has the characteristics of an international civil war in the sense that the managers of military, political, economic, and social communications in the North define and pursue their foreign policies in terms of horizontal rival bloc relations and vertical collaborative elite networks. The collaborative networks (for example, West/China in relation to Mugabe in Zimbabwe, compared to the Soviet Union in relation to Nkomo) have grown since 1945 into a worldwide phenomenon. This growth is based on subnational elite competition in the South (which seeks external partners to win local power struggles), the supply capacities of the northern partners of southern subnational elites, and the material and cultural partnership between international/domestic collaborators. The real meaning of nonalignment is not that the subnational actors in the South wish to break up the domestic/international collaboration, but rather they wish to promote it if they are likely to be the beneficiaries. In this sense nonalignment is power politics of the weaker subnational actors who are able to function on the world scene. In a world where material and cultural development is the name of the game, nonalignment is a struggle by the weaker subnational actors or elites to organize and mobilize the intellectual, material, and coercive resources of the international and domestic environments for group interests.

NOTES

1. Generally speaking, international and regional cold wars share a pattern of constant and variable elements. The

constant elements are: arms racing; military technology development; attitude of mistrust; war avoidance and peace avoidance,
crisis management; and continuous communication between foreign
enemies. The variable elements are: shift in public diplomacy
between cold war and detente or normalization; shifts in size of
military budgets; shifts in size of military forces and the theaters
of deployment; shifts in the amount of tension over a period of
time; and the practice or otherwise of brinkmanship.

    2. Power politics is loosely defined as: the expansion of
state power in regional and international relations; and the
presence of military force as an important element in national
strategy. Reliance on force rather than adherence to military
alliance is the hallmark of power politics. Our definition stresses
expansion of state power, and not necessarily its maximization,
so that defined state objectives can be satisfied.

    3. Culture is defined as a set of political symbols—adopted
by a group of people in relation to other groups—which assert
concepts of reality, human destiny, and global order. Culture
expresses a system of beliefs and values derived from historical
experiences that call for action to resist, induce, or force change.

    4. "C" includes ideology, nationalism, will, culture: i.e.,
it refers to an intranational social mobilization and communication
system that separates the in-heres from out-theres. "M" refers
to scientific, technological, economic, and military capabilities
and society's human resources, which include those capabilities
of a state that can be used in interstate conflict. "S" refers to
the external strategy (strategies) of a state. It is a technique
to exploit international divisions and organize international
divisions of power.

    5. To engage is to be exposed to risk; to be committed;
to induce a change; to gain; to win; to attack; to entangle; to
bring into conflict with the enemy. As such, engagement implies
a wide spectrum—from attraction on the one hand to risk taking
and conflict on the other.

    6.

The most important development in international
relations since Columbus has been the emergence
of a global economic system. The world that Columbus left behind soon came to be dominated by a new
mode of production that divided mankind into a
variety of new social classes and nations. This mode
of production—capitalism—was able within a few short
centuries to penetrate almost every corner of the
globe. The conquest of the world by the capitalist

mode of production meant that capitalism was no longer merely a European phenomenon. Capitalism systematically destroyed older civilizations and cultures and subdivided the world into new political units; the nation-state became a major political instrument of capitalist change. The nation-state, which first predominated in Europe as a political form, soon took hold in the Americas, Asia and Africa. Even while the political form tended to lag behind the economic form, capitalism preceded the nation-state in much of the world.

The Non-Aligned Movement, which began as a broad anticolonialist movement seeking world peace by exhorting the powers to avoid a nuclear holocaust, has become the advocate for a new political and economic order on a global level. The world's resources must now no longer be the private resources of a few countries. The world's resources belong to the world's peoples. The Non-Aligned Movement has put [forth] the question of redistribution on the agenda of world politics. . . . Most of the Non-Aligned countries are experimenting with non-capitalist paths of development. The search for a New International Economic Order (NIEO), then, is simply a demand by the Non-Aligned nations to rectify the present imbalance that exists among states.

A. W. Singham, The Nonaligned Movement in World Politics (Westport, Connecticut: Lawrence Hill, 1977), pp. iii, x-xi. 7.

In the search for the sources of non-alignment, one has to go back much further in time than determined dates. These sources have to be sought, primarily, in the processes that created conditions for changing the existing system of international political and economic relations. These processes were ushered in by the October Revolution. Later, in the course and within the context of the Second World War, they led to the mighty struggle of peoples for emancipation.

D. Belovski in Singham, op. cit., p. 7.

6

Elements of Northern and Southern Strategic Approaches

INTRODUCTION

"There is no longer any such thing as strategy, only crisis management," said Robert McNamara, former U.S. secretary of defense and former president of the World Bank.[1] This view is debatable. The task of strategy is to create the potential for power and influence, to mobilize and apply power with a view to achieving desired outcomes that alter the distribution and organization of local, regional, and international power structures. As such, strategy remains relevant today, perhaps more so than during the period of rigid or high bipolarity from 1947 to 1953. The McNamara view is limited and possibly irrelevant for the study of evolving northern and southern strategies.

Specific relationships that constitute "strategy" are changing, and a contrast between northern and southern strategies is discernible in general terms. Strategy ought not to be narrowly defined as military strategy in the nuclear age, or even even more narrowly defined as nuclear strategy. In its true sense, the purpose of strategy is to create the movement of ideas, materials, and human resources for desired ends. By these measures, the North is becoming frustrated and the South appears to be moving. The development of strategy in the 1980s lies in the South assimilating the lessons of northern strategic experience and thought. These are derived through South/North interactions since the 1800s, particularly as a consequence of colonial and postcolonial (including neocolonial) experiences. The rapid militarization and nuclearization of the international environment beyond the northern world (that is, beyond the northern strategic alliance systems and cores—North America, the two Europes, the Soviet Union, China, and Northern Asia) occurred after the 1960s. This phenomenon is accompanied by the formulation of a competing framework of strategic ideas and policies that justify the militarization and nuclearization of the South. Finally, southern militarization is taking place in a complex and evolving security setting for southern decisionmakers, that is, in a framework of regime instability, hostile military neighbors, and the danger of great power intervention in regional power politics and crises. These are products of postcolonial and neocolonial relations, and therefore have local, regional, and international sources and implications.

This analysis benefits from the study of crisis management by Coral Bell. She categorizes crises as follows:

1. Adversary crisis of the central balance;
2. Adversary crisis of the local balance;
3. Intramural crisis of alliances;
4. Crisis of attempted reunification or secession;
5. Crisis of colonial or postcolonial relationships; and
6. Crisis of domestic political consensus.[2]

The Bell framework will be used in this study with modifications. In the first and third crisis types, northern actors are the primary participants and beneficiaries. Bell separates the second crisis type from the first. Presumably, the difference is that the first one is a "high intensity, high stake" crisis, which concerns the future of the superpower balance, whereas the second one is supposedly of "low or medium intensity, and low or medium stakes." It makes conceptual sense to distinguish between the first and the second crisis type, but it is not always an accurate description of reality. To the extent that the adversary crises between the central balance players can be, and should be (according to the central balance players) "played out" in third world regions, there is a fusing between a medium-intensity or low-intensity great power crisis and its location in a third world region. Precisely because the risks are lower in crises outside the northern strategic core areas, it makes sense to execute the power play outside the northern core areas. That is, it makes sense to test the efficiency and the limits of northern policies, doctrines, and military equipment in the South.

In this case crises may originate as a consequence of Bell's fourth and sixth crisis types but they can, through the existence of postcolonial and neocolonial relationships, introduce great power intervention into crises of local balances. Thus, the linkage between the first and the second crisis type is more prevalent in the contemporary world system than may be readily apparent. The formulation of the linkages could be the result of forces operating at two ends. Great power intervention in local balance crises may be a product of great power competition—where international power evokes international rights; containment of the enemy at every opportunity is the norm; the globalization of superpower presences is achieved by establishing overt and covert relationships with competitive factions in different parts of the world. These are the types of superpower activities that bring them into local balance considerations. Then, on the other end, is the old basis of colonialism; namely, the local feuding princes invited the external powers to enter the local fray and help a particular prince win the power play. The external power was rewarded materially and politically in return for the support. To the extent that great power interventions transform local relationships, there is a connection between adversary crises of the central balance in the North and in the South. The point could be enlarged in the following sense: when local balances are unstable because of regime instability, there may be a close fusing between Bell's first, second, fourth, fifth, and sixth crisis types—that is, of all crises except the intramural alliance crisis.

The interplay between these crisis types requires close scrutiny in the context of developments concerning post-1945 international, regional, and local power structures—particularly with regard to third world societies. This chapter takes a step in that direction by reformulating and enlarging Bell's treatment of crisis diplomacy. This is done by raising questions about the hidden premises of crisis diplomacy. The implication of this inquiry is that crisis diplomacy is an essential part of northern strategic thought, but it has more to do with the goal of preserving the preeminence of the northern managers of international security than it has with crisis resolution or the creation of conditions of regional peace and security. The following questions will be explored: Who are the main players or managers in each crisis type? What are the basic factors in each crisis type? Who are the main beneficiaries of crisis management, particularly in the second, fourth, fifth, and sixth crisis type? Is the primary task of crisis management to freeze North/South and South/South conflicts and power relationships—between states and within societies? In that sense is crisis management a desirable strategy, the premise being that frozen conflict is better than anarchy? Alternatively, it is less desirable in the sense that frozen conflicts are less preferable to a strategy of conflict resolution? If a crisis is defined as activity that "threatens to transform the nature of that relationship,"[3] does northern-inspired crisis management, which involves third world parties, create an incentive for third world elites to resist crisis management and to formulate a strategy that precludes future crisis management by northern states? By freezing conflicts and the prospect of conflict-resolution (which requires getting at the root causes of disputes and finding a strategy that accommodates competing interests), does crisis management produce "structural violence"? Finally, is there a fundamental difference between northern and southern strategies in the sense that the North seeks to avoid a substantial transformation of "structurally violent" postcolonial (and neocolonial) relations, whereas the aim of southern strategy, in select cases, is to transform the historically formed North/South power relations; to strengthen and transform the power structures, the internal weights of societies, which contribute to the establishment of local and regional power balances in the secondary conflict zones of world politics (namely, the Middle East, Northern and Southern Africa, Central and South America, South and Southeast Asia)? Table 6.1 outlines the players, the motives, and the consequences of Bell's different crisis types and helps to explain the conceptual bases and normative implications of northern and southern strategic thinking.

RELEVANCE OF STRATEGY AND ITS CHANGING NATURE

Strategy—its development, use, and study—is not only relevant (contrary to McNamara's view), but the specific relationships that constitute strategic thought and policy should be studied because strategic thought and national strategy is the result of a pentagonal relationship between five elements.

The five elements of strategy are as follows. First, militarization of the domestic and international environment of states and society is constantly taking place, and now the process is truly global in scope. Militarization is the development of military power, military organization, and military culture of the actors in the international system. Second, the development of bureaucracies—domestic and international—is taking place along ethnocentric lines. Bureaucratic development implies, on the one hand, a proliferation of bureaucracies and bureaucratic empires in terms of Parkison's law. But on the other hand, it also implies that the international system is becoming organizationally divided along specialist lines. Overall, organization expansion and divisiveness is the pattern of bureaucratic development. The policy aim of bureaucratic development is elite accommodation via intrabureaucratic bargaining rather

TABLE 6.1

The Northern Perspective on Crisis Management

Type of Crisis	Main Actors	Motives of Actors	Consequences	Remarks
Adversary crisis of central balance	U.S./USSR; states are primary actors	Reduce probability of war Retain the power position (weight) of both super-powers in the inter-national system, i.e., preserve the present distribution of world power and the military-industrial basis of power	Arms control and crisis management are necessary and generally have been achieved in superpower rela-tions	Conflict resolu-tion is not the relevant aim of superpowers' activity
Adversary crisis of local balances	Lesser powers located in conflict zones; states are primary actors	Alter radically the existing distribution of power in conflict zones beyond the NATO/WTO areas Weaker local states seek external protection and invite foreign intervention into regional life	War is an acceptable method to alter the regional power position of a local power Arms control and crisis management are not primary policy and cul-tural values	Same as above; for the local powers also conflict resolu-tion is not a relevant policy aim

(continued)

139

(Table 6.1 continued)

Type of Crisis	Main Actors	Motives of Actors	Consequences	Remarks
		Stronger local powers seek indigenous solutions for indigenous problems and they wish that natural military imbalances could prevail without foreign interference		
Intramural crisis of alliance members	Alliance members; states are primary actors	Preserve alliance relationships	Intra-alliance interactions concerning military policy and diplomacy are primary means of alliance bargaining	Conflict resolution is not relevant policy aim of alliance members
		Increase the weight of a particular alliance member		
		Challenge the dominant position of the bloc leader		
Crisis of attempted reunification or secession	Competing groups or factions in states with weak power and authority structures are primary actors	Gain power for the group or individual	Coups, foreign interventions, center-periphery relationships are the normal pattern of relationships	Without strong local power structures, conflict resolution is not possible; to the extent that conflict management freezes
		Strengthen the domestic-international factional ties along center-periphery lines	"Change" is an evolution from a	

Crisis of colonial of postcolonial relationships	Competing groups and institutions in states with established power structures, but which lack viable authority structures, are the primary actors	Motives are the same as in above crisis type	condition of local anarchy toward the development of local power structures	social conflict, it is undesirable in the third world today
		Since center-periphery relationships persist in the postcolonial period in many third world states, foreign intervention takes the form of arms transfers to local enemies, the use of aid and trade to reinforce or punish particular local elites according to the interests of the external power		Management of center-periphery ties is the dominant framework of domestic/ international group interaction, particularly in North/ South relations
Crisis of domestic political consensus	This crisis type has major attributes of attempted reunification or secession crisis type			

Source: Compiled by author on the basis of C. Bell's work. See note 1.

than the development of creative solutions or conflict resolution.4
Third, an essential element of strategic practice is to manage
social psychology—domestically and internationally—by utilizing
international and intranational communications to foster fear
and images of public enemies. Image management of enemies
(who enjoy a clear public identification) is an essential tool of
bureaucratic and elite behavior. Fourth, since it lacks central
authority or a universal government, the international system
is managed and developed on the basis of self-help, by the
avoidance of anarchy, general war, general peace, and meaningful conflict resolution. These aims are achieved by the development of strategies that freeze strategic conflict and foster tactical,
limited, and organizational conflict (structured conflict). Fifth,
a crucial strategic purpose is to promote material prosperity
and commercial exchange in interstate and international elite
networks. These aims are the basis of the material and organizational development of the dominant groups in the international
system.

These five elements interact and reinforce each other and
provide the sense of a "system" of interstate and subnational
behavior. They are constants in foreign policy and military
thinking in the North and South, in democratic and authoritarian
regimes, in developed and developing societies and economies.
The international strategic system is dynamic in the sense that
the presence of these five mutually supportive elements is irrevocable, and yet actions must be undertaken to prevent the
stagnation and deterioration of this system. The first element
reflects the quest for a military and technological development
of the world environment. The second reflects the quest for a
bureaucratic development of state and society. The third reflects the need for cultural mobilization and development and
integration of social forces in a state. The fourth reflects the
conceptual development of security policy and conflict theory.
The fifth reflects the need for the material development of state
and society. Figure 6.1 outlines the five elements of strategic
thinking. Thus construed, strategy is a dynamic activity. It
is not dead. There is such a thing as strategy, and it is more
than crisis management. It is, of course, true that crisis management is an essential part of northern strategy. To the extent
that it is northern in origin and used because it serves northern
ends, its advocacy and prescription for the southern states by
northern states implies the use of strategic doctrines for policy
ends. In this sense, strategic doctrines can be deceptive exer-
cises. Their aims are to confuse an adversary into adopting
postcolonial and neocolonial thought.

FIGURE 6.1

The Pentagonal Aspects of Modern Strategy

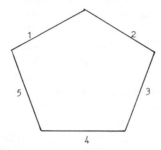

1. The development of modern military technology through
a process of technological determinism, and the continuous
process of militarization of the northern and southern environments since 1945.

2. The bureaucratic development of societies, which points
to the growth of organizations (their size and jurisdiction).
This implies also the growth of conceptual and organizational
disunity as a result of the emergence of competing bureaucratic
interests and because decisionmakers suffer from the problem
of ethnocentrism and the impact of past historically and culturally
conditioned "memories" that permeate organizational and decisionmaking apparatus.

3. In the age of modern communications and nationalism,
strategy requires evidence of skill by elites to create and manage
the base of social psychology in support of elite goals. The
size of population and the level of ideological cohesiveness are
essential to the formulation of national power.

4. The international system since 1945 has developed
several tacit rules of the game, namely, self-help, not morality,
is the basis to organize and distribute or redistribute world
power; general war and general peace are both to be avoided.

5. Strategy requires the development of the material base
of society in part to support the militarization process and in
part to achieve material prosperity for the public. Both aims
require participation in internal and international commerce.
In this sense, strategy and commerce must work hand-in-hand.

In a fundamental sense, foreign policy and military policy should be studied as the practice of deception—as the creation of images and illusions that are meant to confuse the enemy (or to change the enemy's thought structure). As noted above, strategic doctrines that are cast in cool, analytical, and logical terms have a role to play in the promotion of deception in the international arena. The utility of strategic deception is, of course, not a post-1945 phenomenon. Ancient international relations (Chinese and Indian) and international practices in the Middle Ages (Italian and Byzantine) included the use of strategic deception for policy ends. Strategic doctrines of the North are deceptive not necessarily because they are intended to be so, but because their adoption has the effect of confusing the enemy by the creation of illusions and images about the strategists who disguise or distort reality. Strategic doctrines are deceptive because the cool, analytical doctrines do not provide fair warning about the hidden prescriptive policy ends; they are the equivalent of "intellectual or academic colonialism." The practice of strategic deception exists on two planes: first, as selective advocacy of a particular strategic doctrine by a non-governmental, intellectual community that has hidden policy ends; and second, as the advocacy of a particular strategic policy by a government that has hidden policy ends.

It is not the intent here to say that deception is "bad," only that it exists. The notion goes back to ancient strategic thinking. According to the Chinese strategist Sun Tzu, the mind, not the enemy force, is the main object of strategy.[5] Thus conceived, strategy is psychological warfare. Sun Tzu advocated that, on the one hand, there is a strategy to directly and obviously engage the enemy (akin to modern-day containment) but, on the other hand, there is the strategy that uses indirect means to disorient the enemy. The strategist wins by making the enemy's strategy and mind vulnerable. The first priority, says Sun Tzu, is to attack the enemy's strategy; the second is to disrupt its alliances. The third best strategy is to attack the enemy's army. The worst possible strategy is to attack the enemy's cities.[6] Sun Tzu's strategy implies that it is essential to create the image of an enemy so that the public will identify with the policies of the strategists. Without an enemy there is anarchy in social thinking; an enemy integrates society, or at least the significant sectors of society.

The cold war between the superpowers may be studied as a strategy of deception. It makes sense to inquire if the obvious picture of reality is also the significant reality of world politics. The Soviet practice of detente diplomacy may be studied as a deceptive ploy and a successful one to the extent that it has disrupted U.S.-West European relations. American cold war policy is successful deception in the sense that cold war rhetoric has polarized the East-West environment by increasing the Western threat vis-à-vis the Soviet Union and its allies. If the Soviet response to U.S. cold war rhetoric is to increase its military preparation against the "imperialist" threat, the militarization of the Soviet and East European economies and body politic is tied to the goal of "defending socialist gains". This response reduces social expenditures in communist states and disrupts nonmilitary productiveness that could satisfy consumerism in the socialist world. In other words, increased military and political "preparedness" by the Soviet Union and its allies against Western (particularly American) "provocations" increases internal dissension in the Soviet camp. The failure to satisfy basic consumer needs implies an increase of social dissatisfaction and a weakening of the base of domestic social support for Kremlin policies—which in turn requires more external and internal policing.

The point of this discussion is that in a curious way the direct U.S. cold war containment strategy is both deceptive and successful. It is deceptive because it is cast in ideological terms—as a U.S. response to the Soviet threat—when it is just the opposite—an American challenge and provocation to the Soviet system that justifiably (according to this viewpoint) requires a Soviet response. At the same time, the U.S. cold war strategy is successful because it achieves its primary indirect aim, which is to distort the allocation of resources in the Soviet system. By lessening the Soviet elite commitment of resources for developmental purposes and consumerism, the polarization within the system is likely to continue and to retard the full development of the Soviet Union's internal weight. Both superpowers appear to be successful (during at least the period from 1945 to 1980) in terms of Sun Tzu's second priority (disrupt enemy's alliances) and in avoiding the third and the fourth contingencies (do not attack an enemy's army or cities).

Deception in strategy is also necessary because most states, at one time or another, were conceived in violence: consider the American revolution, the Bolshevik revolution, the French and Chinese revolutions, the bloody English history, 4,000 years of regime instability in the Middle East, and the troubled and violent beginnings of many third world states. The critical distinction, however, is that established power and power structures evoke rights that are enforceable (that is, rights and responsibilities flow from an established power structure within the state and in the international system); but on the other hand, weak internal and international power structures beget further power struggles and inconclusive and unenforceable demands for rights. So it may be argued that strategy as deception operates in two different ways, depending on whether or not the power structures are established. In the former instance, the purpose of strategy is to formulate regimes and rights that flow from established power. In the latter instance, the purpose is to prevent regime formation by the stronger powers until local and regional power structures affecting the weaker members of the international system are established to accommodate the interests of the weaker elites. In the former instance, strategic deception formulates doctrines, ideas, and norms of stability and responsible behavior that meet the interests of the satisfied and established powers. In the latter instance, strategic deception opposes the formulation of such doctrines and regimes that are injurious to weaker states' interests; the opposition is usually cast in the name of high principles, but the essential underlying factor is that the weaker, unstable members claim to be potential power centers and do not wish to be frozen out of a future opportunity to establish their claims. In both instances, the strong and the weak usually try to evoke symbols, norms, myths, and doctrines that serve their own ends, and both try to oppose rather than to accommodate the other.

THE UTILITY OF POLARIZATION AND THE FUTILITY OF ACCOMMODATION

Accommodation usually is not a sound strategy because the task of an elite is to divide power in its environment and prevent the emergence of a winning coalition against itself. Given this, a strategy of accommodation is not helpful; a strategy that facilitates polarization is. To promote international and domestic divisions it is essential not simply to have preponderant strength, but also to have a strategy that fosters divisions in the enemy camp. Thus construed, the central aim of strategy is to foster and manage polarization, short of inducing a system breakdown in one's strategic environment. Strategy should both manage an already divided world and induce external and internal divisions that the strategist can manipulate to his own advantage. Divided power is better than unified power in enemy hands. It creates a setting for power sharing among competing groups and an opportunity to participate in decisionmaking by consensus.

The strategy that creates and manages a divisive domestic and international environment stems from external and internal considerations. Externally, divisiveness leads to the balancing of power.[7] However, strategy is not mainly or exclusively a product of external competitiveness[8]; it is also a product of ethnocentrism and groupism.[9] Furthermore, policymaking is not entirely a question of finding rational means to specific policy ends, as expressed mainly by external military threats. Enemies and divisive policy situations help foster group cohesiveness. External policies are the products of internal or self-inflicted insecurities[10] and of bureaucratic politics, which include motives like careerism, intrabureaucratic bargaining, information manipulation, and so on.[11] As a veteran of the U.S. Department of Defense points out, national security decisions reflect the bargaining power, the internal weight of the competing components of the national decision structure, rather than a purely creative and rational process to respond to threats.[12] In other words, the internal dynamics of a country's foreign policy and military establishment reveals divisiveness, groupism, ethnocentrism, and subnationalism as the organizational bases of strategy formation and implementation.

External Incentives to Create and Foster
International Divisions

Two different imperatives—one conceptual and the other policy-oriented—account for a country's external policy to encourage controlled divisiveness in the strategic environment. First, conceptually and normatively, international divisiveness is better than an international system where power is consolidated in a single center and there is a danger of empire. Balance of power (however that idea is defined) stems from a normative preference of divided power. Martin Wight, as noted earlier, provides several different meanings of balance of power: as a self-operating tendency toward balance in international relations; as a policy that seeks a margin of strength to achieve stability; as a normative principle that favors equal distribution of power among all major participants of the system; or as a policy of a powerful, detached, third party that seeks the role of a balancer—working against a potential aggressor. The last three meanings require a dynamic policy or strategy by individual countries with two aims in mind: to divide international power so that a balance is maintained, and to stabilize the international system by developing its capacities to promote the material well-being and the cultural development of its principal constituents.

The notion of the utility of divided power in international relations was expressed in ancient international relations theory. The Indian strategist and political scientist Kautilya, in the seminal work Arthasastra (estimated to date from around 300 B.C.), notes the utility and presence of four types of state actors.[13] The first type is the principal or the conqueror, an expansionist state that is the center of the system. However, its expansion is not unlimited and this central power is not ethnocentric. Its behavior is presumably guided by the norms of stability and prosperity of the system. The second type of state actor is the major enemy of the central power. This essential actor (enemy) provides the challenge to the central power. It creates an incentive for the central power to remain dynamic as a role model in the system: by promoting the system's prosperity and stability, and by guarding against the stagnation and deterioration of the system's essential actors. In a sense, the enemy is a catalyst toward progress in the system. The third type of state actor is a potential ally that must be courted by the principal power. Finally, the fourth type is the neutral, distant, and powerful state whose neutrality is to be encouraged. By modern usage, this detached and powerful state could be a balancer.

The second imperative toward balance via divisiveness flows from the perception that the post-1945 political, military, and territorial map of the world is divided into readily identifiable strategic cores or rings of influence.[14] The relationship within and among these cores can change, depending on how and whether the individual cores make material and cultural progress. The corollary of this perception of the existence of divided power is that the present organization and distribution of world power ought to be managed in desirable directions—and what is desirable, of course, depends on the eyes of the beholder.

This second imperative visualizes the state as a living organism rather than as a mere legal and political idea. As a living thing that consists of land, people, ideas, resources, cultures, and body politics, it contains tendencies that can produce the movement of human beings, material resources, and ideas in the international arena. Thus defined, a particular state, and the system of states, will either grow, stagnate, or deteriorate. (Growth, stagnation, or deterioration is reflected in the following elements of power: the will and good judgment of the authority structure, including the quality of advisers; military strength; economic viability; territorial security; and finally, the existence of a domestic social base of support for political authority.) It is unlikely that all states at a given time will collectively be in a condition of growth, stagnation, or deterioration. The chances are that states will be in different conditions of growth, stagnation, or deterioration with respect to their economic, political, and cultural life. As such, international power is likely to remain divided.

The key unit of analysis in the second imperative is not the division of the world into territorial nation-states, but into key strategic cores of power. These cores have regional and international influence. In the relationships within and among these strategic cores, the elements of power and influence are not static. They must be employed to ensure the primacy of these cores in the international system.

In the policy imperative, the aim of strategy is to defend the territorial frontier—the lines of physical control of a state's political authority—and to enlarge the political, commercial, military, and cultural influence of the constituents in the strategic cores (that is, beyond each core and into the international environment). In other words, the policy imperative is to manage progress or to prevent deterioration and stagnation. This imperative must constantly operate within the realm of two types of frontiers: the territorial and the strategic (the latter being the line of aspiration of political, commercial, military, and cultural influence beyond the territorial frontier). The aim of strategy is to move from the defense of the first frontier to achievement of access to the second one, and to create movement between the two frontiers by demonstrating an ability to move men, ideas, and materials. "Men" includes social migration and the movement of armies. Movement of materials is expressed by commerce and military force. Furthermore, to achieve movement it is essential to urbanize and centralize the components of power and strategy and then to project them.

The expansionist tendency is motivated by an urge to go beyond the territorial frontier and toward the strategic and cultural frontier. But on the other hand, this tendency is moderated by the expansive pressures of competing powers and by the requirement of system stability and progress (that is, by some sense of the interests of the collectivity).

The policy imperative is a dynamic one. Suppose that the communist states are in the center (Eurasia) of a system of concentric circles, and the Western states in part surround the center with their strategic (including naval) power and their policy is to contain the outward flow of the power of the center. The neutral and nonaligned states are scattered in between the

"inner communist circle" and the "outward containment circle"
(in between the two circles or cores of strategic power). Thus
conceived, the neutrals and nonaligned states function as strategic buffers. The general strategy is to challenge the economic
and cultural foundations of the communist bloc and to gradually
find ways to dismantle or at least to erode the Soviet empire.
In the meantime, the strategy is to prevent the domination of
the strategic buffers (Austria, Scandinavian countries, the
Middle East, South Asia, Southeast Asia, the Horn of Africa,
Northern Africa, and Southern Africa) by any power. For the
weaker states, the strategy is to escape diplomatic isolation and
forcible intervention, and to strengthen their status as strategic
buffers that absorb East-West rivalry.

For these weaker states in particular, their geographical
location limits their strategic choices: they can either become
great power satellites (like Afghanistan) or they can try to
maintain themselves as strategic buffers (as is the attitude and
policy of most of the states in the Indian Ocean littoral area).
In this sense geography shapes the strategy of the buffer
states. This strategy is in the context of unequal distribution
of international power between the North and the South, between
developed and developing states, between the industrialized
North and the advanced industrializing (developing) southern
states. The commitment of the northern powers and the secondary states to preserve strategic buffers is widespread. It suggests the importance of strategic buffers for the stability of the
entire international system. Since the principal strategic buffers
are located on the rim of northern strategic cores (an exception
being Southern Africa), the importance of environmental determinism is indicated. The communists deny this and focus instead
on historical determinism. However, environmental determinism
appears to be more important than historical determinism in
describing how international power has been divided and organized since 1945, and this is likely to be valid in the future also.
At present, for most of the weaker strategic buffers, the territorial and strategic frontiers are probably the same in the sense
that their immediate aim is to manage their own limited space
and resources. For the superpowers, however, the strategy
is to manage the space and resources beyond their respective
territorial frontiers because their strategic frontiers are infinite—
extending into outer space and theoretically into all points of
planet earth.

The policy imperative to manage international divisions is
reflected in contemporary world conditions in the organization
and distribution of world power since 1945. The veteran diplomat
George F. Kennan described these accurately:

Our own North American community constitutes one
such center of military-industrial strength. There
are only four others in the world. They are all in
the Northern Hemisphere. Two of them, England
and Japan, lie off the shores of the Eurasian land
mass. . . . The other two have their seat in the
interior of the Eurasian land mass. One of these
last two is made up of Germany and the industrial
regions immediately contiguous to Germany. . . .
The other is represented by the Soviet Union
proper. . . . nowhere outside these five areas can
military-industrial strength be produced in this
world today on what we might call the grand
scale. . . . China, for example, is not one of these
five key areas; her resources do not nearly come
up to this class. And it means that the heart of
our problem is to prevent the gathering together
of the military-industrial potential of the entire
Eurasian land mass under a single power threaten-
ing to the interests of the insular or maritime
portions of the globe.[15]

Furthermore, says Kennan, the Soviet Union does not seek
general war.[16] The implication is that the U.S. containment
of Soviet power is meant to prevent the expansion of Soviet
power beyond the single power core it already controls. Containment is a consequence of the Soviet isolation in the world
power structure and exists despite the Soviet reluctance to
seek war or to rely on military force to achieve a fundamental
change in the distribution of the world power structure. Finally,
Kennan envisages the shrinkage of Soviet power. To facilitate
this aim, he advocates peaceful engagement of the Soviet Union.[17]
        Given the normative and policy-oriented imperatives to
foster and create divisiveness in the international environment,
it appears that the best approach for a strategist is to freeze
strategic conflict. This is done by pursuing an arms race,
acquiring nuclear arms, and, at the same time, managing the
international alignments by political, economic, military, and
cultural diplomacy, particularly among the strategic cores. All
this is done with the declared purpose of achieving the stability
and prosperity of the strategic cores. In an abstract sense,
of course, the strategist has a choice. First, he could opt for
anarchy or tolerate permanent conflict in an unstructured form.
Second, he could try to freeze strategic conflict permanently
by running the arms race at a high level—higher than a potential
adversary coalition could expect to maintain. The underlying

approach in the second option (ably expressed by K. N. Waltz) is that arms racing leads to structuring of conflict and this is integrative. Structured conflict increases attentiveness to an adversary's interests and views. Hostile pairs are careful with each other; the greater the danger of punishment, the greater is the caution between enemies. In other words, structured conflict helps to define responsibilities of conflict-prone parties. It helps to define the permissible limits of conflict. It shows how much the "traffic can bear" and it helps to establish tacit rules of the game.[18]

In effect, the second option seeks peace through preponderance and controlled arms racing. The third option is to seek peace through conflict resolution—by sorting the causes of war and conflict. The premise is that if the causes of conflict are understood, then rational people can be persuaded to negotiate, compromise, and accommodate opposing viewpoints and interests. Of these three options, the second is usually the most widely favored and practiced in the northern industrial-military world, in East/West relations, and in the North's security policies vis-à-vis the South. The strategic aim of the second option is to freeze international conflict, indeed, to freeze the present distribution and organization of world power. The strategic thought that derives from the second approach is expressed by concepts like "peace through strength or preponderance," "arms control," "crisis management," and "intervention" to achieve stability and equilibrium—and not by "disarmament," "arms reduction," "nonintervention," or an approach that encourages the development of "indigenous solutions for indigenous problems". The latter is objected to on the ground that it amounts to anarchy.

The second option is the only real one for northern strategists since 1945. It expresses itself in the form of arms racing in a controlled manner. The nature of the arms race has been altered. In its traditional pre-1945 sense, arms racing had four attributes: competitive amassing of troops and armament; each side tried to gain an advantage through superior armed force; arms races were recurrent; and when they intensified, they led to war.[19] Today arms racing has in part the first attribute— an increase in the quality, type, and quantity of arms—but there is not necessarily an increase in the size of troop levels; indeed, in select circumstances arms acquisitions may become a substitute for troops. The second attribute—seeking an additional advantage—is debatable because arms racing by both sides may cancel out the likely gains by one side. The third attribute— recurrence—is, of course, obvious in contemporary superpower arms racing and among regional rivals, but the fourth attribute—

recurrence leading to war—is not an inevitable consequence of the recurring arms buildup worldwide.

A study of the nature and significance of contemporary arms racing should assess the social and economic utility of arms racing. Arms races develop international prestige for the armed state, although the extent and permanence of the prestige gained is debatable. Arms races help with territorial defense. They develop the military-industrial complex and, to the extent that an MIC freezes internal social and political conflict in a society, the MIC keeps domestic peace—at least temporarily. Finally, arms racing freezes international conflict by preventing the use of violence to change the established distribution of world power. The existence of peace since 1945, defined by the absence of violence in the North, is significant in this regard. (As is well-known, the incidence of interstate violence has shifted to the South in the past century, with the exception of civil violence in a few cases like Northern Ireland.) If the choice is between anarchy or frozen and structured international conflict (given that the international system operates according to the norm of self-help), arms racing is helpful if it is self-controlled, moderated by a sense of international systemic stability, and guided by a concern to promote the material prosperity that comes from continuation of production lines of the northern industrial state. Arms races are wasteful in purely economic terms in that military expenditures could be used for productive social expenditures. But on the other hand, arms races are social institutions in the sense that some see frozen, structured, and limited international conflict as better than unstructured, unlimited, and anarchical conflict. The utility or otherwise of controlled arms racing seems to turn on the normative choice between these two possibilities in conflict, on an assessment of the likely sources of conflict, and on one's own anxieties and insecurities derived from historical memory and images of real or imagined enemies.

The preferred northern strategy then is to freeze strategic conflict rather than to try to resolve the causes of conflict or to permit anarchy. To be successful, this strategy requires the satisfaction of several preconditions. First, it requires nearly universal acceptance of the territorial status quo, particularly among the superpowers and the regional powers. With the exception of the unsuccessful secession attempts in the Congo (by Katanga) and in Nigeria (by Biafra), and the successful one in Bangladesh in 1971, there is a universal belief in the importance of the territorial status quo even though the territorial map of the world—particularly in the third world—is a product of colonial settlements. Second, the northern strategy

requires that the distribution of power among the northern strategic cores remain divided and that diplomacy be used to institutionalize the responsibilities among the core members. Since
the 1950s, the core members have been engaged in a process
that defines rules and responsibilities. Specific rules of the game
have emerged: wars that could become a general war are to be
avoided; territorial status quo is to be maintained; local and
regional powers are to be encouraged to remain in a "no war no
peace" situation with their local or regional rivals, and neither
side should achieve complete victory over the other; peaceful
penetration of the enemy's society and sphere of influence is
permissible, but the use of force to alter the distribution or
organization of power of any northern core member is deplorable;
intervention in the gray areas or the strategic buffers is acceptable (that is, the United States, China, South Africa, and the
Soviet Union can intervene in Angola); the Soviet intervention
in Afghanistan is tolerable, as was the American one in Vietnam;
and so on. According to these rules, a manageable cold war is
tolerable; indeed, it is the prefered medium of interstate communication. These tacit rules include a consensus among the
major powers against disarmament. The acceptance of the primacy
of national means of verifying arms control agreements makes
spying and self-help respectable means of national security.
Despite the high pitch of the cold war rhetoric since the late
1940s, despite the history of East/West crises (Berlin, Korea,
Cuba, Vietnam, African interventions, Afghanistan, Poland,
and so on), note that the power structures of the northern
strategic cores have grown politically, economically, and militarily. The basic viability of these cores is not at issue in contemporary strategic policy and thought. (Contrast this with
the shakiness of regimes in the South.)

The third precondition underlying northern strategic thinking implies the availability of strategic buffers beyond the core
areas, so that the cores can work out their tensions and test
the successes, failures, and limits of their policies and doctrines.
At different points in recent history, the Middle East, South
and Southeast Asia, and select points in Africa, Central America,
and the Caribbean have served as buffer areas for the superpowers. The international system since 1945 has been generous
in its supply of strategic buffers as playthings for the superpowers. The presence of strategic buffers implies that the
authority structure of these buffers is strong enough to escape
forcible domination and isolation by one or more superpower,
but is not strong enough to escape foreign intervention (that is,
the authority structure in the buffer area is weak in comparative

URSS strategy avec T.M. *avec E.U* EU se renforcit adopte sa faiblesse.

STRATEGIC APPROACHES / 155

terms and is open to external penetration). However, the buffer
areas recognize the need to become strong. They are gradually
developing norms and institutions to regulate the flow of foreign
power in their areas. So, in a sense, international change today
is really change in the organization and distribution of power
and authority in strategic buffer areas. International change
refers to the evolution of power relations in areas marked by
"crises of local balance," and crises concerning reunification
and secession attempts, postcolonial and neocolonial relationships,
and domestic political consensus or regime instability.

These crises are objects of Coral Bell's crisis management.
It is arguable that, in terms of northern strategic interests,
the existence of such crisis opportunities are desirable since
they preserve opportunities for northern access to the strategic
buffer areas in the South. The greater the failure of the southern societies (the buffer states) to develop strong and viable
power structures that limit or exclude foreign intervention, the
greater is the opportunity—with tolerable opportunity costs for
the northern strategic managers—to intervene in the aforesaid
crisis types and to manage resources of the southern areas for
northern ends.

In this perspective, the lessons of the Soviet intervention
in Afghanistan are: for Moscow, the diplomatic and military costs
of intervention are tolerable; and for Washington, Afghanistan
is no longer the buffer it had been. With the probably irrevocable extension of Soviet power into Afghanistan, Pakistan, and
Iran are now more than ever exposed as strategic buffers. This
calls for a stronger U.S. commitment to the new buffers. This
example illustrates that crisis management is essential to northern
strategy more to test the limits of interests of competing northern
states than to put out local fires, achieve regional peace, or
reduce human suffering. In this sense, intervention and crisis
management are inseparable instruments of northern interests
and strategy vis-à-vis the South. The availability of unstable
power structures is essential to the success of northern strategy—
which is to define the responsibilities of the northern strategic
cores through the development of structured conflict in areas
where the status quo does not yet exist. In other words, the
nature of strategy depends on the inner strength and organization
of the power structure, or the power context in which a strategist functions. When the power structure is established, and
responsibilities among the core members of the structure—in
relation to their respective territories—are defined, then the
residual competition among the core members must be channeled
toward the strategic frontiers of the expansive core members,

that is, channelled beyond the territorial frontiers of the strategic core areas into the buffer zones. Such expansion is achieved
by a combination of the following elements:

The possession of preponderant power that can be directed
toward the country's strategic frontier and used for national
defense;

The formulation of strategy—involving diplomatic, military,
economic, and cultural intervention—whose task is to engage
the enemy in the buffer areas;

The assertion of the need for arms control and disarmament
of strategic buffers—which is roughly analogous to the colonial
practice of disarming the natives. But "disarmament for others"
does not include disarmament (defined as zero-level arms) of
the strategic core members; and

The norm of stabilizing the strategic buffers through crisis
management (Bell's third through sixth crisis types) is expressed.
Such crisis management has little to do with regional peace making
or conflict resolution.

The central aim of arms control and crisis management is
not simply to define rules and responsibilities on an East/West
basis, but also to prevent or stall the transformation of the
power relationships between the northern strategic cores and
their respective strategic buffers in the southern world. The
probability of war and the successful resolution of crises are
secondary considerations compared to the retention of the power
position of northern strategic cores and the availability of southern buffers for northern ends. Moreover, the effect of crisis
management on the power position of northern strategic core
members is not at issue because their power position is a result
of their internal military, economic, and political weight (including
the strength of the body politic), and is not affected by the
"loss" of Angola or the "gain" of Afghanistan.

Internal Factors in Foreign Policy

Whereas the external imperatives in foreign policy are to
freeze strategic conflict and to participate in limited and local
conflict, the internal imperatives are to increase the internal
weight of a country in the international system, and to increase
the weight of the competing political and bureaucratic players
in the national decisionmaking system. Seen from "inside out,"
the approach to policymaking is to make the system work, whether

or not it produces good policy.[20] Western writings point to the impact of organizational behavior on the policy process. An attempt should be made to integrate these views in the study of the meaning of strategy.

Kennan describes how foreign policy is the product of a "single dominant political faction":

> But let us recall now a most fundamental fact in the nature of governments. Every government has a dual quality. It is in one sense the spokesman for the nation at large. Yet at the same time it is always the representative of a single dominant political faction or coalition of factions, within the given body politic, and thus the protagonist of the interests of the political element over and against the interests of other competing political elements in the respective country. The aspirations and pretensions it voices on the international level therefore do not necessarily reflect only the actual desiderata of the totality of the people in question; they may also be the reflection of the internal political competition in which the respective governmental leaders are engaged. That goes for every country in the world, including our own.[21]

Sanders, a veteran of the Department of Defense, cites the literature that points out that policy is the product of elite accommodation; it is less than creative thinking, and it is more a result of outcomes that reflect the internal weight of the in-house (intragovernmental) competing bureaucracies.[22] Gelb and Betts offer a discussion of nine explanations of the basis of foreign policy behavior, using U.S. decisionmaking about Vietnam as the case study. These explanations are not mutually exclusive and may be described as follows:

First, the arrogance of power produces idealistic imperialism. When enormous power exists, it can be used at every opportunity; conversely, the desire to engage the enemy at every opportunity requires the creation of enormous power. Arrogance stems from the belief that a country can do anything it wishes with its awesome power, and that power equals right.

Second, special interest groups manipulate the government into external intervention. Here foreign policy is economic imperialism.

Third, foreign policy is the result of bureaucratic bargaining, which includes these factors: a macho appearance; foreign

policy is like any kind of bureaucratic behavior where inertia
is a dominant element behind administration (defined as standard
operating procedures), and when change occurs it is a product
of incrementalism rather than a radical departure from past
practices; foreign policy is information manipulation—by field
agents who mislead their superiors and by national security
managers who claim that information is power; finally, foreign
policy is the consequence of elite accommodation.

Fourth, foreign policy is a product of domestic politics—
external adventures are meant to fend off domestic challenges,
usually from the right (such as McCarthyism).

Fifth, foreign and national security policymaking is the
product of an attitude of problem solving. There is a constant
weighing of evidence (including inconclusive data), and tough
choices have to be made on the available evidence.

Sixth, foreign policy is the result of self-centeredness
and misperceptions about the enemy's attitude and behavior.

Seventh, foreign policy is like a slippery slope: there is
an incremental decline. Mistakes are like lies; one leads to
another.

Eighth, foreign policy is primarily a reaction to external
events and trends, and it is meant to contain expansion of
foreign powers. International relations is a struggle of competing
wills of enemies. Containment of foreign aggression is necessary
because failure to contain is to tempt the enemy to become an
aggressor; failure to contain in one place could have a spillover
effect elsewhere.

Ninth, foreign policy is an expression of an ideological
attitude against communism (or capitalism).[23]

Although in the Vietnam case Gelb and Betts regard the
eighth and ninth explanations as the more relevant in the study
of U.S. behavior, it is noteworthy that all other explanations
point to the role of internal factors. The first explanation
stresses the consequences of the internal weight of a country
in several ways: the greater the internal weight, the greater
will be its international expression via containment and intervention; the greater the perceived need to contain public international enemies at every opportunity, the greater is the need
to have internal strength; the greater the need for internal
military strength, the greater is the need to have a strong
economy that can support diversions into economically and
socially unproductive military expenditures; and the greater
the need for a strong national security economy, the greater
is the need to exploit the international economic environment

for the benefit of the national economy. The quests for a
stronger internal military and economic weight and international
intervention are mutually supportive and necessary.

The second explanation obviously reflects the impact of a
coalition of powerful domestic factions on the foreign policy
process. But whereas the second explanation stresses the
primacy of economic gain of the domestic coalition, the third
explanation stresses the importance of bureaucratic power—
collectively and individually—as the basis of decisionmaking
about external events. The fourth explanation is obviously
domestic in nature. The fifth is domestic in the sense that the
bureaucratic problem-solver weighs in evidence not only concerning developments, trends, and tendencies in the international
environment, but also political and bureaucratic considerations
concerning his superiors and the domestic system. The problem-
solver is essentially a bureaucratic player and a rationalizer
who can intelligently use the evidence to justify a particular
choice. So a distinction should be made between the evidence
that forms the basis of a decision, and the evidence that is in
part a basis of a decision, but the decision is a consequence
of other relevant political and bureaucratic considerations.

The sixth explanation stresses the impact of self-
centeredness, of a sense of moral and intellectual superiority
of the decisionmaker, of a lack of curiosity about enemies. To
the extent that a decisionmaker seeks comfort in his own kind
and makes us-them distinctions, decisionmaking is inner directed,
not outer directed. Its purpose is to reinforce the group's
attitudes and behavior, rather than to change the enemy's. In
this sense the inner system is the system, and decisionmaking
is the management of the inner system's beliefs, values, and
policy goals. It is concerned with the organization and distribution of these beliefs, values, and goals between the inner system
and the outside environment. The seventh explanation expresses
the consequences of mistakes rather than factors that lead to
erroneous decisionmaking in the first instance. It does not
show how the decisionmaker first reached the slippery slope
before the slipping started.

The eighth and ninth explanations imply the preeminence
of external imperatives in foreign policy decisionmaking—somewhat
along the lines noted earlier in this chapter. However, Gelb
and Betts provide a clue that links the domestic with the external,
showing how external policies and strategic doctrines can be
instruments to maintain and strengthen the distribution of
bureaucratic and political power within a country. Their explanation of U.S. policy in Vietnam is that the system worked

FIGURE 6.2

Gelb/Betts Model (Modified)

1	2	3	4
Strategic/Ideological Doctrine	Political System	Bureaucratic System	Policy Outcome
↓	↓	↓	↓
Containment and Anticommunism	Decisionmaking should be by consensus of competing U.S. groups	Finds means to serve ends given in column 1	"Bad" Policy

Source: Compiled by the author.

even though it produced bad policy. Figure 6.2 is adopted from their thesis.

In Figure 6.2, the goal in column one is processed by the political and bureaucratic systems outlined in columns two and three, resulting in column four. This is the Gelb and Betts perspective. Let us revise the perspective and consider the first column as the post-1945 consensus that accommodates the ideological diversity represented under the second and third columns. Accommodation of ideological diversity among competing interests is accordingly the overriding aim of the political and the bureaucratic systems. Our premise is that there is no dominant group in this figure, and the forces represented by columns two and three are the dominant groups Kennan may be referring to. The process outlined in the figure is successful to the extent that it accommodates the competing forces represented in the second and third columns. Thus construed, the management of intrapolitical and intrabureaucratic competition is the essential basis of external policies. Management is preferable to anarchial and self-destructive intrasocietal competition. The development of domestic bureaucracies and political avenues of elite accommodation is to domestic politics what military force (particularly nuclear weapons) is to international conflict. Both channel tactical conflict and freeze strategic conflict. The management of conflict is achieved by the formulation of symbols, myths, and code words that have a clear public identification, address obvious and hidden audiences, and have clear purposes. Table 6.2 provides an overview of the role of international communications in freezing domestic political-bureaucratic conflict.

Overall then, strategic weapons are meant to freeze strategic conflict. The establishment of viable political symbols in domestic and international communications also helps to freeze conflict in the sense that these communications create an attitude against anarchy and conflict resolution. In other words, public communications by the elites are meant to prevent both a peaceful accommodation in the global environment and a system breakdown. The concepts and political symbols in public communications usually reinforce the approach of peace through preponderance. The principal northern concepts—international security, arms control, and crisis management—all flow from the notion of peace through preponderance. In this sense, public communications freeze intellectual rethinking of alternative methods to achieve security; indeed, they freeze thinking about the meaning of security and about the relationship between economic and military dimensions of security for states outside the NATO/WTO framework.

A distinction must be drawn between national security of the superpowers and international security. There should also be a distinction made between security that stems from the preservation of a system of military preponderance and over-armament of a few powers in the North, and a system that seeks arms reduction. In the latter, the central concept is that of peaceful economic exchange; "security" is organized around the notion of economic security. The prevailing northern definition of international security fails to distinguish between the interests of the superpowers and their allies and the security interests of the rest of the world. The constant reiteration of "international security" and related political symbols, strategic doctrines, and international communications by those in the North who have a vested interest in the military form of security, in effect blocks understanding about ways to rethink norms and methods to increase security for many states.

The employment of strong international communications for the purpose described above is deliberate and necessary for those who have a vested interest in promoting their view of national security. It is not, as has been mistakenly claimed, a result of a "can do" myth, if "can do" means problem solving or conflict resolution. It is not simply activism for activism's sake. It is not an impulse to improve a bad situation with a good solution. It is a quest to seek new bureaucratic and political frontiers. It is not a question of taking action instead of staying out of trouble. Rather, it is a strategy to deliberately not allow indigenous solutions to emerge for indigenous problems.

To "let things be" would be to encourage the stagnation and deterioration of the available surplus bureaucratic and

TABLE 6.2

The Instrumental Nature of Public Communications

Public Communications*	Audience	Policy Purpose
Formula 1. Peace can be best achieved by nonalignment, neutrality, and avoidance of entangling alliances. Nations should mind their own business	The audience is external and internal. The rigid image of the perpetual, irrevocable enemy does not dominate public communications of elite groups	Behavior modification of the enemy is not central policy aim
Formula 2. Peace is best achieved through cooperation and accommodation with enemy	Both external (enemy) and internal audiences are addressed by this message. The intent is to seek agreement and conflict resolution rather than a prolongation of hostility	The purposes of the message in Formula 2 are: to modify enemy's intransigent conduct; to modify enemy's hostile attitude; to modify the intransigent behavior of internal groups; and to modify the hostile attitude of internal groups

Formula 3. Peace requires preponderance of military strength. There is no alternative to reliance on military strength against a dangerous and unreliable enemy

The obvious audience is external; military preparedness is seen as the obvious answer to an enemy's threat. The message in public to the enemy is to seek peace. However, the significant audience is at home. Formula 3 helps organize and integrate domestic factionalism against a public foreign enemy

In Formula 3 the primary purpose of foreign policy and military strategy is to reinforce the behavior and attitudes of one's own constituency rather than to help secure the modification of an enemy's behavior and attitudes

---

*Refers to the use of ideas, symbols, myths, and code words that are meant to evoke emotion from the audience. The obvious audience and purpose may not be the significant audience and purpose.

Source: Compiled by the author.

political energy that exists in the northern military-industrial world. Just as the economic market must either expand or stagnate and deteriorate, a bureaucratic-political system must either expand its organizational weight in the domestic and international systems or stagnate and deteriorate. As experts are beginning to recognize, foreign policy has little to do with external dangers; it has more to do with internal insecurities and psychological needs.[24] Foreign policy appears to be a reaction to a sense of "psychological crowding" by the decision-makers. To the extent that this sense can come into being irrespective of the presence of an actual military danger, one's inner fears rather than actual external threats motivate foreign policy actions. In other words, to escape "psychological crowding," organization and strategic men not only require a clear definition of rights and responsibilities (jurisdictions), but they also require buffers where competing bureaucracies can attempt to enlarge their spheres of influence. The buffers' function is to accommodate competing forces through coexistence and select rules (no dominance by any) to govern access by a few rather than a single power.

In other words, overseas arenas accommodate domestic competition—which is constant and irrevocable. Domestic bureaucracies have a tendency to grow according to Parkinson's law. When domestic fights are extended overseas, the domestic polarizations are also extended to the international environment. The organized domestic constituencies are, in other words, trying to organize the anarchial international environment according to their requirements and priorities. At the same time, the polarization of the international environment is necessary to reinforce domestic polarization and group loyalties at home. Reinforced groupism creates an organizational and value framework for the extension of domestic factionalism abroad to favored constituencies. In short, external intervention, and deception about its real basis, is essential to preserve the nature of the domestic political and bureaucratic systems. In these systems, domestic peace depends on the ability to accommodate competing interests. The international environment is the only channel of accommodation. Washington and Moscow are too small to accommodate the competing elite groups and ministries—all of whom have little competing tzars and empires to protect and promote.

NORTHERN STRATEGIC OVERDEVELOPMENT AND
SOUTHERN STRATEGIC UNEVEN DEVELOPMENT:
A CONTRAST

Northern strategic thinking flows from the five elements of strategy described earlier. The rapid evolution of military technology accounts for the militarization of the northern environment. Table 6.3 summarizes the North/South distribution of military expenditures on a global aggregate basis. The gap between North and South is tremendous. The northern strategic picture is clearly one of overarmament. Northern military forces can defend and deter not only their own territorial frontiers, but they also can project power into their strategic frontiers. Yet, it is clear that overarmament does not necessarily buy more security. Arms are needed for security, but more arms do not necessarily buy more security; there are gaps between the ability to acquire military means and the ability to enforce the will of the "stronger" power. Insecurity could be a consequence of gaps between potential power and mobilized power and between mobilized power and applied power. The emergence of the European peace movement and the unwillingness of European governments to increase their commitments to NATO are signs of popular concern about overarmament. They reflect a desire to stop an arms race that is unproductive in social and in military terms. The European questioning of the military and social utility of an infinite arms race (not of arms racing per se) is mirrored also in the tendency in Rumania and Poland to freeze or reduce their defense spending levels. Although Soviet military and civil economics are parallel, there is an emerging view that the Soviet economy may not be able to run the arms race on the levels of the past, and that economic restraints may slow its military build-up.[25]

The phenomenon of overarmament is the child of insular, ethnocentric elites. Overarmament, or vertical stockpiling of nuclear and conventional arms, appears to be a consequence of a proliferation of organizational interests, popularly known as the military-industrial complex. This includes the military establishment, the military industries, civilian strategists (who shape and rationalize organizational interests), and arms control agencies (which operate within parameters set by organizational interests and avoid disarmament like the plague). There appears to be fierce competition among different organizations dealing with strategic policy. This is reflected in debates about strategic doctrines, military force structures, the nature of the enemy threat, and so on. These debates are intense and as yet unsettled.[26]

TABLE 6.3

Distribution of World Military Expenditures, 1955 to 1980 (percent)

Groupings	1955	1960	1965	1970	1975	1980
Nuclear weapon states[a]	81.4	78.9	76.0	75.8	67.1	64.6
Four leading arms exporters[b]	76.2	73.3	67.4	65.8	57.4	55.8
NATO and WTO	86.9	85.4	80.5	77.4	70.5	68.8
of which:						
United States and USSR[c]	(68.7)	(63.7)	(48.9)	(47.4)	(31.9)	(27.1)
Other developed[d]	9.8	10.1	13.6	15.4	16.0	15.1
Developing countries						
of which:						
Middle East[e]	0.6	0.9	1.3	2.2	7.3	7.8
South Asia	0.6	0.6	1.1	0.9	0.9	1.1
Far East[f]	1.0	1.4	1.4	1.6	1.9	3.6
Africa[g]	0.1	0.3	0.8	1.2	1.8	1.7
Latin America	1.0	1.3	1.3	1.3	1.6	1.8

aUnited States, USSR, France, United Kingdom, China.

bUnited States, USSR, France, United Kingdom.

cAs recognized by the international community dealing with these matters, official military budget figures for one of these countries are not directly comparable to those of most other countries, owing to differences in coverage and difficulties with currency conversion rates. SIPRI estimates (percent) for the share of the United States and the Soviet Union in world military expenditures are as follows: 1955: 66.0; 1960: 62.6; 1965: 58.2; 1970: 58.7; 1975: 50.1; and 1980: 48.0. The well-known difficulties in comparing military expenditures over time and among countries are being addressed by several U.N. and national bodies. Further help in overcoming the difficulties would be provided by the wider participation of states in these efforts and the sharing of their information on technical aspects (see Economic and Social Consequences of the Arms Race and of Military Expenditures [United Nations publication, Sales No. E.78.IX.1], footnote 63, pp. 33, 36).

dEurope, excluding NATO and WTO, plus Australia, China, Israel, Japan, New Zealand, and South Africa.

eExcluding Israel.

fExcluding China and Japan.

gExcluding South Africa.

Sources: World Armaments and Disarmament, SIPRI Yearbook 1981, pp. 156-69 (for all footnotes except c).

United Nations General Assembly, A/36/356, Oct. 5, 1981, p. 68.

167

As a result of the divisiveness of internal debates in policy circles in the northern societies, the third dimension of strategy listed in Figure 6.1 (namely, elite management of the domestic social base of strategic policy and the creation of ideological cohesiveness and consciousness for elite policies) is problematic. The public is confused and divided, as is evident from ongoing debates between the Warnkes and the Nitzes of the U.S. establishment. Moreover, it appears that the public is bored with military strategy because the elites have failed, as a result of overspecialization in debates and overkill in their communication of fear, to educate the public. So a gap is now emerging between overarmament and organizational divisiveness on the one hand, and the lack of a clear public identification with the orthodox view of strategy on the other. This dilemma is well expressed in recent writings by Henry Kissinger, who is now reduced to arguing that foreign policy and military policy depend on "unprovable assumptions".[27] Trust me, says Kissinger in effect. It is ironic that the plea to the U.S. public to depend on "unprovable assumptions" is coming from a former Harvard professor and secretary of state.

In the past, a close link existed between armament and commerce in the sense that armament secured the international environment and made it safe for the commerce of stronger economic powers. Today, this link is tenuous. Overarmament in the hands of the stronger powers does not prevent, say, revolutions in Angola and Iran. There is a further link between armament and commerce in that commerce provides the inflow of necessary resources for military production and the financial support for unproductive military expenditures. On both counts the North is becoming vulnerable. First, the military cannot guarantee peace and order in the international environment; it cannot mind much of the world particularly, where minding is needed such as the third world. It can intervene on behalf of its clients; it can give economic and military aid; it can destabilize unfriendly regimes; but it cannot create a peaceful, disarmed environment for peaceful commercial (perhaps unequal) exchange. Second, with trade imbalances in several major northern military powers, the economic base of military policy has become shaky. The tension between the military, commercial, and social goals of even the greatest power is hard to accommodate these days.

As such, only self-help, the last element on the strategic pentagon, appears to be functioning. Self-help remains the basis of the process of distribution and organization of power, but to demonstrate self-help it is necessary to achieve balance among the pentagonal relationships outlined in Figure 6.1. This is problematic when overarmament implies a loss of control by the elite over the organizational and social bases of strategic policy, as well as over the international environment.

The Southern security perspective flows from a condition of underarmament. Underarmament presents three kinds of security problems: fear of superpower intervention, fear of hostile neighbors, and a continuous concern with regime instability. The gap between northern and southern arms levels and military expenditures is significant. It seems unlikely that this gap can be bridged soon. The shift in the incidence of conflict to the South from the North was noted earlier. The overwhelming majority of wars and conflicts in global aggregate terms since 1945, and particularly since the 1960s, contain elements of the three kinds of security problems mentioned above. As such, southern conflict cuts across Coral Bell's different crisis types (with the exception of intramural alliance crisis); that is, southern crises since the 1960s have involved local balance, superpower balance, and regime instability considerations. Usually southern crises involve a mixture of all three considerations in varifying degrees. In other words, intrasocietal conflict is linked with horizontal interstate regional conflict and with vertical involvement of the superpowers in local conflict. In this sense, South/South conflicts are integrated with East/West conflicts, and the integration yields a North/South focus.

The other element that differentiates southern from northern strategy is that the organizational and domestic social bases of strategic policy processes in the South are in some sense unevenly developed, or underdeveloped, or underdeveloping—with the prospect of further stagnation and deterioration. "Unevenly developed" implies that some sectors of strategic policy development are well developed in comparison with northern capabilities (such as conventional force), while others are less so (such as nuclear and space capabilities). "Underdeveloped" implies that all sectors of strategic policy are less developed in comparison with northern capabilities, but there is a recognized need to alter the condition of unequal distribution of power between the North and the South. "Underdeveloping" implies that societal decay has already set in and the curve is likely to go downward rather than upward in the future. Of these three categories, the challenge to the North comes from states that are unevenly or underdeveloped. These societies are regional and middle powers because, despite their strategic weakness measured in terms of capabilities, they are able to escape forcible intervention and still have residual and growing power to influence the shaping of international regimes, such as through regional crisis manage-

ment, by stressing indigenous bilateral solutions for local disputes, or by interfering with the Nonproliferation Treaty and
International Atomic Energy Agency (NPT/IAEA) safeguards-
type regimes. The latter are meant to increase international
supervision and access into third world policy circles, and
thereby to preclude modernization and development of indigenous
capabilities that challenge the power and rights of superpowers
and external powers.

The common element in southern states' strategy is that
they seek economic and military development, not disarmament,
during the 1980s. Figure 6.3 shows the upward trend in the
South's rearmament. They do not seek to engage the North by
aspiring toward a preponderance of power. That is neither
achievable nor necessary. The case of Chinese strategy is
instructive in this regard. China has successfully engaged the
superpowers by: adopting a model of minimum strategic deterrent
based on liquid-fuelled missiles; avoiding a quantitative and
qualitative arms race, in either strategic or tactical arms, of
the nuclear and conventional types, with its principal adversaries;
and its defense machinery continues to depend on a poorly
equipped, and yet credible, people's army. Vast territory and
a large standing army enable China to absorb enemy offensive
action. In other words, China's military force is credible because it can absorb punishment by a stronger adversary. It
can also inflict some credible punishment; this is a deterrent
because no Soviet general can offer an ironclad guarantee against
Chinese retaliation.

India, Egypt, Israel, and South Africa are other examples
of countries able to engage in limited self-help in medium intensity
crises. Note that they share a common element; their military
means have to police limited strategic frontiers. In each case
the strategic frontier is somewhat greater than each country's
territorial frontier, and national security policy is not limited
to waiting for the enemy to strike one's own ground. Rather,
national defense implies the use of strategic (political and military)
and tactical (military) surprise and deception in regional crises
to achieve some sort of "initiative" in regional security matters
and to engage the superpowers from a position of weakness (for
example, Indira Gandhi in 1971 vis-à-vis Nixon and Kissinger,
and Sadat in 1973 vis-à-vis the Soviet leadership and the United
States). In these instances, Southern strategy is to achieve
some impact on northern thinking and policies by entering the
"big picture" as a factor in Northern planning. Second, the
achievement of strategic surprise, deception, and initiative
restricts the diplomatic and military fields of maneuver of

FIGURE 6.3

Military Expenditure as a Percentage of GNP, 1963 to 1978

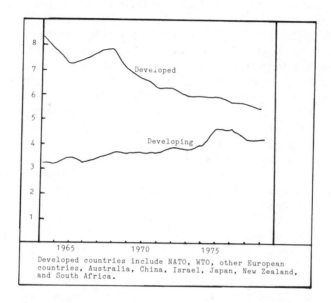

Developed countries include NATO, WTO, other European countries, Australia, China, Israel, Japan, New Zealand, and South Africa.

Sources: United States Arms Control and Disarmament Agency, World Military Expenditures and Arms Transfer, Washington, D.C., various years. UN General Assembly, A/36/356, Oct. 5, 1981, p. 70.

the superpowers. Restricting superpowers' freedom of movement is a sign of regional and middle power status and is a cardinal aim of southern diplomatic-military strategy. So even if the superpowers have missiles with global reach, if an element of uncertainty is introduced into their thinking by the development of the military capability and diplomatic skill of a regional state, then, despite its weakness, the southern strategic practitioner meets the test of Sun Tzu's first norm: disrupting the enemy's thinking rather than engaging the enemy's military forces.

It could be argued that the real challenge from the South in the 1970s came more from OPEC's oil diplomacy and Islamic fundamentalism than from southern military behavior. This view is shortsighted. "Islamic fundamentalism" is an imprecise term. It obscures the considerable infighting in the Arab world among believers of many faiths. The meaning of "fundamentalism" remains to be explained by Middle East experts. Second, "Islamic fundamentalism" received its muscle from OPEC oil diplomacy rather than from Islam in the sense that the oil weapon created a crisis for Western industrial development and third world economies. Without the oil weapon, the impact of Islam on international political and military thinking would have been limited. Islam may be assessed as a cultural force that has been released as a reaction to modernization and materialism. In that sense it is worthy of study, say, with regard to Iran in recent years.[28] But as a factor of change in the distribution and organization of world power, its influence cannot be assessed independently of the oil weapon. And to the extent that OPEC is now in disarray, it may be argued that the impact of the oil weapon during the 1970s has already been absorbed by actors in the international system and in that sense the crisis has been managed. In other words, although the Islamic belt extends from North Africa through the Middle East to South and Southeast Asia, it appears that during the 1980s Islam alone is unlikely to alter the framework of regional and international security. Military diplomacy is likely to remain as relevant, if not more so, for a study of the strategy of southern states.

The primary factor underlying change in southern strategy is that the underdevelopment of the military machinery of southern states is being remedied by the modernization of third world armies, as is evident from data published by the Stockholm International Peace Research Institute, the International Institute for Strategic Studies, and other sources. This allows the regional middle power to stabilize its immediate environment and to limit foreign military intervention. Furthermore, the bureaucratic development of the strategic constituency in third world states is increasing, although it is clear that, as a collectivity, the southern world is unevenly developed on this scale. India, Pakistan, Israel, Egypt, Nigeria, and South Africa have fine military establishments that have absorbed modern military equipment and fighting doctrines and have established international reputations. However, the armies of many Arab and African states are in shaky condition and are unlikely to arouse fear or respect anywhere.

There are a number of reasons why the bureaucratic development of strategic communities in the South is unevenly developed. First, these states have yet to acquire the technical means to gain complete strategic and tactical intelligence concerning the global strategic environment. Second, to the extent that postcolonial relationships between the North and South are really hidden neocolonial relationships between politically nationalistic (in the South) and "open to persuasion and accommodation"

(North/South) elites, the problem is not one of ethnocentricity in southern decisionmaking. Rather, it is that "cosmopolitanism" also implies receptivity to foreign strategic doctrinal and tactical advice, which could be a form of deception. (By deception is meant that the flow of advice and communication from the North to the South is cast as if it is in the South's interest, but in fact is not so, and is not intended as such.) Third, inasmuch as it is mainly preoccupied with issues of survival, the mass public is unable to provide social input into foreign policy and military policymaking in noncrisis periods. Mass apathy creates a great opportunity for domestic and international elites to manipulate mass social psychology in the third world states for the interests and ends of the concerned elites. As such, there appears to be a link between the management of scarcity by third world leaders so that their own domestic publics can be kept dependent on elite goodwill for survival, and the management of information and mass psychology by international and domestic elites in support of elite goals. To the extent that the material development of the country and of elites groups is the material base of policy development in southern states' strategic behavior, southern strategy is not based on consumer and mass satisfaction. Rather, it is based on the avoidance of mass satisfaction as this would deprive the governing elites of the opportunity to manage the politics of survival and to manage their own precarious position in a world of competing and unestablished (or not fully secure) factions.

So southern military strategy appears to rest primarily: on the development of civil and military bureaucratic power in society (reflected by increased centralization and urbanization of the bureaucratic centers of power); on the avoidance of complete mass satisfaction; and on the use of political nationalism among many people living close to the survival level. This is an ideal setting for the use of ideology as a tool of social control. It also means that a considerable amount of rhetoric in the South is a consequence of insecure or unstable (meaning not firmly established) power structures in southern states. In other words, the five pentagonal elements are constants in both northern and southern strategy development, but their interplay varies between the practitioners.

NOTES

1. Cited in C. Bell, "Crisis Diplomacy," in L. Martin, ed., Strategic Thought in the Nuclear Age (Baltimore: John Hopkins University Press, 1979), p. 168.

2. Ibid., pp. 159-60.

3. Ibid., p. 159.

4. R. Sanders, "Bureaucratic Plays and Strategems: The Case of the U.S. Department of Defence," Jerusalem Journal of International Affairs 4, no. 2 (1979):1-15.

5. Sun Tzu, The Art of War, trans. and ed. S. B. Griffith (London: Oxford University Press, 1963, 1971), p. 41.

6. Ibid., pp. 77-79.

7. See M. Wight, Power Politics, eds. H. Bull and C. Holbraad (New York: Penguin, 1978), ch. 16 for different definitions of balance of power.

8. John Garrett, "Disarmament and Arms Control Since 1945," in L. Martin, ed., Strategic Thought in the Nuclear Age, op. cit., pp. 202-03.

9. Ken Booth, Strategy & Ethnocentrism (London: Croom Helm, 1979).

10. Gary Wills, "The Kennedy Imprisonment," Atlantic Monthly, February 1982, pp. 52-66.

11. L. H. Gelb with R. K. Betts, The Irony of Vietnam: The System Worked (Washington, D.C.: Brookings, 1979), pp. 14-23.

12. Sanders, op. cit.

13. R. Shamasastry, Kautilya's Arthasastra (Mysore: Wesleyan Mission Press, 1923); and R. Choudhary, Kautilya's Political Ideas and Institution (Varanasi: Chowkhamba Sanskrit Series Office, 1971).

14. For a particular discussion on the idea of cores see S. B. Cohen, Geography and Politics in a World Divided, 2d ed. (New York: Oxford University Press, 1973).

15. George F. Kennan, Realities of American Foreign Policy (New York: Norton, 1966), pp. 64-65.

16. Ibid., pp. 69-70.

17. Ibid., p. 78.

18. K. N. Waltz, The Spread of Nuclear Weapons: More May be Better, Adelphi Papers, no. 171 (London: IISS, Autumn 1981).

19. Wight, op. cit., p. 239.

20. Gelb/Betts, op. cit.

21. Kennan, op. cit., p. 43.

22. Sanders, op. cit.

23. The following are the author's formulations adopted from Gelb and Betts study, op. cit., pp. 14-23.

24. Eugene H. Rostow in Gary Wills, op. cit., p. 58.

25. T. R. Cusack and M. D. Ward, "Military Spending in the United States, Soviet Union and the People's Republic of

China," Journal of Conflict Resolution 25, no. 3 (Sept. 1981): 429-69.

26. For instance, see McGeorge Bundy et al., "Nuclear Weapons and the Atlantic Alliance," Foreign Affairs 60, no. 4 (Spring 1982):753-68.

27. Cited in Max Frankel, "Memoirs of a Master of Survival," review of H. Kissinger, Years of Upheaval (Boston: Little, Brown, 1982), in New York Times Book Review, April 4, 1982, p. 25.

28. K. Pakravan, "The Political Economy of Middle Eastern Oil and the Islamic Revival," in C. K. Pullapilly, ed., Islam in the Contemporary World (Notre Dame: Cross Roads Books, 1980). G. H. Jansen's Militant Islam (London: Pan Book, 1979) is a highly recommended study.

7

The Changing Strategic Environment of the Indian Ocean World

INTRODUCTION

Since the 1970s the Indian Ocean world has emerged as a focal point of military and nonmilitary crises. Zbigniew Brzezinski has described the Northwestern Indian Ocean-Gulf area as the "arc of crisis".[1] This crisis was perceived after almost two decades of neglect by the United States. Up to the mid 1970s, the U.S. attitude about Indian Ocean regional power politics was one of neglect and preoccupation with great power relations in the North.

When the Nixon-Mao handshake triangularized great power politics, this made both Moscow and Peking look up to Washington as the center of international political communications. There was euphoria in American thinking about the implications of triangular diplomacy for the U.S. position in world affairs. "Detente" became the code word for "negotiation from a position of armed strength," for arms control, for crisis management of primary East/West and marginal North/South relations. The perception of the utility of detente had started to emerge in the 1950s, but it took almost two decades to give it the status of established policy.[2]

Just when detente became codified in international diplomacy, the ground started to slip from under this U.S. policy. The Soviet intervention in Africa and the Red Sea area in the mid 1970s raised questions about Kissinger's Africa policy and his general position on detente; it also raised questions about Soviet intentions in the third world.[3] The blow by OPEC countries in 1973 revealed the impotence of military power and the emerging power of oil and Islamic culture in Middle Eastern relations with the rest of the world. Sadat's brilliant military initiative and diplomatic victory in 1973 released Egyptian diplomacy from the

straitjacket of superpower-controlled relations.[4] It showed how
a poor third party could participate in international crisis diplomacy; how third parties could potentially not only start an international crisis but also, to an extent, manage its parameters
and eventual outcome. The stakes in the Middle East were (and
remain) high: the future of the oil weapon and of Arab economic
and political power; the future of Israel in relation to Arab states;
and the future of superpower relations and cooperation in the
Middle East. Finally, there was the larger question: Was security
in the Middle East a matter of finding a solution to the Palestine
issue, or was it that of achieving Arab development by the year
2000?

During the 1970s the Middle East agenda had the potential
to alter the structure of world power relations, particularly in
economic and cultural aspects. In comparative terms, the victory
of India in the 1971 Bangladesh crisis was of less consequence.
A crisis is defined as a high threat to high values, a pressure
that creates surprise and must be addressed in a short time.
The year 1971 was important because it revealed the fragility
of U.S. decisionmaking when the unexpected happens in a
regional crisis.[5] The fact that Indira Gandhi outmaneuvered
Henry Kissinger and Richard Nixon in the Bangladesh crisis
was remarkable but less important than the fact that South Asia
per se did not loom large in the U.S. policy focus; the capacity
of South Asian elites to introduce rapid systematic change in
the international system was less so than that of select Middle
Eastern elites. Nevertheless, the South Asian crisis revealed
that some advanced developing countries could engage the great
powers in a middle-level crisis.[6] The lessons of Vietnamese,
Egyptian, and Indian regional crisis behavior have generalized
significance. Secondary states in crisis regions can and do
engage the superpowers. They can escape forcible intervention
and diplomatic isolation. They can affect crisis outcomes if
they play their cards right. They have the power to shape
events, policies, attitudes, and processes in regional life. They
can, at a time and place of their choosing, manage active or
latent conflicts, and use these two forms of conflict to engineer
systemic change.

The changes initiated by regional powers in the Indian
Ocean environment in the early to mid 1970s released several
tendencies. After the oil crisis of 1973, European, Japanese,
U.S., and third world economic and financial experts found it
necessary to work in particular with Iran and Saudi Arabia—
the twin pillars of OPEC. Egypt's diplomatic behavior paved
the way to a peace treaty with Israel, the revival of U.S. diplo-

macy in the Middle East, the neutralization of the Israel-Egypt military front, and the polarization of the Arab states in relation to Israel. Subtle shifts emerged in Israel-Arab relations. The agenda continued to stress the issue of the Palestinians, but it changed from an issue about refugees to that of Palestinian rights and homeland. At the same time, the Arab drive appeared to center more against the return of territories occupied by Israel since 1967 and less toward driving Israelis into the sea. Peace was not at hand in the Middle East but neither was there a mood to start a general war in the region. The aim of diplomacy was to formulate the small meaningful move, not to engage in grand strategy.

Behind the "small-move diplomacy" was a desire to institutionalize the North/South dialogue between the rich industrial nations and the rich oil producers in the Middle East. Economic exchange and political stability seemed to reinforce each other as desired values as long as a clear public identification could be created about social and economic change in the Middle Eastern states. The shah of Iran became dispensable when he forgot to keep the balance between modernization and tradition; when his ambition to police the region exceeded his capacity to do so; and when it became clear that being too friendly with the United States could be the kiss of death to a third world leader. Unsettled, competitive subnationalism in a developing country could undermine the grand strategy of a shah.

The mid to late 1970s was a period of considerable turbulence in the Indian Ocean world. The fall of the shah in the late 1970s pointed to the hidden impact of Islam as a major factor in the developmental process and in the formulation and application of military strategy in the area. The Iranian revolution showed how a coalition of diverse social, economic, and foreign-inspired forces could come together against a common internal enemy: the shah. Yet the restraint of the superpowers—initially at Soviet urging—revealed how detente worked despite the outward hostility between the superpowers. Moreover, if the Iranian revolution revealed instability in the Gulf, Sadat's visit to Israel in 1977 revealed that diplomacy was at work. Its form was bilateral but its context was multilateral. The Soviet Union took the front seat in mediating the Indo-Pakistan war in 1965, which led to the Tashkant agreement, and Washington signaled its willingness to take the back seat. In the Israel-Egypt negotiations, the Soviet Union took the back seat. The United States did the public work of establishing a no-war regime while the Soviets acknowledged, through U.N. resolution 242, that Israel had a right to exist. So even though it did not have a seat at the formal table, the Soviet Union nevertheless was a party. It had its voices in the Arab world, and these voices could not be ignored by the major participants in the area.

Sadat's visit to Jerusalem was a positive development in the sense that it took place. But to the extent that his assassination in 1981 revealed elements of Egyptian hostility to either peace with Israel and/or to the U.S. presence in Egypt, the unfinished peace process contained an element of instability. Two other developments added to the sense of instability in the Middle East and Gulf areas: the Soviet invasion of Afghanistan in December 1979 and the Iran-Iraq war. The Soviet invasion revealed that the West was probably deliberately misled about Soviet intentions; the Soviet Union had used strategic and tactical deception.[7] It was also remarkable because it demonstrated the USSR's ability to move around 80,000 troops in a short period in difficult terrain.

The Soviet action had its hidden use for U.S. diplomacy. It is likely that the possibility of Soviet intervention was known several months earlier and nothing was done about it. It is likely that the intervention occurred because of an emerging cooperative relationship between U.S. authorities and Prime Minister (later President) Hafizullah Amin in Afghanistan. Despite his anti-U.S. posture, Amin personally engaged himself in a serious dialogue with the U.S. government a few months prior to the Soviet invasion of Afghanistan, and it is possible that the Soviet authorities regarded this kind of contact as a sign of "foreign interference" in their backyard. In any case, the Soviet intervention helped President Carter establish a clear public identification against detente. The quest for such an identification could be traced to the first year of Carter's presidency. Carter's indecisiveness and the Washington debate about detente and Soviet intentions seemed to be settled with the Soviet intervention in Afghanistan. It could be argued that Carter's reaction to this had more to do with settlement of policy debates in the U.S. establishment, and was less concerned with facilitating the Soviet withdrawal from Afghanistan. In other words, foreign crises are welcome when they solidify or settle domestic policy debates.

The Iran-Iraq war was similarly important because it shifted the headlines away from the Israel-Arab dispute. It showed that a war in the Middle East did not necessarily have to become a general crisis, that Middle East crises were not simply Israel-Arab conflicts, but also stemmed from regime instability in the Arab-Persian Gulf area. This war, therefore, also has had its uses in policy debates.

THE SIGNIFICANCE OF CONFLICT IN THE
INDIAN OCEAN WORLD

Indian Ocean international relations appear to be products
of an extensive amount of regime instability and local and regional
conflicts in the Middle East, Persian Gulf, Africa, and South
and Southeast Asian states. Furthermore, there is evidence
of a considerable enlargement of the Soviet, East German, and
Cuban political-military-economic presence in Indian Ocean areas.
There is also evidence of a considerable military buildup by
both superpowers, apparently in reaction to each other. It is
debatable if the superpowers are in the Indian Ocean areas
because of the presence of the other side or primarily because
of their own interests—which presumably would continue even
if the other side left. Whatever the motives, and these are
complex, it is obvious that since the late 1960s the superpowers
have been in the process of shaping East-West detente in northern
international relations; at the same time, their navies were
attempting to institutionalize their presences in the Indian Ocean
itself.

The rationales varied, thus lending credibility to the notion
that enemies are always available to provide temporary excuses
for the institution of new programs in bureaucratic debates.
Once a program is in place, it is likely to continue even if the
original reason for it has changed. For instance, the U.S.
navy first started periodic patrolling of the Indian Ocean in
the early 1960s, ostensibly to protect the Indians against the
Chinese. This rationale did not carry much weight with India,
China, or the Indian Ocean states. Then the entry of the Soviet
fleet in the late 1960s created a new and better rationale for the
U.S. naval presence.

To the extent that enemies justify each other's presence,
they complement and make each other essential. Moreover,
since the late 1960s, the pattern of interaction between the
superpowers' navies warrants the conclusion that they have
practiced de facto naval arms control in the Indian Ocean in
the sense that their relationship is devoid of surprise or deception. The U.S. naval force structure in the Indian Ocean has
been relatively constant, with periodic but predictable upgrading
of naval forces to match crisis contingencies. Under these
circumstances, formal de jure arms control is unnecessary as
expectations are regularized and behavior is predictable and
hence stable. In any case, trends in U.S.-Soviet naval
operations do not reveal an excessive preoccupation with the
Indian Ocean compared to other areas of naval concern (see

FIGURE 7.1

Trends in U.S.-Soviet Naval Operations (ship days out-of-area)

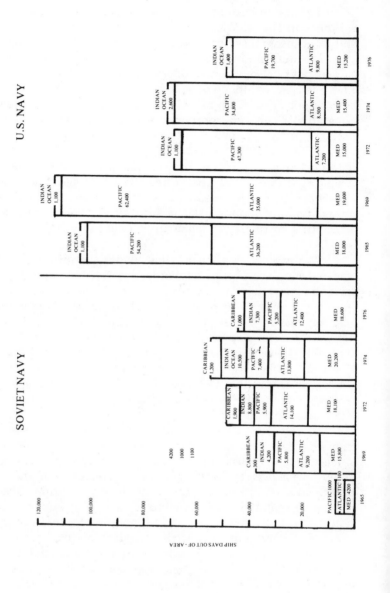

Figure 7.1). Therefore, the establishment of superpowers' naval capabilities in the Indian Ocean world should be treated as an evolving process that originated in the early 1960s, and is not simply motivated by events in Angola, the Horn of Africa, or Afghanistan. At issue is not the enlargement of the U.S. and Soviet naval presence in the Indian Ocean world, but its significance. [8]

There is also considerable evidence concerning the enlargement of the Soviet bloc presence in the Middle East and Africa. Consider the following data. Table 7.1 lists the Soviet Union's friendship treaties with third world states. Table 7.2 reflects the Cuban and East German presence in the third world. Again, at issue is not the fact of the intrusion of the Soviet bloc into third world regions and the singular erosion of Chinese presence on a comparative scale. This is remarkable since it is the view of Western experts that the Soviet entry into Africa was a consequence more of Sino-Soviet rather than Soviet-American competition. [9]

There were estimated to be about 4,000 East German military and civilian personnel in Africa. Their primary involvement appeared to be with internal security and police work. The East German news agency ADN is generally active in third world countries. East German aid and trade appear to be limited: less than $200 million in Africa (mostly North Africa), compared to Soviet aid of at least $2,000 million, and more than double that amount from Western sources. The aid component of GDR activity appears to be growing since the late 1970s.

Some experts argue that the obvious point about the growth of superpowers' activities in the Indian Ocean world is that the world is becoming, or has already become, a single strategic stage. [10] This observation makes sense, first, as a description of superpowers' perceptions of each other's military might and behavior and, second, if superpower behavior in the third world, particularly since the breakdown of detente in the mid 1970s, is treated as an extension of East-West confrontation into the southern world. The notion of the world as a single strategic stage stems from U.S. geopolitical thinking. Henry Kissinger was one of its foremost practitioners. Note, however, that to Kissinger "geopolitical" had a particular meaning. It

---

Source: Understanding Soviet Naval Developments, Office of the Chief of Naval Operations, Department of the Navy, Washington, D.C., January 1978, 3d ed., p. 14.

TABLE 7.1

Soviet Friendship Treaties (up to 1980)

Nation	Date of Treaty
UAR (Egypt)	27 May 1971, unilaterally abrogated by Egypt on 15 March 1976
India	9 August 1971
Iraq	9 April 1972
Somalia	11 July 1974, unilaterally abrogated by Somalia on 13 November 1977
Angola	9 October 1976
Mozambique	31 March 1977
Vietnam	3 November 1978
Ethiopia	20 November 1978
Afghanistan	5 December 1978
South Yemen	25 October 1979
Syria	8 October 1980

Source: Compiled by the author from various sources.

did not mean that geographical elements shaped military strategy and international relations. Rather, to Kissinger it meant that U.S. foreign relations must go beyond the old attitude of legalism, moralism, and problem solving on an ad hoc basis. The new emphasis, according to Kissinger, was to formulate a system of great power (triangular) international "equilibrium". Hence, the tendency was to see the third world or the South primarily in East-West terms. (The major exception to this statement concerns Israel's special status in U.S. political life.)

Like many other American intellectuals, James Schlesinger, former defense secretary, energy secretary, and Rand Corporation thinker, also dismisses the third world as an independent factor in contemporary international relations. He sees that the world today is undergoing a transition, but he notes that "the evolution of the third world during this period of transition will be determined to a large extent by forces impinging on it from outside."[11] He maintains that "shifts in the third world . . . are unlikely in themselves to be decisive."[12] Schlesinger's seven basic points deserve a close scrutiny.[13]

TABLE 7.2

Cuban Activities (up to 1979)

Country	Military	Civilian
Angola	19,000 (mostly combat troops)	6,500
Ethiopia	about 15,000 (mostly combat troops)	450
Guinea	350	50
Congo	up to 300	75
Mozambique	200	600
Equatorial Guinea	200 (until recently)	50
Guinea Bissau	50-100	30
Zambia	up to 100 military advisers (with ZAPU)	—
Tanzania	up to 50	150
Sao Tome and Principe	up to 50	100
Madagascar	up to 50	—
Benin	up to 50 (security advisers)	—
Sierra Leone	up to 50 (security advisers)	—
Cape Verde	—	10-15

Source: Compiled by the author from various sources.

First, the prospects are for increased turbulence and instability for the balance of the century. The reason is simple: the decline of U.S. power.

Second, the "ultimate outcome" depends, says Schlesinger, on the following forces: realism of third world leaders—their willingness to limit their ideological posturing in exchange for limited advantage; whether the post-Brezhnev Soviet leadership will be moderate or aggressive; whether the People's Republic of China will resist following the example of Soviet exploitation of third world instability and align itself with the proponents of stability; whether Europeans will abandon the Atlantic relationship as a consequence of U.S. and European parochialism, and seek an independent Europe; and whether the United States will become realistic or remain moralistic and withdrawn.

Third, as U.S. (military) strength decreased so did its influence, says Schlesinger. The erosion of the U.S. security framework increased instability worldwide, particularly in the Arabian Gulf because of the dependence of the world on its oil supply:

> The dominance of the strategic nuclear forces of the United States and the clear-cut superiority of her naval and mobility forces provided adequate deterrence for outside threats to the region. Now, with the disappearance of strategic nuclear superiority, the Gulf area is open to pressures from the North.

Fourth, in security matters, it is more appropriate to describe the third world as "gray areas". In the North, if Europeans, Chinese, and Japanese were to shift sides, that would imply "a major if not decisive, swing in the equilibrium of power." In, say, Berlin, there is no "grayness". (A critic could say that although military commitments are firm in Berlin, it nonetheless is losing its people, its spirit, and its cultural entity.) In Berlin, says Schlesinger, the military risks are high, but in the "gray areas" the risks are low, and subversion, conflict, pressures may occur "without any major impact on the overall balance of power."

Fifth, in the gray areas, the areas of tension:

> The key ingredients of policy will be the proximity to the sources of Soviet and American power, residual influence by European states (as in Francophone Africa) and the presence or absence of a locally dominant military power.

(Schlesinger notes Vietnam, Israel, and South Africa as locally dominant military powers but not India—a strange omission.) In Africa and Southeast Asia, but not in the Persian Gulf, the fundamental interests of the superpowers are not obviously engaged. Consequently, there is a degree of permissible tolerance of unrest and shifting ties, says Schlesinger. Angola and Cuba fit into this description of national interest.

Sixth, the low potential gains and risks make third world regions (Africa and Southeast Asia, for example) susceptible to low-level military hostilities.

Seventh, the world is now in transition, says Schlesinger, and it is moving toward a new geopolitical equilibrium. This new equilibrium will be determined by the more influential players on the world scene—the major ingredients being the policies of the Soviets, the Europeans, and the "most critical ingredient is the future direction of American policy."

There are several major deficiencies in Schlesinger's thesis. In relation to Indian Ocean international relations, the notion of the world as a single strategic stage is only half-true. Strategic unity exists in the formal or technical sense that the military might of the superpowers can be projected worldwide; but "can be" does not mean that it "effectively is" in a manner that provides the system maintenance or system change desired by the superpowers. Moreover, as the following discussion will show: there is no conceptual unity between superpowers' means and ends; there is no necessary unity between the military, political, commercial, and cultural aims of the superpowers; and there is no necessary unity between the northern patrons and their southern clients. If the military means (strategic power) are in ample supply (as measured by the phenomenon of superpowers' overarmament), but when the ends (goals) are diffuse, open to debate, negotiation, temporary compromises, and renegotiation, then means and ends are not complementary. The North must deal with the South to organize southern markets and resources, to organize and maintain northern access to southern policy circles in exchange for limited (economic, political, and military) advantages for insecure or unstable local elite power structures that require external buttressing. But in doing so, the helpless northern giants cannot separate economics from politics, or economics from military strategy.

Third world instability is an invitation to foreign intervention; it is also an invitation to frustration. The gray areas have diffuse power structures that have a high tolerance of ambiguity. Indeed, they require ambiguity rather than neatness in the power structure. Ambiguity facilitates patron-client bargaining. In these circumstances there are many obstacles against the easy flow of U.S. military power into the third world. The United States seeks access and control over foreign markets. It seeks to manage both the distribution of third world resources and the elites who have the formal power to allocate third world resources. However, third world politicians recognize the utility of ambiguous and diffuse local structures both as a defense against foreign domination and as a recognition of local political cultures. Under these circumstances, the notion that a global equilibrium of power—a military balance—can be formed and maintained by U.S. military strength ought to be debunked as a conceptually flawed proposition.

The point can be approached from another angle. There is a major paradox in superpowers' diplomacy vis-à-vis the third world or southern states. The paradox exists because of the compulsion in U.S. and Soviet behavior toward globalism. The compulsion is not to define limits to the globalism, but to seek globalism by military means. Yet, the patterns of economic, cultural, political, and military diplomacy in the Indian Ocean areas give Indian Ocean countries a position in world politics. The point is not that all third world elites behave identically, but that they all share a common approach: to induce the involvement of the North into southern affairs on the South's own terms. The norm is to achieve North/South engagement from a position of southern weakness. Lenin and Mao were among the foremost practitioners of the strategy of acquiring influence from a position of weakness. It is an irony of history that this norm is being applied against the Soviet Union, the first country to demonstrate that power and influence could be gained despite weakness. Furthermore, third world nations seek temporary alliances with their northern partners. The North recognizes that as third world nations become stronger, the original economic, political, and security bargains can and will be renegotiated on terms that are better for the South. Finally, as noted earlier, another element that gives some conceptual unity to third world behavior is that its elites practice ambiguity and use it as a tool of political and cultural communication between and within states. Ambiguity in third world power structures is the minefield northern elites have to cross if they are to make an impact on third world thinking and policies.

These are the kinds of elements that give the Indian Ocean world--despite its varieties of economic, political, and sociocultural systems—a sense of connectedness with world politics, a sense that the centers of international communications in the North (the policy centers) now cannot avoid emerging local and regional power centers in the third world. World politics can no longer be studied simply in East-West terms, military terms, superpowers' rivalry terms, or in terms of geopolitics defined as a great-power-managed equilibrium.

Despite the variety of social, economic, and political phenomena in the southern areas, despite the different levels of organization and distribution of power in the southern world, despite the difficulty of describing the Indian Ocean as a single "region" that has shared values and institutions, there are three conceptual justifications for the study of the Indian Ocean world. First, the superpowers' detente is of limited and paradoxical character. Second, historically there has been a process of continuous decline of the superpowers' capabilities to project power—defined as the ability to control the patterns of regional

power. There is organizational disunity and paralysis in superpowers' decision structures that inhibits their flow of power.
Third, with the emergence of regional and local powers in the
Indian Ocean world, new power structures are gradually emerging
to the detriment of superpowers' interests.

Detente is of a limited character. This became evident in
the reactions of the superpowers to crises in the Indian World,
including Angola, the Horn of Africa, the Middle East, the
Persian Gulf, and Afghanistan. Therefore, international relations
history after 1945 should be studied in terms of the following
developments. Crises in the northern world—Berlin, Korea,
Cuba—reveal a low tolerance in the policies of the principals for
ambiguity, challenge, and prolonged crises. Responsibilities
and limits must be fixed quickly, as they were in each northern
crisis. Once these are fixed they must be respected as accepted
norms, as they have been in northern cases. Yet, at the same
time, because Northern crises must be avoided, it is necessary
to find outlets for northern powers to test the limits of their
strategic doctrines, policies, and equipment in low and medium
intensity crises in areas beyond the established spheres of
operation of the NATO and Warsaw Pact areas (namely, beyond
the North Atlantic area, the two Europes, the Sino-Soviet or
Eurasian landmass, and Northeast Asia). On the one hand, it
is necessary for the northern powers to find southern outlets
for the testing and probing of enemy intentions; on the other
hand, testing the enemy carries the danger of publicizing the
limited character of detente.

The necessity to expand and test the limits of detente is a
consequence of a philosophy of globalism. But when the limits
of detente are discovered in the South, the failure of detente
creates repercussions in East-West relations and, more important,
in intrabureaucratic and interelite debates in the United States
and Soviet Union. If detente in the 1960s and early 1970s was
meant to secure temporary advantages in East-West relations,
the failure of detente in a southern crisis erodes the utility and
image of detente in the North. The problem is not so much with
the notion of detente, which is to find temporary accommodation
among adversaries by eschewing the use of force for international
change. Rather, the built-in problem of detente is that superpowers have not asked themselves: How much military and economic expansion is enough? What are their strategic frontiers
beyond their territorial frontiers? What are the measurements
of policy success or failure? What is the relationship between
superpowers' globalism and their detente commitment? Is detente
the means to promote globalism, or must limits to superpower

globalism be established in an identifiable fashion before detente
can be come a viable proposition? In the latter instance, would
detente be a consequence of identifiable limits to globalism?

In part, the problem with detente—as an idea and as a
policy problem in the 1970s—is that it reflects a Soviet claim
to be recognized by the United States—the only country that
can invest such a claim with legitimacy—as an equal, as a superpower. Detente is the vehicle to satisfy the Soviet demand for
legitimacy. This is deep-seated; bear in mind that the Bolshevik
leaders are the products of a brutal system and are seen widely
as the successors of the tzars. Their system does not command
the voluntary support of its publics, say, in Central Asia and
among the Soviet Muslims and Jews. The treatment of the Soviet
Union by the United States depends on the prevailing political
mood of the U.S. administrations at different times. The status
accorded to the Soviet Union depends on the pattern of politics
in Washington and this creates an uncertainty in Soviet elite
thinking about its status in U.S. eyes.

The problem is that if the U.S. establishment's commitment
to detente is weak and subject to internal debate (as it always
has been), and if the Soviet claim to globalized legitimacy is
also weak (as it always has been since 1917), Soviet expansionist
threats are needed both to impress on U.S. elites the need to
negotiate with the Soviet leaders, and to prove Soviet potency
through the only instrument that has a chance of success in
Soviet experience: military force. This points to the paradoxical
nature of detente: the greater the divisiveness within the U.S.
establishment and between the superpowers about the existence
of detente, the greater is the need for the doctrine of negotiation
from a position of strength, and the greater is the opposition
within the United States to the notion of East-West collaboration.
So on the one hand, the superpowers—to persuade skeptics at
home and abroad—need to project threats to the world system
to underline the need for crisis management and detente. But
on the other hand, deterioration of East-West relations increases
superpowers' hostility—at least in the public realm. It increases
domestic pressures toward rearmament, reduces the prospects
of arms reduction in the foreseeable future, and increases
superpower competition in the third world. The deterioration
raises demands for an increased commitment to anticommunism
both at home and abroad, and for rearmament, which in turn
produces a call for arms control and detente, accommodation,
or reduction of international tension. The circle is joined and
the game goes on. The basic questions regarding the utility
of military arms for security and the limits of superpower globalism remain unanswered.

Schlesinger dismisses the independent power of the gray areas in the Indian Ocean world—including the arc of crisis from Angola to Afghanistan. His style of thinking is symptomatic of the self-centeredness and confusion in U.S. policy circles; therefore, it is worth considering the deficiencies in his analysis and advocacy.

The notion that third world instability has increased because of a decline of U.S. military power abroad is wrong. Turbulence in the third world is at least 2,000 years old. There was turbulence in ancient international relations of the East—present-day China, Southeast Asia, South Asia, the Middle East, and the Mediterranean world—in the sense that local and regional power structures were not firmly in place; empires were conflict-prone; the idea of sharing power between and within societies was more or less missing.[14] Turbulence in the Indian Ocean world is an old story; it came into being before the ancient princes ever heard of anything called "America".

In the contemporary context, to the extent that third world turbulence is a consequence of third world domestic and regional rivalries, of unsettled domestic and regional power struggles, of struggles between Zionism and Arab nationalism and other regional rivalries (such as struggles between Iraq-Iran, Iraq-Syria, and so on), the presence or absence of a dominant U.S. military power is inconsequential to the fate of these ongoing struggles. At best, the U.S. presence can provide temporary relief to local rivalries, buying time and freezing local conflicts. If realism means an exchange of limited economic advantage for a lessening of third world ideological posturing—which Schlesinger advocates—then the U.S. offer of a limited economic exchange to its local clients is to provide an incentive for ideological posturing; that is, local rulers should start with ideological posturing and agree to limit it in exchange for a good but temporary bargain with their U.S. patron. Nevertheless, the intrusion of the U.S. presence inhibits the search for local, bilateral, or regional-multilateral solutions for indigenous issues. In that sense, the offer of limited advantage to the local elites postpones conflict resolution and freezes interstate and intrasocietal conflict.

The availability of U.S., Soviet, or European foreign aid is helpful to the local elites in the Indian Ocean area, but the elites should not be viewed merely as clients of external patrons. Conceptualization about the dynamics of international power relations could be advanced if culture-bound preconceptions were dismissed and regional and local powers were seen as more than neocolonials who are locked into patron-client, dominant-subordinate, center-periphery relations. It is worth considering them as the weaker states who actually manipulate the external patrons.

The lesser powers include "pariahs," and these should be studied in terms of their ability to move about in a world of isolation, and in a world of actual and latent conflict. Pariahs can and do manipulate states and environments that possess superior military force; they must do so if they are to survive a hostile world. The most interesting pariahs are located in the South, outside formal alliance relations. In this sense there is a conceptual connectedness between the Indian Ocean world and the North—and the connections lie through the study of Pariah-Patron relations. Pariah-patron relations reveal the impact of the pariahs on the international system. Pariahs are smart and influential if they are able to identify the availability of potential, temporary partners for select issues; if they appreciate the limits of the partnership; if they can anticipate international and regional trends and are able to offer a deal to their potential clients—the formal patrons; and if they know when the limits of the relationship have been reached and it is time to move on. Pariahs possess technology, economic and military resources, and have considerable ideological and organizational unity—as is evident in the cases of Israel and South Africa. The innovativeness of a pariah state lies in turning a formal patron into a client, in locking a patron into a relationship that is mutually beneficial.

Many believe that East-West conflict should be curbed and not allowed to spill over into the Indian Ocean world. But southern elites are able to manipulate their northern "masters" precisely because the northerners have failed to find limits on their globalism that satisfy their political and bureaucratic constituencies, precisely because neither superpower has so far succeeded in integrating its interventions in the third world into an overall strategy, and precisely because the superpowers may not even follow a fully thought out policy in individual cases.[15] High-level, high-intensity regional crises in the Indian Ocean world are also crises in northern bureaucratic and policy debates. When East-West elites view each other through the prism of the other's actions in the third world, and when the other side's boldness is assumed to be a sign of its strength,[16] then regional conflict impacts on the perceptions of key elite members (like Kissinger and Brzezinski). It reveals a connection between elite and organization behavior in the North and events in the Indian Ocean world. In other words, to the extent that northern behavior in the South becomes a test of East-West relations, the

southern crises impact on the North by increasing the divisiveness and paralysis in northern security organizations. When
such connections are made in organizational memory banks, they
are hard to erase.

The Indian Ocean pariahs thrive on crises. Indeed, they
need crises to establish their power position and international
credibility. For the regional and local pariahs, Soviet intervention and U.S. reaction (or vice versa) in East-West terms is an
opportunity to relate to their patrons and to manipulate them to
their own ends. So if the United States were to increase its
power projection into the Indian Ocean world—particularly into
the Gulf region—the pattern of the East-West relationship would
imply a further Soviet power projection into that or a related
area. From the point of view of a local elite or a pariah state,
the greater the power projection into third world regions of
instability, the greater is the opportunity to gain influence with
their external patrons.

Schlesinger emphasizes three key elements for policy in
the gray areas: the proximity to U.S. and Soviet power; the
limited influence of the Europeans; and the absence or presence
of a locally dominant military power. However, three variations
should be introduced into Schlesinger's scheme:

A. The greater the proximity of competing U.S. or Soviet
elites to the source of U.S. and Soviet power, the greater is
the internal competition among the various constituencies, and
the greater is the paralysis of power within the superpower
establishment. In other words, the projection of power overseas
is not simply the consequence of "military power possessed";
it is a consequence of available military power and organizational
unity in a decision structure. Without organizational unity,
power projection can be retarded and paralyzed.

B. Because U.S. and Soviet establishments fail to comprehend the nature of instability in the Indian Ocean world, the
intellectual and cultural distance between the superpowers and
the crisis spots is a vast one. The greater this distance, the
greater is the likely loss of applied power, even when there is
a considerable amount of available or possessed power. In A,
the proximity of competing elites to the center of power and
constant organizational infighting and overspecialization often
produce temporary bureaucratic and political consensus, but
this is subject to a constant drive to redefine and renegotiate
issues within the government and between governments of allies
and enemies. This drive results in paralysis because of the
constant infighting. Here, paralysis is a consequence of the

failure to comprehend the nature of local rivalries in the crisis spots. Consequently, "proximity" to the power centers and "distance" from the crisis spots interact constantly. The interaction results in a paralysis or retardation in the flow of organized and effective power from the superpower to the crisis area. This is a sign of weakness, not restraint.

C. Schlesinger fails to consider the implications of the above elements in conjunction with the growth of the military capabilities and regional influence of the local military powers in the Indian Ocean area: South Africa, Israel, and India. Historically there has been a process of continuous decline of U.S. and Soviet power-projection capabilities that shape the patterns of regional power, combined with slowly increasing capability of local and regional military powers. Soviet military intrusions into the arc of crisis suggest the opposite of this hypothesis. However, at issue is not the ability of the superpowers to project their military power, but the impact of their organizational behavior on their available military capabilities in crises, as well as the consequences of the growing interaction between the factors described in A and B. The deterrent impact of the growing internal military weight of the local and regional military powers merits attention in the context of the problems in superpower planning as a result of the factors outlined in A and B. As such, the issue is not whether East-West detente works or not; it does not and it cannot because of its paradoxical character. The real issue is whether the present-day superpowers can escape the implications of the increasing limits to their actions in the third world. These limits are a consequence of their organizational paralysis, which itself reflects an interplay between a number of elements. Military power possessed is not the same thing as military power applied, and it does not assure impact over crisis outcomes. The third world is essential to northern prosperity as it provides essential markets and natural resources to the North. Finally, the pariah states and the secondary states (including the neocolonials) have learned the art of manipulating and managing their so-called patrons.

The strategic unity of space has been broken by the emergence of pockets of autonomy in select regions, particularly in the Indian Ocean arc of crisis. The world is not a single strategic stage except from the point of view of strategic force deployment. There is discontinuity in space, and it exists in terms of the political and strategic developments in the Indian Ocean world. Discontinuity is the consequence of inhibitions against northern projection of military power and other forms of influence into the South. The inhibitions against power projection are the result of organizational disunity within elite power structures in northern strategic cores. The militarily strong are organizationally weak and divided. Unending and inconclusive political and bureaucratic debates about foreign and military policy result in "action," not in strategic movement (defined as the creation of viable international regimes).

On the other hand, attempts are being made to create some sort of strategic unity in select parts of the Indian Ocean world. Regional and bilateral dialogues are currently under way to find alternatives to "international security". There is a reaction to the extension of superpower norms into regional life as these inevitably bring superpower tensions into regional issues. Regional strategic unity is still an aspiration rather than a reality, but it is gaining momentum. Regional strategic unity is being sought on the basis of a geographical sense of identity, ignoring existing ideological diversities. Methods should be found to bring together, say, India and Pakistan, Israel and Egypt, South Africa and black Africa. The sense is growing that geographically continuous states are in most instances "core actors". (A core actor is a state that has influence merely because of its presence in an arena of conflict, rather than by its size or level of military power.) It is significant that the core actors have historically been enemies. The presence of enemies should be studied as a catalyst of change in regional international relations.

An enemy not only helps structure a conflict, but it also serves as a catalyst for conflict management. The idea here is that conflict is integrative and this is the central lesson of regional conflict in the Indian Ocean world. Most major wars in South Asia, the Middle East, Angola, and the Horn of Africa have produced caution and attention to the enemy's concerns. Wars have led to enemies reassessing each other. This observation applies to those regional conflicts where the primary core actors are the hostile regional or local powers and they, not the superpowers, are shaping the origin, development, and outcome of the regional conflict.

Consequently, conflicts in the Indian Ocean world should be viewed as positive elements in the sense that they have helped to shape a strategic process that could eventually result in real regional cooperation. If the Indian Ocean world is studied in the context of 2000 years of disorganized military and cultural conflict among a variety of local and competitive power centers, the emergence of a few local or regional power centers (such as India, Israel, and South Africa) should be studied as an evolutionary process. This process is moving away from anarchical conflict and toward establishment of stable local or regional power structures that can expect to gradually create strategic unity in select geographical areas, and without heavy dependence on northern states.

This process is a far cry from the prescriptions of those experts who seek to promote international security. "International security" is itself a vague term and open to different interpretations. It could be primarily a code for the continued primacy of the superpowers in the current international power structure. In this sense, it could be a self-serving doctrine for the superpowers. It could also be interpreted as the doctrine that promotes the security of NATO and WTO alliance members without necessarily accommodating the vital interests of southern states. In its pure form, it should mean the security of many states, including weak southern states, rather than only the security of the fully armed or overarmed North.

In the Indian Ocean world—the world beyond the one controlled by northern alliance members—international security does not enjoy much credibility because of the misuse of this concept by ethnocentric northern elites. So the operative norm in the thinking of select Indian Ocean states is to stress the idea of a collective interest that is distinguishable from that of the pure selfishness of local power. In the present setting, a sense of collectively is being pursued in the form of bilateral and trilateral dialogues: such as interactions among India-Pakistan-Saudia Arabia; South Africa-Southern African black states-Western contact group; Israel-Egypt-United States. These are the best examples at present of "regional cooperation" This has a dual meaning. First there is a quest to establish effective local and regional power structures that are in a position to organize power, manage communications, and negotiate both intensively and extensively. Progress has been made in the sense that anarchial conflict has already been converted into structured conflict. Second, there is agreement that the lines of communications must be kept open among enemies at all times, even if these do not readily yield a negotiated solution that enjoys a clear public identification. Enemies, therefore, are helpful as catalysts of change.

The inclination to change, to rethink the causes of conflict and the desired solutions, comes into being when violence has been tried and has failed to achieve its desired ends. But the resort to force must first occur, as must its failure, before the attentive publics in the conflict zones can recognize the importance of moving from unstructured, anarchial conflict to structured conflict that opens the possibility of inching toward ad hoc, meaningful agreement. This is already happening in the Indian Ocean world. The local military powers are helpful as organizers of regional conflict and of small meaningful steps toward informal agreement and norm building among hostile regional pairs. This is the contribution of the Indian Ocean regional powers to international security thinking. Organizing the failure of superpower grand strategy and facilitating the development of a diplomacy that takes small but meaningful steps is the new game in international relations in the 1980s.

NOTES

1. See Time, September 22, 1980, pp. 28-30, and News-week, July 14, 1980, pp. 30-36.

2. Kissinger saw the Soviet Union as a traditional power, and this emerged as the basis of superpower detente. See C. Gati, "Mr. X Reassessed," in C. Gati, ed., Caging The Bear: Containment and the Cold War (New York: Bobbs-Merrill, 1974), p. 52.

3. C. Bell, The Diplomacy of Detente: The Kissinger Era (New York: St. Martin's Press, 1977).

4. M. Heikal, The Road to Ramadhan (London: Fontana Collins, 1976).

5. H. Kissinger, White House Years (Boston: Little, Brown, 1979), Chapter 11; Roger Morris, Uncertain Greatness: Henry Kissinger and American Foreign Policy (New York: Harper and Row, 1977); and Jack Anderson with George Clifford, The Anderson Papers (New York: Random House, 1973).

6. D. Haendel, The Process of Priority Formation: U.S. Foreign Policy in the Indo-Pakistan War of 1971 (Boulder: West-view Press, 1977).

7. Jiri Valenta, "Soviet Use of Surprise and Deception," Survival 24, no. 2 (March-April 1982):50-60.

8. See note 1.

9. Colin Legum, After Angola: The War Over Southern Africa (New York: Africana Publishing, 1976), author's note.

10. J. R. Schlesinger, "The International Implications of Third World Conflict: An American Perspective," in Third-World Conflict and International Security, Part I, Adelphi Papers, no. 166 (London: IISS, Summer 1981), p. 5.

11. Ibid.

12. Ibid.

13. The seven points are derived from Ibid., pp. 5, 8, 9, 10-11, and 12.

14. A. Bozeman, Politics and Culture in International History (Princeton, N.J.: Princeton University Press, 1960).

15. R. Legvold, "The Super Rivals: Conflict in the Third World," Foreign Affairs (Spring 1979):772, makes this comment about Soviet intervention in the third world in the 1970s. I have extended his ideas to include the United States also.

16. Ibid., p. 756.

8

A Concluding Note

This book has been an exploration of changing tendencies in the Indian Ocean area, tendencies that are of generalized significance for contemporary international relations. A study of the southern world, particularly the Indian Ocean world, is important for a number of reasons. The major crisis points in the world are presently in the South. Recent political, military, and economic developments, particularly in the second half of the 1970s, drew international attention to the Middle East. World attention was also focused on Southern African issues in the aftermath of the Soviet intervention in Angola, in the struggle for Zimbabwian and Namibian independence, and in the attempt to alter the political regime of South Africa.

The South African regime is likely to be able to contain internal and external pressures for at least a decade; at present, the momentum to change South Africa's preeminence in Southern African international relations appears manageable. In the Middle East, however, there are strong tendencies to "do something" about the Palestinian issue and to recognize the central importance of Arab development by the end of the century. The military, political, and psychological setting in the Middle East is such that a variety of forces have been engaged in talks and selective negotiations. The Jewish and Islamic worlds are actively seeking constructive solutions for pressing problems. Military-strategic conflict in the Middle East is becoming frozen. There is reluctant coexistence between Israel and Arab states. The primary focus now is not simply on Israel-Arab relations; it has broadened to include the issue of intra-Arab and Persian-Arab conflict. The phenomenon of regime instability points to the central role of competitive subnationalism in the foreign policy and military decisionmaking of many Arab states. Foreign and military policies of many Arab states are a consequence of internal power struggles.

Peace does not necessarily mean social harmony. In state relations, "peace" implies the existence of a process and of a consensus that the process should continue. The process means a situation, a dynamic one, where: strategic conflict is frozen and a ceiling against further escalation is established; and at the same time, cultural, political, and economic forces are able to flow in different directions in search of a power structure, and an authority structure, which accommodates competing forces. In other words, and this is particularly relevant in the study of third world international relations, when rights and responsibilities are not fixed and accepted, the first step in the peace process is to identify the enemies, and then encourage the enemies to accept others' rights and their own responsibilities.

The problem here is not the existence of enmities. Enemies are important because their presence helps to codify relations and to provide focal points for the establishment of relations and of power and authority structures. Rather, the problem arises if the presence of enemies is not followed up by the definition of rights and responsibilities between enemies. In this sense enemies are good and necessary. It could be argued that in the Middle East, the first step in the peace process has been taken in the sense that enemies exist, are well known, and now the second phase is under way: to define and induce acceptance of rights and responsibilities between enemies.

The Middle East is ahead of Southern Africa in another sense. Not only do visible and viable enemies exist, but the region has also undergone the trauma of social and military conflict on a constant and pervasive scale. The Middle East has a record of an ability to absorb large-scale military, political, economic, and cultural crises. Like India and Pakistan, the psychological mood or tendency is to say, "enough is enough." The tendency now lies in the argument that war does not yield military victory, military machines are socially and economically costly, and the primary norm for the year 2000 should be to move toward meaningful social and economic change and development. The Middle East has a long history of conflict and regime instability. But there is also a recent, albeit a tentative, history of slow and painful accommodation or reluctant coexistence between Israel and Egypt, between factions in Lebanon, and now the Saudis are speaking the language of a peace offensive.

In southern conflict zones, the process of military confrontation and reluctant coexistence occurs in parallel fashion. Accommodation is not the alternative to military conflict; in most cases of successful mediation and peacemaking, it is the consequence of an unsuccessful or inconclusive military adventure. When the costs of military adventure and military power outweigh the potential benefits, when the elites perceive this to be so and also perceive that the use of force is militarily, economically, and socially costly, then the setting for accommodation exists.

The Middle East appears to be in this frame of mind. This is a qualitative change in Middle Eastern thinking rather than merely a change in interstate tactics. The fear of high crisis and the experience of high crises and war in the past are the bases for the change in attitude and behavior. This is not to argue that accommodation between Israel and Arab states, between Jewish Palestinians and Arab Palestinians, and between Arab states themselves is around the corner. It is not so because to accommodate one must negotiate, and to negotiate the negotiators must know who their opposite number is, whether the enemy negotiator has a strong domestic social base so that he is able to engage in risk taking and in making concessions, and generally is in a position to deliver on his promises.

The setting for accommodation in the Middle East has come into being because past crises have revealed the limits of the role of force (its impermanence) and have provided test cases that have displayed the true nature of the enemy's behavior, something that low-risk conduct and political rhetoric cannot reveal. So military risk taking to test the limits of enemy intentions and behavior is a prerequisite for diplomatic risk taking. The Middle Eastern states are locked into changing patterns of military and diplomatic relations. On the one hand, the limits of enemy behavior have been determined (and still are being determined) through regional and local crises; on the other hand, an environment favorable to diplomatic risk taking has been created since 1973, and some risks have already been taken (for example Israeli return of the Sinai).

The Indian Ocean world is important because of the movement of military conflict and societal instability from the North to the South—away from the strategic cores in the upper half of the globe where military, political, and industrial power are at present effectively organized. In part, this reflects the desire of northern states to test East-West doctrines, policy, commitments, and equipment in the South; it also reflects the southern states' own instability. The southward flow of international conflict in the last century is a phenomenon that poses a challenge to our way of thinking. Although our thinking, as a result of laziness, flows along East-West lines, the direction of international change is North-South and has been so for some time. East-West relations are stable in the sense that they are predictable. They are also stable in that political, military, and territorial relations are now defined and accepted, as are relationships between enemies; rights and responsibilities are mostly known. The public disputes between Washington and Moscow concern atmospherics. Whatever the intensity of the rhetoric is at times, East-West communications and threats are no longer likely to alter the organization and distribution of East-West power or the pattern of political and military organization in the North. The South, however, does not lend itself to easy codification of rights and responsibilities. In the world beyond the North, in the world beyond NATO and WTO countries, the local and regional power structures have yet to emerge in stable and publicly explicit form. The definition of rights and responsibilities between enemies must await the emergence of power and authority structures.

Despite the differences between the permanence of northern strategic cores (with the implication that northern power structures are able to project power in their respective spheres) and the southern world (where the struggle is still to formulate effective strategies that foster desirable tendencies), it would be wrong to be pessimistic about southern international relations. International conflict has moved southward—as is evident by the incidence and location of international conflict in the world beyond the northern strategic cores. Yet, this is not to say that instability is the inevitable fate of the South and its international relations. Our view is that southern elites recognize the implications for their future if "historical conflict" or inevitable conflict in the third world is not transformed into a condition of "frozen strategic conflict," which in turn is meant to open up a process of increased cross-cultural communications between military enemies and hostile societal pairs. Thus, toning down or freezing strategic conflict usually implies first the use of military force and then the recognition that such force does not settle anything and is socially and economically wasteful. The use of force may be functional in that it creates a sense that it is wasteful; this recognition then becomes a basis for putting a lid on military conflict.

The point here is not that frustration in the use of force in a regional setting is likely to lead to disarmament. Rather, that frustration is likely to produce an awareness of the futility of further escalation and use of military force, and of the potential utility of opening up a dialogue with the moderates in the enemy camp. It is in this sense that one could assert that the seeds of regional detente have been sown during the 1970s in South Asia and the Middle East (perhaps also in Southern Africa, but to a lesser extent).

Detente presumes the existence of enemies, not their elimination. Enemies are essential actors and detente is based on
this reality. Enemies are catalysts for system building and
system maintenance. Without enemies there would be no useful
role for governments and professors. Political diplomacy is
not an alternative to the use of force or to conflict management
by the use of force; it is a consequence of the failure of force
to settle a dispute. In a sense, political diplomacy is a consequence of frozen strategic conflict. Political diplomacy also
benefits from the ability of military force to soften the enemy
up by letting it know that beyond certain limits it should expect
punishment.

The lesson of South Asian international relations after 1971
has a bearing on the notion of regional detente. In South Asia,
particularly between India and Pakistan, regional detente exists
in the sense that military and political diplomacy are both at work.
The pattern of power and the nature of the bilateral relationship
at present (and as it is likely to be in the 1980s) appear to be
a consequence of wars since 1948. The India-Pakistan analogy
is relevant to the study of Israel-Egypt relations (and perhaps
to other hostile pairs) in the coming years. In each case, although specific circumstances vary, there are tendencies toward
accommodation, or at least toward thinking about accommodating
competing interests. One can hypothesize that the toning down
of strategic-military conflict (as measured by the incidence of
war) is usually accompanied by continuation or even intensification of cross-cultural hostile communications, as between Hindus
and Muslims, Jews and Arabs, and whites and blacks. Both
tendencies are to be applauded if they lead to a release of pent-
up, deep-seated feelings and to an eventual accommodation of
these feelings.

In studying regional detente tendencies, it is worth noting
that the cohesive norm of hostile pairs is not to formulate international relations on the basis of a concept of "international
security" or of "regional security". These norms lack precision
and are impractical in a world of competing groups and states.
The tendency toward a regional detente is not a product of a
globalized consciousness about the utility and practicality of
international security. "National security" as perceived by concerned elites is still the operative and cohesive norm; at the
same time, an element of change has entered the national security
framework. The enlargement of the national security framework
represents a growing recognition among elites that there is a
link between strategic and cultural conflict. Strategic conflict
has a cultural base and cultural consequences. Unfortunately
these connections are not reflected in prevalent contemporary

strategic thought, such as crisis management, arms control, and conflict management. The enlargement of the national security framework is taking place in an environment of a growing need to improve other-directedness and to recognize that lasting national security is a matter of the economic and military development of a state.

The new approach to national strategy formation is to stress the utility of some sense of collective interest. The process to formulate collective interest is presently being conducted along bilateral lines—for example, normalization between India and Pakistan according to the Simla agreement (1971) explicitly excludes superpower or third party diplomatic intervention. The Israel-Egypt peace process and the Camp David agreement seek bilateral normalization with the help of a third party (United States) and exclusion of another (Soviet Union). Indo-Pakistani normalization in the 1970s was assisted by the diplomatic and financial assistance of Iran and now by Saudi Arabia.

As such, it appears that a sense of collective interest is gradually taking shape in the form of bilateral and triangular dialogues. But the collective approach is not necessarily a departure from the national security framework, and it does not reflect adherence to the idea of international security. "International security" could mean the security of the superpowers or it could mean a global consensus. The first definition of the term is not acceptable to a majority of countries and the second one does not exist. The tendency toward regional detente exists in that there is movement to broaden the national security framework by seeking bilateralized and triangular forms of consensus building and by seeking to explore the cultural bases and consequences of strategic-military policies. Yet, the bilateralized and triangular consensus-building processes are described in this study as "regional detente" because these activities tend to have ripple effects throughout the region; that is, even bilateral activities can have system-changing effects and in that sense, even though the form is bilateral, the consequences may be regional and international.

The rise of regional powers that have some impact on the attitudes, events, processes, and policies that shape the world today is a new phenomenon. At issue is not the possibility of their impact on the world, but rather the scope and significance of the impact. The emergence of regional powers and the development of middle power-superpower interactions in the broad context of South/North interactions is not the same thing as "regionalism," which, in its traditional sense, was measured in terms of growth of regional institutions and subordinate systems.

Nothing like the neatness required by the traditional literature on regionalism may be found in the conflict zones, the strategic buffers, or in the behavior of the regional powers and middle powers that shape regional international relations in the Indian Ocean world.

The Indian Ocean world was for over 300 years a plaything of the Europeans and then of the superpowers. For the northern states, interventions of all kinds were within the rules of the game. Indeed, it was necessary to export northern rivalries to the South so that northern peace could be preserved. The balance-of-power principle was applied in defense of European intervention in the South. Thus, the South was essential for northern international system maintenance. The South was peripheral in the sense that the organization and distribution of international power was essentially located in and managed by northern states. But the South, although peripheral as an international actor, was not peripheral as a source of resources, land, manpower, and as a playground for the northern powers.

In the post-1945 international system, the Indian Ocean world wished to avoid being a plaything of the northern powers. Until recently, the wish exceeded the power to enforce the wish. The answer to the northern powers came through southern-managed resource diplomacy and militarization and nuclearization of the South. The new third world orientation toward international relations is to create third party (third world) interference in superpower planning, and to create the intellectual and material foundation to strengthen the capacity and the will to interfere. Resource diplomacy, conventional arms proliferation and its use in a crisis, and the diplomatic and potential military value of nuclear weapons options are products of this new orientation. The ability of select states in the South to run interference against the superpowers' planning and thinking is significant not only in the sense that the regional powers can shape crisis origins, crisis development, and crisis outcomes, but also in the sense that regional powers are gradually beginning to engage the superpowers in middle power-superpower interactions in both crisis and noncrisis atmospheres. Whereas crisis diplomacy by the middle powers, and the acquisition of conventional armament and nuclear options by them, is the obvious development in the southern strategic environment, the significant point is that a subtle process is currently under way—through crisis and non-crisis behavior—to arrest the flow and increase the risks of superpower influence in regional politics. In part, this is a consequence of the growth of the material and intellectual bases of third world (economic, military, and bureaucratic-intellectual) strategic development.

The measure of the impact of regional powers and middle powers lies in the recognition that the superpowers are not likely to become global powers—certainly not in the Indian Ocean world or in the southern half of the globe generally. It is not that they lack global military power. Rather, the problem is that they lack a comprehensive and insightful global outlook, and their strategic thought and policy reflect the deficiencies of ethnocentrism and insularity. The persistent organizational and conceptual disunity in the foreign policy establishments of the superpowers accounts for the growth of a gap between super-powers' international presence (as measured by diplomatic and military activity and by speechmaking) and the decline of their international influence (as measured by ability to control out-comes).

It could be argued that, particularly in the arc of crisis, the "radical" and "anarchical" forces (for example, Qadaffi, Khomeini, and the PLO) have overtaken the "moderate" forces and the voices of "order". Such terms are value loaded, impre-cise, unanalytical, or even anti-analytical. They are hard to verify empirically; they neither explain nor predict. They are policy relevant in the sense that they are meant to evoke an emotional response from their audience, and as such serve a propaganda function. In most cases the use of such terms is a misuse of language, and scholars should carefully examine the adjectives. In each instance, the description of the enemy's conduct should be measured against the actual behavior of both the enemy and the propagandist.

Consider some examples. Henry Kissinger, one of the most articulate spokesmen for world order and peace, ordered the destabilization of the democratically elected Salvador Allende in Chile, which is hardly peaceful and orderly conduct. We have the paradox that U.S. advocates of world order are also the noisiest advocates and practitioners of intervention in the name of world peace and order. Qadaffi and Khomeini have often been called irrational. Questions: Who are we to say this? Is there a psychiatric basis for this? If so, what is it? Then there is the example of Islamic "fundamentalism". There is probably no such word in the Koran. Qadaffi is a Sufi, Khomeini is a Shia, and Saudis are Wahabbis. The Saudis are not mentioned as "fundamentalists" in the U.S. media, presumably because the Saudis are "moderates" compared to the "radical" Qadaffi and Khomeini, and perhaps also compared to the "intransigent" Israelis! If Qadaffi and Khomeini are both fundamentalists and belong to different sects and compete with each other, then the use of the term Islamic "fundamentalism" obscures the central facts that politicized and pervasive Islam (a studied fact) is also divisive (a fact also, but not studied as a factor in the Middle East strategic developments). Another example concerns the use of terms for describing guerillas. If one does not like guerrillas, the term used is "terrorist"; if one likes them, they are "liberation fighters". A change in words induces a change in attitude. Language tells us more about the person who mis-uses it than about the phenomenon it is supposed to describe.

The fear of anarchy and radicalization of international processes is a fear of change, fear of the unknown, a fear of new cultural and material realities. The changes taking place in the Indian Ocean world from Southern Africa to South Asia deal with retribalization of policy processes. Retribalized politics and military-political strategies are being released in response to submerged cultural tendencies in changing societies. The territorial and administrative maps of the world were delineated in the past and reflected colonial realities. In some countries, such as Trinidad-Tobago and Guyana, social conflict has been frozen along racial and ethnic lines. The state has been in the hands of one group that could freeze social conflict with the assistance of a foreign power and foreign aid. However, frozen social conflict increases the identification with one's own group, with one's religious, ethnic, racial, and cultural bases of support. When the political and economic structure begins to change—as in the case of Iran under the shah—these latent social forces come to life. The humiliated and oppressed forces break away from the controls of established state institutions. Note that in the case of Iran under the shah (and there are other examples), the image of an external enemy (the Soviet Union) was utilized to keep internal enemies (regionalism, mullas, Kurds) at bay. An external enemy image became the basis for a strategy both to freeze internal social conflict and to shape an alliance with the United States. The social conflict could be frozen, but not permanently.

It would appear that "anarchy" and "disorder" refer to overt, retribalized, competitive subnationalism or groupism (which relates to ethnic, religious, cultural, racial, and tribal sources of psychological comfort for the concerned individuals), whereas "order" and "peace" refer to a world with frozen strate-gic and social conflicts. In the latter instance, a strategy of "order" and "peace" is meant to retain the present organization and distribution of world power, as well as the present advan-tages of the northern power centers. The Soviet Union does not particularly benefit from this scheme of things, but Moscow badly desires the stamp of approval of the West to give it the international legitimacy, status, and respect it so badly craves. Moscow's rulers know that they are the illegitimate successors to the tzars; that the Soviet economic, political, and social system cannot be a base of world revolution or a role model of peaceful change for other countries. Hence, it must have U.S. approval to justify its claim to be a superpower.

As far as the third world is concerned, Moscow's rhetoric appeals to its wish to unfreeze social conflicts and thereby alter the distribution of power. Only thus could a "have-not" hope to become a "have". But the Soviet position is contradictory. To achieve the legitimacy it craves, it must follow a code of conduct the United States insists upon. Broadly speaking, Moscow has accepted Washington's terms. Detente or no detente, the Soviet behavior pattern is parallel to the American one. Both favor world peace and order; both seek to freeze strategic conflict; both seek to freeze social conflict in their respective spheres—the United States in Central America and the Soviet Union in Eastern Europe; both behave as super military powers, stressing at all times their superior material accomplishments; and both are insensitive and inexperienced about coping with foreign ideologies and cultures. Their public differences are obvious, but their shared style of thinking about ways to manage international relations is the more significant point about their behavior.

The new development about the Indian Ocean world is not the danger of Soviet expansion in the so-called arc of crisis. The important new development is that the cultural bases and consequences of strategic behavior of foreign and local ruling elites are now coming to the fore in public thinking. The relationship between strategy and culture is emerging as the central relationship in the study of southern international relations--whether the study is of relationships between the Hindus and the Muslims, between Jewish and Arab Palestinians, between South African whites and black Africans, between Persians and Iraqis, and so on. To the extent that the super-powers are likely to fail to understand the meaning of competitive retribalization and competitive subnationalism as the basic unit in regional life, the irrelevance of their military strategies is likely to grow. Money can buy technology and arms, but it cannot establish a viable authority and power structure that will enlist the voluntary participation of constituents. Nor can money and technology produce sound strategic thought and a viable relationship between strategy and culture in the world today.

Appendix

The Work of
the Ad Hoc Committee on
the Indian Ocean

Since 1971 a U.N. committee has been discussing a declaration adopted by the General Assembly at its twenty-sixth session. This declaration would create a zone of peace in the Indian Ocean from which great-power rivalry and military presence would be excluded, so as to enable the littoral and hinterland states to concentrate on the task of national reconstruction free from great-power interference and influence. In 1981 a conference on the subject was scheduled to meet in Sri Lanka, but due to the absence of a consensus among the participants, the meeting was postponed. To date, no agreement has been reached on the proposal to create an Indian Ocean peace zone and the prospects of such an agreement in the future remain dim.

There is a view that the Western powers and their allies wanted to scuttle the conference and that they achieved this by attempting to broaden the scope of the work of the U.N. committee. Whereas the original mandate and the declared purpose of the committee was to eliminate great-power rivalry and military presence in the Indian Ocean, during the 1970s the deliberations of the committee members revealed a diversity of strategic interests and political positions that could not be constructively blended into a U.N. compromise. A number of salient foreign policy and strategic positions emerged in the period preceding the scuttled 1981 meeting in Sri Lanka. The United Kingdom and Australia took the view that the threat to stability did not come from the sea but from destabilizing activities by conventional military forces operating in neighboring areas and by extraregional forces, such as the Soviet invasion of Afghanistan. Because of this, the two nations felt that strategic relationships in the Indian Ocean had to be studied in the context of global strategic relationships. The Soviet and U.S. positions revealed a polarization with respect to problem definition. Whereas the Soviet Union focused on the "crucial question" of elimination of military bases in nonlittoral states, the United States sought to link the conference to the question of Soviet withdrawal from Afghanistan. In addition to encompassing relevant forces within the region, the United States felt that the committee's work "must take account of Soviet land and air forces in land areas contiguous to the littoral and the hinterland states."

This committee's work merits study because it points to progress on a complicated subject. The absence of a formal arms control or disarmament agreement would seem to indicate failure, but the involvement of so many ideologically and politically diverse and strategically vital countries is a reason for hope. In the context of modern multilateral diplomacy, the existence of continuous talk among competing countries and elites is itself progress; if the participants begin to listen and rethink their respective public positions, that would be significant progress. An agreement that codifies risks and entails meaningful arms reductions would, of course, be a miracle. At present, the work of the Indian Ocean committee should be studied at the level of progress, and not in terms of miracles.

From the outset, the basis of the committee's work has been controversial. The idea of a peace zone in the Indian Ocean came from a Sri Lankan initiative to demilitarize the Indian Ocean. India, among others, opposed this approach and instead sought to focus on great-power rivalry. Still, it has been apparent to experts that India has little faith in a peace zone to promote its security goals. Because the Indian Ocean is India's strategic rear, the failure of peace zone diplomacy sanctioned an intensification of Indian naval development to cope with the escalation of great-power rivalry and military presence. Nevertheless, there is a point to the Indian advocacy that the nonaligned littoral and hinterland states are obliged—in terms of their commitment to the U.N. declaration to make the Indian Ocean into a peace zone—not to facilitate great-power military presence through the provision of military bases and logistical supply facilities. However, despite the validity of this point, the opposition by a number of Indian Ocean states to the strengthening of the Diego Garcia base and the escalation of the U.S. military presence in the Indian Ocean and Gulf areas (as expressed by plans for a rapid deployment force) reflects the political relationships between the littoral and hinterland states and the United States. For example, during Prime Minister Indira Gandhi's visit to the United States in the summer of 1982, the Diego Garcia topic was not an important issue in bilateral talks as it had been in preceding years. India opposes the development of U.S. bases or facilities in the Indian Ocean area but it is willing to subordinate its concern on the subject to improve the prospects of Indo-U.S. relations. The nuances in India's diplomatic behavior suggest that India's Indian Ocean diplomacy reflects its assessment of bilateral Indo-U.S. relations. From the Indian example, one can generalize that in many instances statements by U.N. members at the U.N. have a purpose:

they are intended as a barometer of bilateral relations rather than as statements of fact about the actual naval balance in the Indian Ocean. In this sense, it is arguable that much of the U.N. committee's work is intended to flush out the intentions of friends and foes alike rather than to necessarily foster agreement.

Third world advocacy of an Indian Ocean peace zone has the public appearance of a united front against the two superpowers, but the interests of the littoral and hinterland states vary. From this point of view, the committee's work deserves a full-length study. Many third world countries located in areas of conflict in the Indian Ocean periphery oppose any plan that could lead to their own demilitarization and nonmilitarization. International restraints on conventional arms supply are also opposed as these could jeopardize their security position in a hostile environment. Many littoral and hinterland states face enormous security problems: extraregional intervention, hostile regional states, internal security problems, and regime instability. Considering that many Indian Ocean states started to develop their security establishments from almost a zero-level military-industrial infrastructure, their concern is understandable. Moreover, because of competing elite ties and national interest perceptions, existing North/South ties continually produce cleavages on East/West lines in third world groupings such as nonaligned conferences.

At the same time, the superpowers and other major arms suppliers cannot tolerate arms supply restraints for commercial and political-strategic reasons. Arms supplies to unstable countries not only keep domestic production lines in operation, but arms supply relationships have been known to offer leverage (although the case for this should not be overstated). Furthermore, with respect to the specific question of a peace zone in the Indian Ocean, the superpowers' strategic interests are served by the continuation of low-level (in comparison to other deployments), balanced, and predictable naval relationships in the Indian Ocean. Both superpowers recognize the utility of naval show-the-flag missions as a source of latent or potential political influence and as a form of reinforcement for friendly countries. As such, the deployment of naval force under controlled conditions in the Indian Ocean has become fruitful as an instrument of low-level and medium-level crisis diplomacy rather than as a method of deployment of strategic forces.

The superpowers not only have their own axes to grind, but their diplomacy is two-faced. Publicly, Moscow has criticized the U.S. naval presence in the Indian Ocean, particularly since

the establishment of the base at Diego Garcia in the past decade.
Washington has denounced Moscow for its presence in the Indian
Ocean since 1968 and its interventions in Africa, the Red Sea
area, and Afghanistan. Yet, both superpowers' behavior does
not reveal any panic about the other side's presence. The point
is that even if the Soviets left the Indian Ocean, the Americans
would still stay to pursue their regional and local interests (and
vice versa). In this perspective, the image of a superpowers'
arms race in the Indian Ocean is misleading. Several common
interests unite rather than divide the superpowers in the
Indian Ocean. That is, even when they compete with each
other—as governments and bureaucracies must compete against
each other and against foreign enemies—their mode of behavior
is derived from their positions as superpowers who have developed an Indian Ocean policy in the context of their global,
regional, and local interests and aspirations.

Initially, the United States ignored the work of the U.N.
committee to create a peace zone in the Indian Ocean. The
Reagan administration has taken the line that the real threat
to regional peace comes from the Soviet invasion of Afghanistan
and from regional disputes and arms races. In going beyond
the original framework of General Assembly resolution 2832
(XXVI), which declared the Indian Ocean to be a peace zone,
the United States and its allies have in fact signalled to regional
powers in the Indian Ocean area that the validity of an argument
depends on the power of the country concerned. In that sense,
the U.N. committee's work has legitimized the present tendency
toward the militarization of the Indian Ocean environment.

Selected Bibliography

Adie, W. A. C. Oil, Politics and Seapower. New York: Crane, Russak, 1975.

Agee, P. Inside the Company. London: Allen Lane, 1975.

_____ and L. Wolf, eds. Dirty Work. Secancus, N.Y.: Lyle Stuart, 1978

Allison, G. T. The Essence of Decision. Cambridge, Mass: Little, Brown, 1971.

Alperovitz, G. Atomic Diplomacy. New York: Simon & Schuster, 1965.

_____. Cold War Essays. New York: Doubleday, 1970.

Ambrose, S. E. Rise to Globalism, rev. ed. New York: Penguin, 1976.

Anderson, J. with Clifford, G. The Anderson Papers. New York: Random House, 1973.

Arbatov, G. The War of Ideas in Contemporary International Relations. Moscow: Progress Publications, 1973.

Barnds, W. J. India, Pakistan and the Great Powers. London: Pall Mall, 1972.

Barnet, R. J. Roots of War. New York: Atheneum, 1972.

Bell, C. The Diplomacy of Detente. New York: St. Martin's Press, 1977.

Beres, L. R. and Targ, H. R. Constructing Alternative World Futures. Cambridge, Mass.: Schenkman, 1977.

Beitz, C. R. and Herman, T., eds. Peace and War. San Francisco: Foceman, 1973.

Bohlen, C. E. The Transformation of American Foreign Policy. New York: Norton, 1969.

Booth, K. Strategy and Ethnocentrism. London: Groom Helm, 1979.

Boulding, K. E., ed. Peace and The War Industry, 2d ed. New Brunswick, N.J.: Transactions, 1973.

Bozeman, A. Politics and Culture in International History. Princeton, N.J.: Princeton University Press, 1960.

Brown, S. The Faces of Power. New York: Columbia University Press, 1968.

Buchan, A. The End of the Postwar Era. London: Weidenfeld and Nicholson, 1974.

Cantori, L. J. and Spiegel, S. L., eds. The International Politics of Regions. Englewood Cliffs, N.J.: Prentice-Hall, 1970.

Choudhary, R. Kautilya's Political Ideas and Institutions. Varanase: Chowkhaniba Sanskoit Series Office, 1971.

Cohen, S. B. Geography and Politics in a World Divided, 2d ed. New York: Oxford University Press, 1973.

Cottrell, A. J. and Burrell, R. M., eds. The Indian Ocean. New York: Praeger, 1972.

Donaldson, R. H., ed. The Soviet Union in the Third World. Colorado: Westview, 1981.

Etzold, T. H. and Gaddis, J. L., eds. Containment. New York: Columbia University Press, 1978.

Fainsod, M. How Russia is Ruled. Cambridge: Harvard University Press, 1967.

Falk, R. A. and Mendlovitz, S. H., eds. Regional Politics and World Order. San Francisco: Freeman, 1973.

Franck, T. M. and Weisband, E. World Politics. New York: Oxford University Press, 1971.

Fox, W. T. R. The Superpowers. New York: Harcourt, Brace, 1944.

Gati, C., ed. Caging the Bear. New York: Bobbs-Merrill, 1974.

Gelb, L. H. with Betts, R. K. The Irony of Vietnam. Washington, D.C.: Brookings, 1979.

Gorshkov, Admiral S. A. Red Star Rising at Sea. Annapolis, Md.: Naval Institute Press, 1974.

____. Seapower of the State. New York: Pergamon, 1979.

Gurtov, M. The United States Against the Third World. New York: Praeger, 1974.

Haendel, D. The Process of Priority Formation. Colorado: Westview, 1977.

Halle, L. J. Cold War As History. New York: Harper, 1975.

Harrison, S. S. The Widening Gulf. New York: Free Press, 1978.

Heikal, M. The Road to Ramadhan. London: Fontana/Collins, 1976.

Jackson, R. South Asia Crisis. London: Chatto & Windus, 1975.

Janis, I. L. Victims of Groupthink. Boston: Houghton Mifflin, 1972.

Jukes, A. The Soviet Union in Asia. Sydney: Angus & Robertson, 1973.

Kennan, G. F. Realities of American Foreign Policy. New York: Norton, 1966.

Kirkendall, R. S., ed. The Truman Period as a Research Field. Columbia, Mo.: University of Missouri Press, 1974.

Kissinger, H. White House Years. Boston: Little, Brown, 1979.

Klien, R. The Idea of Equality in International Politics. University of Geneva Thesis No. 166, 1966.

Kohli, Admiral S. N. Seapower and the Indian Ocean. New Delhi: Tata-McGraw-Hill, 1978.

Kolko, G. The Roots of American Foreign Policy. Boston: Beacon, 1969.

La Feber, W. America, Russia and the Cold War, 1945-1980, 4th ed. New York: Wiley, 1980.

Lebedev, N. I. A New Stage in International Relations. New York: Pergamon, 1976.

Lefever, E. W. Nuclear Arms in the Third World. Washington, D.C.: Brookings, 1979.

Legum, C. After Angola. New York: Africana Publishing, 1976.

_____ et al., eds. Africa in the 1980s. New York: McGraw-Hill, 1979.

Lifschultz, L. Bangladesh: The Unfinished Revolution. London: Zed Press, 1979.

Lippmann, W. U.S. Foreign Policy. Boston: Little, Brown, 1943.

Luard, E. Conflict and Peace in the Modern International System. Boston: Little, Brown, 1968.

Martin, L., ed. Strategic Thought in the Nuclear Age. Baltimore: Johns Hopkins University Press, 1979.

Mazrui, A. A. A World Federation of Cultures, New York: Free Press, 1976; The African Condition. London: Cambridge University Press, 1980.

McGwire, M., ed. Soviet Naval Developments. New York: Praeger, 1978.

_____ and McDowell, J., eds. Soviet Naval Influence. New York: Praeger, 1977.

Miller, J. D. B. The Politics of the Third World. London: Oxford University Press, 1967.

Morris, R. Uncertain Greatness. New York: Harper & Row, 1977.

Nicolson, H. The Evolution of Diplomatic Method. London: Constable, 1954.

Nitze, P. H. et al. Securing the Seas. Colorado: Westview, 1979.

Nixon, R. U.S. Foreign Policy for the 1970s, Message to U.S. Congress, Feb. 25, 1971.

Nogee, J. L., ed. Man, State and Society in the Soviet Union. New York: Praeger, 1972.

_____ and Donaldson, R. H. Soviet Foreign Policy Since World War II. New York: Pergamon, 1981.

Odell, P. R. Oil and World Power. New York: Penguin, 1979.

O'Neill, R. J., ed. Insecurity. Canberra: Australian National University Press, 1978.

Payne, J. L. The American Threat. Chicago: Markham, 1970.

Potholm, C. P. and Dale, R., eds. Southern Africa in Perspective. New York: Free Press, 1972.

Pullapilly, C. K., ed. Islam in the Contemporary World. Notre Dame: Cross Roads Books, 1980.

Radovanovic, L. V. The Non-Alignment Policy Today. Belgrade: Medunūrodna politika, 1966.

Rapoport, A. The Big Two. New York: Pegasus, 1971.

Roosevelt, K. Countercoup. New York: McGraw-Hill, 1979.

Rosen, S. J. and Jones, W. S. The Logic of International Relations, 3d ed. Cambridge, Mass.: Winthrop, 1980.

Rosenau, J. N. et al., eds. World Politics. New York: Free Press, 1976.

Rothstein, R. L. Alliances and Small Powers. New York: Columbia University Press, 1968.

Russett, B. M. International Regions and the International System. Chicago: Rand McNally, 1967.

Schelling, T. C. Arms and Influence. New Haven: Yale University Press, 1966.

Schwartz, M. The Foreign Policy of the USSR. California: Dickenson, 1975.

Service, J. S. The Amerasia Papers. Berkeley: University of California Press, 1971.

Shamasastry, R. Kantilya's Arthasastra. Mysore: Wesleyan Mission Press, 1923.

Singh, K. R. Politics of the Indian Ocean. Delhi: Thompson Press, 1974.

Singham, A. W. The Nonaligned Movement in World Politics. Westport, Connecticut: Lawrence Hill, 1977.

Spanier, J. American Foreign Policy, rev. ed. New York: Praeger, 1962.

Stockwell, J. In Search of Enemies. New York: Norton, 1978.

Stoessinger, J. G. Nations in Darkness, 3d ed. New York: Random House, 1978.

Tarcouzio, T. A. War and Peace in Soviet Diplomacy. New York: Macmillan, 1940.

Triska, J. F. and D. A. Finlay. Soviet Foreign Policy. New York: Macmillan, 1968.

Truman, H. Memoirs, vol. 2. New York: Doubleday, 1956.

Tungendhat, C. The Multinationals. Markham, Ont.: Penguin, 1971, 1973.

Tzu, Sun. The Art of War, trans. and ed. S. B. Griffith. London: Oxford University Press, 1963, 1971.

Vital, D. The Inequality of States. Oxford: Clarendon Press, 1967.

Wallace, H. A. Toward World Peace. New York: Reynal & Hitchcock, 1948.

Wight, M. Power Politics. New York: Penguin, 1979.

Williams, W. A. The Tragedy of American Foreign Policy, rev. and enlarged ed. New York: Dell, 1962.

Yanov, A. Detente After Brezhnev. Berkeley: Institute of International Studies, University of California, 1977.

ARTICLES AND DOCUMENTS

Brecher, M. et al. "A Framework for Research on Foreign Policy Behavior." Journal of Conflict Resolution 13 (1969).

Bundy, McGeorge et al. "Nuclear Weapons and the Atlantic Alliance." Foreign Affairs 60, no. 4 (Spring 1982), pp. 753-68.

Cusack, T. R. and Ward, M. D. "Military Spending in the United States, Soviet Union and the People's Republic of China." Journal of Conflict Resolution 25, no. 3 (Sept. 1981).

Indian Ocean Arms Limitations & Multilateral Cooperation on Restraining Arms Transfers. Hearing before a panel of Committee on Armed Services, House of Representatives, 95th Congress, October 3, 10, 1978.

Legvold, R. "The Super Rivals: Conflict in the Third World." Foreign Affairs, Spring 1979.

"Military Industrial Complex—Russian Style." Fortune, August 1, 1969.

Newsweek, July 14, 1980, pp. 30-36.

Sanders, R. "Bureaucratic Plays and Strategems: The Case of the U.S. Department of Defense." Jerusalem Journal of International Affairs, October 4, 1979.

Schlesinger, J. R. "The International Implications of Third World Conflict." In Third World Conflict and International

Security. Adelphi Papers, no. 166. London: International Institute for Strategic Studies, Summer 1981.

Sivard, R. L. World Military and Social Expenditures, annual.

Time, Sept. 22, 1980, pp. 28-30.

UNESCO Courier, April 1974.

Valenta, J. "Soviet Use of Surprise and Deception." Survival 24, no. 2 (March/April 1982).

Waltz, K. N. "The Spread of Nuclear Weapons." Adelphi Papers, no. 171. London: IISS, Autumn 1981.

Wills, G. "The Kennedy Imprisonment." Atlantic Monthly, February 1982.

Index

About the Author

DR. ASHOK KAPUR is an Associate Professor of Political Science at the University of Waterloo, Waterloo, Ontario. He is the author of India's Nuclear Option (Praeger, 1976), International Nuclear Proliferation (Praeger, 1979), and several scholarly articles on foreign policy and security issues.

During 1980-81 Dr. Kapur served as a member of the United Nations Committee on Israeli Nuclear Armament and co-authored a report on the subject. He has lectured at the Israeli National Defense College (Tel Aviv) and the Canadian Defense Forces College (Toronto). He has testified before the House of Commons Standing Committee on External Affairs and Defense on disarmament and security issues.